The R

Italy

Rough Guides online

www.roughguides.com

credits

Text editor: Barbara Mellor, Matt Milton
Series editor: Mark Ellingham
Production: Julia Bovis, Andy Turner
Cartography: Maxine Repath
Proofreading: Carole Mansur
Picture research: Amanda Russell

publishing information

This edition published May 2003 by
Rough Guides Ltd, 80 Strand, London WC2R 0RL

distributed by the Penguin group

Penguin Books Ltd, 80 Strand, London WC2R ORL
Penguin Putnam, Inc, 375 Hudson Street, New York 10014, USA
Penguin Books Australia Ltd, 487 Maroondah Highway,
PO Box 257, Ringwood, Victoria 3134, Australia
Penguin Books Canada Ltd, 10 Alcorn Avenue,
Toronto, Ontario M4V 1E4, Canada
Penguin Books (NZ) Ltd, 182–190 Wairau Road,
Auckland 10, New Zealand

Typeset to an original design by Henry Iles

Printed in Spain by Graphy Cems

© Jonathan Keates 2003
384 pages includes index

A catalogue record for this book is
available from the British Library.
ISBN 1-85828-836-3

The Rough Guide
History of

Italy

by
Jonathan Keates

series editor
Justin Wintle

contents

introduction

Italy has always been an object of desire. Its history, from the outset, was influenced by its geographical position, that of a fertile peninsula in the central Mediterranean, with an abundance of good natural harbours along its coastline and an imposing northern frontier formed by the Alps. Deeply rooted ideas of it as a place of wealth and prosperity are embodied in the name *Italia*, in use by 500 BC, which derives from a native tribal word meaning 'calf' or 'cattle' (the modern Italian word *vitello*, meaning 'calf' or 'veal', is related) indicating the land's rich pastoral agriculture.

Unified control of the Italian landmass was established by the Romans, who overcame existing Etruscan, Greek and Celtic civilizations in the north and south by the end of the 3rd century BC, and who built up a Mediterranean empire after defeating their principal trade rival Carthage. Republican government in Rome was replaced, after bitter power struggles, by the rule of emperors, increasingly dependent on the support of the army. Invaded by the Goths and other barbarian peoples, the western Roman empire collapsed during the 5th century AD. Italy was claimed by the eastern emperors ruling from Byzantium, but their power in the region was contested by the Longobards, Germanic invaders whose settlement, particularly in the north, had a lasting impact on Italian life at every level. Sicily soon fell to Muslim raiders from North Africa, and a vibrant Islamic culture in the island lasted well beyond its seizure in the 11th century by Norman mercenaries, founders of a Christian kingdom embracing the southern mainland as well. This realm eventually formed the kingdom of Naples, known in the 19th century as the Two Sicilies.

The centre of Catholic Christendom was Rome, where the popes sought to assert their authority over Italian rulers by taking a political role which did more harm than good to their spiritual leadership. Their rivals for control of Italy were the Holy Roman Emperors, heirs of Charlemagne. While papal-imperial struggles threatened to tear medieval Italy apart, its people sought safety in small-scale social units such as the extended family and the independent city state. In such communities prosperity encouraged the patronage of artists by merchants and guilds. During the 15th century, Florence, with its settled government and cultivated bourgeoisie, saw the first flowering of the Renaissance, the name given by historians to a period of unparalleled creativity in the arts throughout Italy, significantly inspired by a rediscovery of the classical world of Greece and Rome.

With its cultural sophistication, technical skills and abundant wealth, Renaissance Italy was studied enviously by European rulers from beyond the Alps. During the early 16th century the north in particular became a continuous battleground between the invading armies of France and the Holy Roman Empire. The power of the popes was weakened by Emperor Charles V's sack of Rome in 1527, which established a Habsburg hegemony that would last in one form or another for three hundred years. During the late 16th century economies of once flourishing Italian states such as Venice entered a slow decline, but Italy began a fresh incarnation as 'the paradise of travellers', a place whose art treasures attracted a peaceful tourist invasion which has never slackened since.

The appeal of their past to others made Italians yearn for a revival of the impetus which produced the achievements of ancient Rome and the Renaissance. After Napoleon's invasion of Italy in 1797 showed how easily rulers of its patchwork of sovereign states could be overturned, agitation began for national unity, eventually delivered via war and

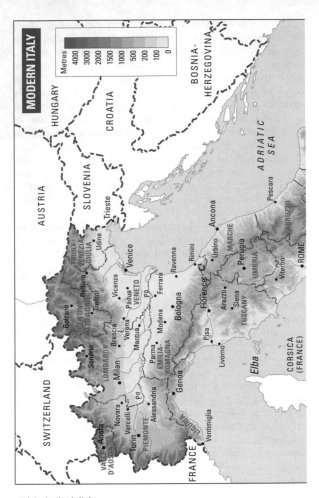

MODERN ITALY

Metres
4000
3000
2000
1500
1000
500
200
100
0

HUNGARY

CROATIA

BOSNIA-
HERZEGOVINA

ADRIATIC
SEA

AUSTRIA

SLOVENIA

Trieste

FRIULI
VENEZIA
GIULIA

Udine

Belluno

TRENTINO
ALTO ADIGE

(Trento)

Bolzano

Vicenza

Venice

VENETO

Padua

Po

Ancona

MARCHE

Urbino

Rimini

Ravenna

Ferrara

Bologna

Perugia

UMBRIA

ROME

Viterbo

SWITZERLAND

Sondrio

Brescia

Verona

Po

EMILIA
ROMAGNA

Modena

Florence

Arezzo

TUSCANY

Siena

Pisa

Milan

LOMBARDY

Mantua

Parma

Novara

Vercelli

Alessandria

Po

Genoa

Livorno

Elba

CORSICA
(FRANCE)

Aosta

VALLE
D'AOSTA

Turin

PIEMONTE

LIGURIA

Ventimiglia

FRANCE

Pescara

ABRUZZO

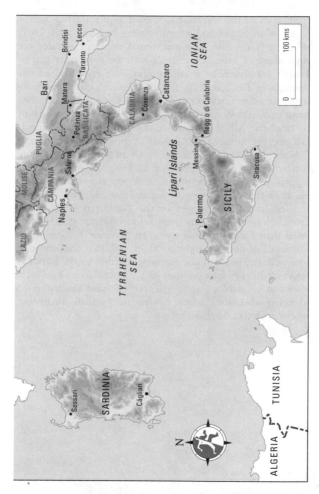

revolution in the movement known as the Risorgimento. Many of its hopes and promises were betrayed after 1870, when Italy became a constitutional monarchy under the royal house of Savoy. Discontent with the rewards reaped by Italian involvement in the Great War encouraged the triumph of Fascism, initiating another and more disastrous sequence of expectation and betrayal. Catastrophic involvement in World War II was followed by Nazi invasion of Italy to stem the Allied advance, and a prolonged and bloody campaign culminated in Mussolini's capture and execution.

Since 1945 Italy has become one of Europe's wealthiest nations, but its age-old problems endure. The south remains a jigsaw of corrupt fiefdoms, the country as a whole is cynical as to the effectiveness of big government, the idea of a unified Italy is challenged by the Northern League, and crowd-pleasing politicians with simple answers gather more votes than those seriously trying to persuade Italians of the virtues of democracy and the rule of law. In a country so in love with the modern and the new, whether in fashion or in football, history involves not just a complacent backward glance at Leonardo, Dante, Michelangelo and Galileo, but a 'damned inheritance' whose burden many Italians are unable, or else reluctant, to shake off.

list of maps

list of illustrations

1
Earliest beginnings to Julius Caesar

3000–44 BC

I n Virgil's great Latin epic poem the *Aeneid*, written during the 1st century BC, it is the gods who inspire the Trojan warrior Aeneas, ancestor of the Romans, to make his home in Italy. Archaeology more prosaically suggests that Italy's earliest communities were drawn to it by its natural resources. In the north, the fertile Alpine foothills and broad flood plains of the principal rivers encouraged the growth of agriculture, while in Tuscany and on the island of Sardinia mineral deposits were exploited for iron-smelting and the making of weapons and ornaments in copper and bronze. The oldest culture of any significance was the **Villanovan**, dating from the 10th century BC and taking its name from Villanova, near Bologna, where one of its cemeteries was excavated in the 19th century. During the 9th century BC, Sardinia was visited and colonized by the **Phoenicians**, among the most adventurous of Mediterranean trading peoples, whose home territory lay in the area now known as Lebanon. They established commercial centres along the Spanish and North African coastlines, and created a western mercantile empire ruled from Carthage, near modern Tunis. While the Carthaginians built up a trade network in Sardinia and Sicily, **Greek** colonists from cities such as Athens and Corinth settled in the thinly populated southern Italian mainland during the same period (800–600 BC). Greek civilization soon established itself in the Italian peninsula's 'toe and heel', which was to become known to the Romans as Magna Graecia ('greater Greece'). Further colonies sprang up along the Sicilian coastline, with **Syracuse** being the fastest growing and most influential among them.

Meanwhile, in central and northern Italy, two very different peoples gained control of both territory and trade routes. By around 600 BC the **Etruscans** (whom some scholars believe to have been indigenous to Italy, although evidence suggests they migrated from the Near East), dominated the whole area between the northern Apennines and the Tiber basin, which became known as **Etruria**. Sometimes establishing new cities, sometimes building on existing Villanovan settlements, they set up trade routes with Carthage and the Greek colonies, as well as with the native peoples of southern France, Spain and the Dalmatian coast. In northern Italy, the **Celts** settled in the Alpine slopes from the 6th century onwards, having crossed the mountains from overpopulated areas of southern Gaul (modern France) to challenge the Etruscans for mastery of the fertile, wooded Po valley. Ancient historians referred to this northern region as **Cisalpine Gaul** ('Gaul this side of the Alps').

It was not only in the north that the Etruscans were threatened. Pushing south to attack the Greek cities, they were turned back at **Cumae**, near Naples, in 524 BC: a defeat which effectively checked their territorial ambitions for good, and ambitious tribes and communities back in their central heartland threatened to shift the balance of power. Chief among these were the inhabitants of **Rome**, originally a scattering of small villages on hills above the River Tiber in the region known as **Latium**. A thriving trade centre by the end of the 8th century BC, Rome was a monarchy for hundreds of years. **Tarquinius Superbus**, Rome's last king, was overthrown in 509 BC by a group of aristocrats who established the **republican government** under which Rome would prosper, so laying the foundations of a great empire that would endure for the next four centuries. Whilst they absorbed elements of Etruscan civilization, the Romans had their own language, **Latin**, and they underpinned their government with a clearly defined legal system and rigid social hierarchy. The early decades of the new republic's existence were marked by unavoidable conflict with nearby Etruscan cities and with the peoples of the mountainous interior, whose migration to the richer coastal plains had to be curbed if Roman trade beyond Italy was to survive. A further threat presented itself in the early 4th century BC, when **Celtic tribes** from Cisalpine Gaul started raiding Etruria and pushed down into Latium to reach Rome itself. The Gaulish army preparing to attack the city was driven off (probably with the aid of bribes), eventually to be overwhelmed by an Etruscan force as it moved northwards.

Over the next hundred years, Rome successfully overcame the Etruscans and gained territory from the **Sabines** and **Samnites** in a sequence of hard-fought wars. As it pushed its frontiers ever further outwards, the republic found itself involved in disputes between the cities of Magna Graecia, which culminated in 280 BC with the arrival from Greece of **Pyrrhus**, king of Epirus, at the head of a huge army. Pyrrhus failed to dislodge the Romans from southern Italy, where they gradually annexed the Greek cities and founded new colonies.

A head-on collision with Carthage became unavoidable as the expanding Roman republic sought commercial outlets in the wealthy island of Sicily, and in 264 BC the first of the so-called **Punic Wars** (*Punicus* being the Latin for Carthaginian) erupted between these two major trading rivals. The Second Punic War, fought mainly in Italy against an army of Carthaginians and their allies under **Hannibal**, at first went badly for the Romans. But despite inflicting two major defeats on the Roman forces, Hannibal failed to reach Rome itself and was eventually forced back to Africa, where the Carthaginians were finally vanquished at the battle of **Zama**. A brief Third Punic War, some fifty years later (149 BC), resulted in the total destruction of Carthage itself and the annexation of **Africa** to the Roman empire.

The devastating effect of the Punic Wars changed southern Italy forever, both physically and psychologically. The peasant economy was replaced by a system based on *latifundia* (large estates worked by slave labour). This major increase in the **slave population** was to have serious consequences for Roman society over the next hundred years: issues of personal freedom, citizenship and the distribution of land became the central concerns of Roman government during this period, erupting in 90 BC in a revolution known as the **Social War**. In the wake of international conflict and the nation's successful struggle for survival, the *plebs* (common people) demanded a greater say in administration and a fairer redistribution of resources, while the **patricians** (nobility) grew correspondingly more dogged in seeking to defend their privileges. Reforms introduced by the brothers **Tiberius** and **Gaius Gracchus**, intended to remedy abuses of power while preserving the status quo, succeeded instead in antagonizing vested interests within the Senate.

The rise to power from 87 BC onwards of **Lucius Cornelius Sulla**, overcoming his military rival Gaius Marius, showed how vulnerable the republic was to the ambitions of a dictator. It was one of Sulla's younger political opponents, however, whose meteoric career was to culminate in his becoming king of Rome in all but name. Having proved his skills as a commander in Asia Minor, **Gaius**

Julius Caesar combined a still more successful campaign in Gaul with the shrewd manipulation of useful political alliances, especially with the wealthy **Marcus Crassus** and **Pompey** (Gnaeus Pompeius), an equally experienced if less self-disciplined military leader. The death of Crassus in battle against the Parthians left Caesar and Pompey the only rivals for supreme control of the Roman state. Victorious over Pompey in Greece and loaded with honours by the Senate, Caesar became the single most powerful figure in the history of Rome up to this point. Though his murder by disaffected patricians in 44 BC was motivated in part by a desire to restore the republican system, Caesar's personal rule had set the example for a new style of **imperial government** which Rome would impose on its empire for the following 500 years.

> **" ** The study of history is the best medicine for a sick mind; for in history you have a record of the infinite variety of human experience plainly set out for all to see; and in that record you can find for yourself and your country both examples and warnings. **"**
>
> Livy, *History of Rome*, Book I, trans. Aubrey de Selincourt

8000 BC Palaeolithic communities, using stone tools, begin to develop in Italy, concentrated largely in the mountainous areas of Piedmont, Liguria and the eastern Alpine foothills.

3000 BC Settlers begin to put down roots in the foothills of the Alps and the Po valley, taking advantage of fertile flood plains and trade routes along rivers such as the Ticino, Adige and Piave. Early settlements in western Tuscany and Sardinia begin to mine copper and iron.

1100–800 BC The **Villanovan** culture, named after the village near Bologna where 19th-century archaeologists excavated one of its cemeteries, flourishes in northern Italy. The Villanovans cremated their dead, burying the ashes in ceramic urns decorated with imitation helmets or made in the form of small wattle-and-daub huts. Such pottery and the accompanying grave-goods make this Italy's earliest identifiable civilization.

In **Sardinia**, the abundant basalt boulders of the island's volcanic landscape are used without mortar to build *nuraghi*, cone-shaped houses, forts and shrines. **Phoenician** traders from the North African city of **Carthage**

Syracuse and Greek culture

Sicily was one of the leading cultural centres of the ancient world, and evidence of Greek civilization remains strong in the island today. Poetry, drama, philosophy and architecture all flourished in its prosperous merchant cities. Richest of these was **Syracuse**, on a little island off Sicily's east coast. Here the tyrant Dionysius II (b.396 BC) was influenced, and perhaps visited by, **Plato**; and later Hieron (reigned 478–466 BC) patronized poets such as the versatile **Simonides** and **Bacchylides**, famous for his passionate choric hymns, or dithyrambs. Two of antiquity's greatest writers found an appreciative audience among the Syracusans. **Pindar** (b.518 BC) wrote some of his finest odes here, in celebration of the winners of athletic contests such as the Olympic Games, and **Aeschylus** produced his tragedy *The Persians* in the city's theatre. Some years later, the dramatist died while visiting Sicily: ancient tradition ascribes his death to a bizarre accident, when a lammergeyer vulture (which kills its prey by smashing it against rocks), mistook Aeschylus's bald head for a stone, and dropped a tortoise on it. It was during their capture of Syracuse in 211 BC that Roman soldiers killed **Archimedes**, greatest of all Greek scientists, as he was engaged in trying to solve a mathematical problem.

(near modern Tunis) visit Sardinia and found settlements along its coastline. Building up further trading contacts with the **Sikels**, early inhabitants of **Sicily**, these Carthaginians lay the foundations of a major commercial empire in the Mediterranean.

c.800 BC Southern Italy and Sicily begin to be settled by **Greek** colonists from Athens and Corinth. The following centuries are to witness the growth of a significant Greek civilization in the region, which becomes known to ancient historians as **Magna Graecia**, ('greater Greece'). Principal cities include Syracuse, Acragas (modern Agrigento) and Panormus (Palermo) in Sicily, and Tarentum (Taranto), Cumae, Sybaris and Neapolis (Naples) on the Italian mainland.

753 BC According to early historical tradition, the city of **Rome** is founded by **Romulus** and **Remus**. Archaeological evidence suggests that by this time a small collection of villages supported by pastoral agriculture had indeed grown up on the range of seven hills over which Rome was to spread, on both banks of the River Tiber.

750 BC The **Etruscans** begin to settle Villanovan sites between the Tiber and the Po. A people of uncertain origins, they trade mainly with Magna Graecia, Carthage and Greek colonies on the coasts of France and Spain. The Etruscan names of certain eastern Italian cities, such as **Rimini** and **Ravenna**, suggest that they also carried their mercantile activity further afield, and Etruscan artefacts have been found in places as far-flung as Croatia and the Greek islands of the Aegean.

616 BC **Tarquinius Priscus** becomes the first Etruscan king of Rome, previous rulers having been drawn from the Latin-speaking peoples of the surrounding region. The Etruscan kings bring their people's formidable engineering skills to Rome, turning a swamp into the **Forum**, raising

The Etruscans

The origins of the Etruscans have remained an enigma ever since the ancient historian **Dionysius of Halicarnassus** disagreed with the opinion of his precursor **Herodotus**. While the latter believed that the Etruscans had migrated by sea from Lydia in Asia Minor (modern Turkey), Dionysius argued that they were in fact a native Italian people, but that their culture had developed as a result of contact with neighbours such as the colonists of Magna Graecia, whose Greek alphabet they adopted to write their non-Indo-European language. Who were they and how did they live? Etruscan literature has vanished without trace, but the wealth of decorative art that survives in the elaborate **tombs** they created in their rock-hewn cemeteries presents an image of a rich and pleasure-loving society.

Etruscan tombs were equipped with the worldly goods – or representations of them – needed for a happy existence in the afterlife, and their painted murals reinforce this impression of hedonism and sensuality. It appears as if the puritanical Romans were often shocked by the Etruscans' free and easy enjoyment of sex, and by the liberties allowed to women: treated as the social equals of men, they were permitted to drink wine (forbidden to Roman females), were fond of dancing and were often scantily dressed. Yet at the same time the Romans were fascinated by the wisdom of Etruscan priests and soothsayers, the **haruspices**, who practised divination by 'reading' the liver cut out of a recently sacrificed animal.

Etruscan influences permeated numerous aspects of Roman life, from the architecture of temples, gates and fortifications to the triumphal processions of victorious generals. One of the most familiar legacies of the Etruscan civilization is perhaps the **fasces**, the image of an axe blade emerging from a bundles of rods, used to symbolize the concept of firm government at the core of society – and notoriously adopted centuries later in Italy by **Benito Mussolini** to serve as both the name and the emblem of his regime.

Etruscan mural (c. 470 BC) from the Tomb of the Triclinium ('dining room') at Tarquinia, showing a flautist playing a double flute

handsome public buildings in stone and devising a sewage system centred on a main drain, known as the **Cloaca Maxima**.

c.600 BC Aided by an alliance with the **Carthaginians**, the Etruscans reach the zenith of their power in Italy. The city of **Capua**, which they found north of Naples, soon becomes one of the most affluent communities in southern Italy.

540 BC At the battle of **Alalia**, a combined Etruscan and Carthaginian force checks a Greek bid to seize naval control of the western Mediterranean.

524 BC Seeking to extend their frontiers southwards, the Etruscans march on the Greek city of **Cumae**, only to be turned back in a decisive battle which halts any further Etruscan expansion.

509 BC **Tarquinius Superbus**, last of Rome's Etruscan kings, is overthrown after his son Sextus has outraged the Roman nobility by raping Lucretia, virtuous wife of the soldier Collatinus. Led by **Lucius Junius Brutus** and a group of fellow aristocrats, the Romans institute a **republic** based on a balanced hierarchy of patricians, knights and commoners: a system of government which will last, with certain modifications, for another 450 years.

499 BC The neighbouring Latin cities contest Rome's domination of the region. Defeated by the Romans at the battle of **Lake Regillus**, near modern Frascati, they enter into a military and commercial union known as the **Latin League**, in which Rome becomes the major partner.

493 BC Having reached agreement on the equal sharing of booty and captured territory, Rome and the Latin League wage war against neighbouring peoples – the Sabines, Aequi and Volsci – who have migrated from the mountainous hinterland towards the richer coastal pastures.

From this period springs the legend of the rape of the **Sabine women**, which tells of Rome's attempts to remedy its shortage of females by seizing marriageable girls ('rape' here meaning abduction rather than sexual assault)

S.P.Q.R.

The letters 'S.P.Q.R.', found on so many Roman monuments and artistic depictions of military trophies, stand for '*Senatus populusque Romani*', 'the Roman Senate and people'. The **republic** created in 509 BC was founded on an awareness of the division that existed between these two elements in society. The word 'republic' itself derives from the Latin '*res publica*', meaning 'the public thing' or 'public matter', and the original concept of the Roman state focused on the notion of the shared concerns that bound together patricians and people, and that were essential to the city's survival and defences. The **Senate**, drawn from members of the upper class, began as an advisory body but soon assumed key administrative powers. Never more than eight hundred in number, and drawn exclusively from aristocratic families, the senators elected two consuls annually to serve as leaders of the state in both peace and war. The people – *plebs* in Latin – had their own **elected** representatives within the community, known as **tribunes**, who were allowed to veto the appointment of senators and magistrates and to voice the various grievances of the Roman working class. According to the historian Polybius, they were 'bound to carry out the wishes of the people and to devote themselves to this task'. Young men ambitious for a senatorial career often began as **quaestors**, junior magistrates attached to civil and military officials, with special responsibilities in such areas as food supply, tax collection and the drafting of laws. Their fellow law officers, the **aediles**, acted in disputes over matters such as usury or patrician infringements of plebeian rights. This carefully graded administrative hierarchy, with its balance of patrician and popular privileges and duties, was maintained wholesale throughout the thousand-odd years of Roman ascendancy, until the empire's collapse in the mid-5th century AD.

from Sabine families who were visiting Rome for a civic festival. By the time the Sabines mustered an army to attack Rome, the girls had settled into Roman family life and acted as peacemakers between the two sides.

491 BC Gnaeus Marcius Coriolanus, a hero of the war against the Volsci, is expelled from Rome for his severity in dealing with the *plebs*, refusing to allow grain to be distributed to them during a period of famine. He joins the Volsci and leads them in an attack on Rome, but turns back in response to the entreaties of his wife and mother. The Volsci later murder him.

474 BC Following their defeat by a Syracusan naval force off the coast near **Cumae**, the Etruscans lose control of the western Mediterranean.

451 BC Rome draws up its earliest code of laws, based on established customs within the community. They are inscribed on bronze tablets known as the **Twelve Tables**, and placed in the Forum, the city's central public space.

> ❝ You, Romans, must remember that you have to guide the nations by your authority. Let this be your skill, to graft tradition onto peace, to show mercy towards the conquered, and to wage war until the haughty are brought low. ❞
>
> Virgil, *Aeneid*, Book VI

c.450 BC Celtic tribes from the Alpine regions move south into the river plains of the Po, Adige and Ticino, establishing tribal capitals on the sites of present-day Milan, Bologna, Brescia and Verona. The invaders are known to the Romans as **Gauls**, the Galatians to whom St Paul's epistle was addressed, whose name derives from a Celtic root-word found elsewhere in the Gaelic language. Northern Italy becomes known as **Cisalpine Gaul** ('Gaul this side of the Alps').

406 BC The Romans embark on a prolonged siege of the important Etruscan stronghold of Veii. The city's capture in 396 BC (ten years later according to early historians) doubles the territory under Roman rule and enables the victors to pick off remaining Etruscan city states such as Volsinii, Caere and Tarquinii.

399 BC A horde of Gaulish warriors raids the Etruscan lands and defeats a Roman army sent to meet it at the River Allia, eighteen kilometres north of Rome. The Gauls' planned night assault on the city is reputedly foiled only by the cackling of the sacred geese kept on the **Capitol**. Bought off by the Romans (who subsequently invent a story of a sudden counter-attack to save their reputation) the invaders turn north, only to be massacred by an Etruscan force.

343 BC The first of Rome's two wars against the **Samnites**, a powerful tribe with lands in the southern Apennines, leads to further strife with nearby peoples. Roman conquest brings with it colonial rule, with limited rights of citizenship, self-government for towns and cities and the guaranteed maintenance of local religious traditions. This arrangement will form the basis of Roman **imperial rule** as it spreads across Europe, Africa and the East over the next 700 years.

328 BC A Roman colony established at **Fregellae** (Fregene, east of Rome) is given full civic status, provoking a furious reaction from the Samnites. The resulting war, which lasts with brief intervals for 37 years, brings Rome into closer contact with Greek cities of the south, as **Neapolis** (Naples) asks for a Roman garrison to replace the Samnites.

321 BC In a battle at the Caudine Forks, a narrow pass in the hills near **Benevento** (southeast of Naples), a Roman army is forced to surrender to the Samnites.

316 BC Having built up their fighting force once more, the Romans resume hostilities against the Samnites. After initial defeats in Latium, Rome gains the advantage. Pushing further into the central Apennines, the Romans build roads and establish colonies in **Umbria** and the **Abruzzi**. The earliest Roman settlement on the east coast is founded at **Hadria** (Atri), so giving the Adriatic Sea its name.

304 BC Peace with the Samnites gives Rome total control of the fertile coastal region of **Campania**, around the city of Neapolis (Naples).

c.290 BC More cities of Magna Graecia, including the important cultural centres of **Croton** (Cotrone) and **Rhegium** (Reggio Calabria), begin to ask for Roman military protection. Fearing a full-scale takeover, **Tarentum** (Taranto) seeks help from **Pyrrhus**, king of the northern Greek state of Epirus.

280 BC Pyrrhus lands in Italy, leading a massive army including twenty elephants (one of which he later displays to the Roman commander Fabius in a vain attempt to unnerve him), but his successes against the Romans are achieved at great cost – hence the term 'Pyrrhic victory'. After his peace terms are rejected and he fails to make any meaningful alliances with the surrounding enemies of Rome, Pyrrhus returns to Greece. A second expedition, against the Carthaginians in Sicily, is an equally costly failure. The king is eventually killed after a woman throws a roof tile at him to avenge the death of her son during a battle in the Peloponnese.

264 BC The **First Punic War** begins. Invited to help the mercenary garrison in the Sicilian town of Messana (Messina), under siege by the Carthaginians, the Romans drive off the besiegers. Full-scale land war in Sicily and the threat posed by the large, well-equipped Carthaginian fleet force Rome to confront the need for adequate naval support.

260 BC A Roman navy of one hundred warships, fitted out in under a year and led by admiral Gaius Duilius, defeats the Carthaginians at **Mylae**.

257 BC Marcus Attilius Regulus leads an attack on **Carthage**. Though initially successful, he is ultimately defeated by **Xanthippus**, a Spartan mercenary general responsible for the reorganization of the Carthaginian army. Regulus is kept prisoner in Carthage.

241 BC At the battle of the **Aegates (Egadi) Islands** the Romans destroy the Carthaginian fleet. Carthage is forced to sue for peace, surrendering Sicily and paying a huge indemnity to the Romans.

238 BC Crippling manpower losses and problems with raising this indemnity weaken the Carthaginian hold on the western Mediterranean, allowing Rome to seize **Sardinia** and **Corsica**. **Hamilcar Barca**, commander of the defeated Carthaginians in Sicily, makes his son **Hannibal** swear an oath of eternal hostility to Rome.

232 BC Roman forces invade **Cisalpine Gaul**. In military operations over the next ten years, Rome seizes major tribal capitals such as **Mediolanum** (Milan) from the Gauls and distributes the more fertile lands among colonists.

219 BC Carthage's attempt to establish a new empire among the tribes of the Spanish hinterland arouses Roman suspicions. When Hannibal attacks the town of Saguntum, on the Mediterranean coast of central Spain, Rome sends an ultimatum to Carthage. It is flatly rejected.

218 BC The **Second Punic War** begins in spectacular fashion with Hannibal's march from Spain across the Alps. His army, a large and multiracial force including troops from Africa, the Spanish tribes and the Gauls, is accompanied by war elephants.

217 BC Vanquishing Roman opposition in northwestern Italy, Hannibal marches south towards Rome. At **Lake Trasimene** (Trasimeno) he masterminds the crushing defeat of a large army led by Gaius Flaminius.

216 BC Discouraged by his lack of support among Rome's Italian subject peoples, Hannibal advances into Apulia to seek alliances with the Greek cities. At the battle of **Cannae** a Roman army is massively defeated, but despite gaining support from Macedon and Sicily, Hannibal fails in his long-term bid to demoralize Roman resistance. Under its commander **Quintus Fabius Maximus**, known as *Cunctator* ('the Delayer'), a new Roman force evades Carthaginian attempts to engage it in open battle, forcing Hannibal to fight a costly war of attrition.

> Although the Romans were now indisputably beaten and their reputation as soldiers was destroyed, yet it was through the special virtues of their constitution and their ability to remain calm in a crisis that they regained their mastery of Italy, defeated the Carthaginians and in a mere few years became rulers of the entire world.
>
> Polybius, *Universal History*, on the battle of Cannae

215 BC Rome now engages the Carthaginians on three separate fronts. In southern Italy, **Marcus Claudius Marcellus** defeats Hannibal at Nola and forces him back into Apulia. In Spain, the brother generals **Publius** and **Gnaeus Scipio** attack the armies of Hannibal's brother **Hasdrubal**, while also sending envoys to deter Syphax, ruler of the North African kingdom of Numidia, from making an alliance with Carthage. Roman forces are meanwhile sent to the northern Greek kingdom of Macedonia to prevent its king, Philip, from going to Hannibal's assistance.

Around this period, Roman soldiers returning from the various war fronts introduce new **religious cults** into Italy, including several from Greece and Sicily. Often followed in secret at first, these gain a footing in various parts of southern Italy.

211 BC Rome gains the key city of **Capua** from the Carthaginians. An army led by **Marcellus** besieges **Syracuse**, allied with Carthage and defended by machinery devised by the scientist **Archimedes**, including a giant grappling hook capable of levering an entire galley out of the sea. Marcellus's capture of the city returns **Sicily** to Roman control.

210 BC After the death of the two Scipios, killed while fighting in Spain, Publius's son **Publius Cornelius Scipio** is invested with special powers and sent to take over the army.

209 BC Scipio captures the important Spanish city of **Carthago Nova** (Cartagena). **Hasdrubal** manages to evade the Romans, but after leading another army over the Alps is driven back at the **River Metaurus** in eastern Umbria.

203 BC **Hannibal** brings his troops home to Africa, where Carthage itself is threatened by a Roman army under Publius Cornelius Scipio, who has defeated the Carthaginians' African allies.

202 BC Hannibal confronts Scipio's army at **Zama**. Though inferior in numbers, the Romans rout the Carthaginians, stampeding their elephants into the cavalry lines. Carthage sues for peace and is subjected to a heavy tribute over a fifty-year period as well as enforced full-scale disarmament.

200–150 BC Rome takes advantage of its newly won supremacy in the western Mediterranean to establish itself as an imperial power in **Spain**, **Gaul** and **Illyria** (modern Slovenia and Croatia).

196 BC After invading **Macedonia**, the Romans defeat King Philip at **Cynoscephalae**, so gaining control of Greece and its cities.

171 BC War breaks out once more in Macedonia. **Lucius Aemilius Paulus** inflicts a crushing defeat on Philip's son Perseus, bringing home great booty and a thousand hostages from the Greek cities. Greece is subsequently divided into the Roman provinces of **Macedonia** and **Achaea**.

Roman religion

Religious life played an important role within the communities under Roman rule, whether large or small. Central to official worship were the three deities **Jupiter**, **Juno** and **Minerva**, counterparts of Zeus, Hera and Athena in Greek mythology. All Roman towns possessed temples dedicated to these gods, and when Rome extended its empire beyond Italy, any important city would be endowed with handsome temples as a symbol of imperial rule and the benefits of a shared culture and language (all temples were adorned with Latin inscriptions). At least some of the Romans' success as conquerors and colonizers lay in their willingness to incorporate local gods into the traditional pantheon, which also included the war god **Mars** and the harvest goddess **Ceres**. Shrines of ancient Italian **tribal cults** were maintained under Roman domination, as were important centres of worship such as the **Grove of Diana** at Nemi near Rome and the **Temple of Fortune** in the Adriatic port of Fanum (Fano). During the imperial era, the emperor was himself revered as a god, boasting the title of **Pontifex Maximus**, bestowed originally on the head of the Roman college of priests. Rome was the centre of a number of specialized cults and religious offices, including the **Vestal Virgins**, six priestesses charged with tending the sacred fire of the hearth goddess Vesta, and the **Augurs**, a group of priests who practised divination from omens. The strength of popular belief in

149 BC The **Third Punic War** is started by an attack by the rearmed Carthaginians on Rome's African allies the **Numidians**. The Roman writer, orator and senator **Cato**, known as 'The Censor' (a magistrate in charge of public morals), ends all his speeches to the Senate with the words '*Delenda est Carthago*', 'Carthage must be destroyed'.

146 BC Carthage finally falls to **Scipio Aemilianus**, adopted grandson of the victor of Zama, who orders total destruction of the city. The ruins are ploughed up and the site symbolically 'killed' by sprinkling salt over it.

portents and signs certainly endured beyond the official sanctioning of **Christianity** by the emperor Constantine in the 4th century. Just before Rome fell to the Goths in 410 AD, the city's defenders, led by Pope Innocent I, are said to have summoned Etruscan '**haruspices**' (soothsayers), still secretly practising their art, who duly forecast the impending disaster.

The Temple of Ceres (or Temple of Athena) at Paestum, built according to classical Doric principles in around 500 BC

The Punic Wars leave southern Italy devastated: its Greek civilization is destroyed forever and cities such as Locri and Tarentum never fully recover. The surrounding peasant economy collapses, to be replaced by large estates known as *latifundia*. Former arable land is turned over to pasture, and the whole area in the Italian 'toe and heel' – the modern regions of **Basilicata**, **Calabria** and **Apulia** – takes on the oppressed, poverty-stricken, lawless character it will retain for the next two thousand years.

133 BC **Tiberius Gracchus** is elected tribune. With his younger brother Gaius, he proposes a new law limiting the size of landed estates and distributing the surplus to poor citizens. When **King Attalus of Pergamum** in Asia Minor leaves his wealth to the Roman state, Gracchus decrees that it should be divided among these new farmers to help them buy stock and equipment. The Senate resents this challenge to its control of public expenditure and when Gracchus is elected for a second term, a senatorial faction orders its henchmen to murder him and his supporters. The murder eventually leads to a dangerous stand-off between the **patricians**, keen to retain their ancient privileges, and the **people**, angry at government corruption and the misuse of public money.

123 BC **Gaius Gracchus**, as tribune, undertakes **wholesale reforms** designed to streamline the taxation system and redistribute resources more fairly. His efforts to extend voting rights to embrace non-Romans and his reform of the judicial process by the introduction of jury trials are greeted with dismay by vested interests at all levels of Roman society. He and his supporters are attacked and seek refuge on the Aventine Hill, where the Senate, desperate to claw back its authority, has them brutally massacred.

c.114 BC A series of disastrous defeats on the imperial frontiers in **Gaul**, **Thrace** (northern Greece) and **Africa**

undermines popular confidence in the military expertise of the Roman Senate.

107 BC **Gaius Marius**, appointed consul, takes command of the Roman army in North Africa, where he vanquishes the Numidian rebel **Jugurtha**. On the strength of this, he is given free rein to overhaul the army. He creates legions of 4500 men, each divided into ten cohorts. These are further subdivided into three smaller units, led by officers called **centurions**.

102 BC Marius leads the new Roman army in a successful campaign against the **Cimbri** and **Teutones**, Germanic tribes who are attempting to cross into Italy after invading Gaul.

91 BC Tension starts to develop between Rome and the neighbouring Italian peoples and cities brought together under its rule, known as the *socii Italici* ('Italian allies'). Disputes over their subject status, citizenship rights and heavy contribution to the cost of military operations lead to open revolution, known as the **Social War**.

89 BC Having brought the Social War to an end, the Romans concede defeat on the issue of **citizenship**, offering full civil rights to all who lay down their arms.

87 BC **Lucius Cornelius Sulla** is given command of an army sent to punish the rebellious client kingdom of Pontus in Asia Minor, under its ruler **Mithridates**. While the force is mustered in the southern region of Campania, Sulla's old adversary **Marius** challenges his appointment. Sulla marches on Rome and Marius flees to Africa. When Sulla leaves for the east with his army, Marius returns to Italy, marches on Rome and massacres his political enemies. Shortly after being named as consul, he dies.

84 BC Successful campaigns against Mithridates win back support for Sulla, who returns to Italy, mopping up Marian opposition and gaining the backing of two rich and ambitious young patricians, **Marcus Licinius Crassus** and **Gnaeus Pompeius** (Pompey).

82 BC Sulla becomes **dictator of Rome**, embarking on a **reign of terror** in which his opponents, military and political, are systematically executed or exiled, their names first appearing on the dreaded 'proscription lists'.

81 BC Having undertaken a wholesale shake-up of the Roman political and judicial system – including the introduction of special courts, limited powers for tribunes and minimum age requirements for public office – Sulla relinquishes his dictatorship, dying in retirement three years later. His reforms bolster the powers of the Senate and the army, creating a recipe for social discord and laying the foundations of a prolonged **power struggle** that will eventually destroy the Roman republic.

73 BC **Spartacus**, a Thracian gladiator, assembles an army of runaway slaves on the slopes of Mount Vesuvius. Living off the surrounding countryside, they repel successive Roman attacks until overcome by Marcus Crassus, commanding one of the largest Roman forces ever assembled. Spartacus is killed in battle and the captured slaves are crucified along the major road known as the Appian Way.

70 BC In an attempt to check the Senate's misuse of its powers, the consuls **Pompey** and **Crassus** dismantle Sulla's constitution. The lawyer and orator **Marcus Tullius Cicero** exposes the governor of Sicily, **Gaius Verres**, as the most corrupt of public officials. Cicero's two indictments of Verres, accusing him of embezzlement and robbery of artworks, remain classic denunciations of the abuse of power and political influence.

69 BC Pompey begins a series of successful campaigns in Asia Minor and Syria which enhance his reputation with the

Spartacus

Compassion was not a highly regarded virtue in the world of pagan antiquity, and Spartacus (c.109–73 BC) was not a figure likely to be romanticized by historians in his own time. Slaves could expect little sympathy in a society in which unpaid labour was taken for granted and the economy depended substantially on its support. They posed an all too real threat, moreover: the consensus of opinion among early writers is that Rome was lucky to escape destruction by the **slave army** of 73 BC. The size of the opposing force under Crassus certainly bore witness to the seriousness with which the Senate took the threat of a general revolt, and he undoubtedly gained political credit and popularity from his ruthless suppression of the uprising.

It was left to socialist movements of the 19th and 20th centuries to hail Spartacus as the leader of a **proletarian revolt**. Left-wing American writer Howard Fast made him the hero of a novel, later turned by **Stanley Kubrick** into the epic movie *Spartacus*, which famously represents the patricians as venal and decadent. There is no historical evidence to suggest that the rebellion was anything more than an ad hoc uprising by groups of discontented slaves from the *latifundia*, who followed Spartacus for his instinctive leadership qualities rather than for any ideological vision he might have held out to them of radical social change.

army, sparking off corresponding fears in Rome of a new dictatorship.

62 BC Failing to gain election as consul on a populist platform, the disgraced ex-colonial governor **Catiline** (Lucius Sergius Catilina) organizes a conspiracy in a bid for power. **Cicero**, elected consul by patricians who believe him to be a 'safe pair of hands' despite not being of their class, exposes the planned coup d'état to the Senate. After Catiline's death in battle, Cicero has the co-conspirators executed without trial.

58 BC Gaius Julius Caesar, nephew of Caius Marius, embarks on a protracted Roman invasion of **Transalpine Gaul** (France). His campaign memoirs, *De Bello Gallico*, composed six years later, will become one of the earliest classic texts of military history.

© SCALA

Marble bust of Julius Caesar, National Museum, Naples

Julius Caesar

Julius Caesar (100–44 BC) is the most compelling figure to emerge from the turbulent final decades of the Roman republic, the man who, for all future ages, seemed to personify Rome's military might and the inexorable spread of imperial rule beyond Italy. Not for nothing did his family claim descent from **Aeneas**, the Trojan hero who according to legend was a founding father of the Roman people and whose exploits became the subject of Virgil's epic, the *Aeneid*. Making his mark as a soldier in Asia Minor and Spain, Caesar nevertheless also found time to establish himself as a politician, supporting the enemies of **Sulla** (who had tried to thwart his career) and making useful alliances with **Pompey** and **Crassus**. His **invasion of Gaul** took seven years and was the most costly and destructive campaign ever undertaken by a Roman commander. Its impact on local communities and ecosystems was devastating.

After the **triumvirate** formed with Pompey and Crassus collapsed, Caesar was ruthless in fomenting civil war in Italy so as to escape impeachment by the Senate on corruption charges. Having crushed Pompey and his followers he became **dictator of Rome**, dressing himself in royal robes (though refusing the title of king) and receiving honours as the 'divine Julius'. Far from sealing his reputation as a **vainglorious tyrant**, his assassins, Brutus, Cassius and the rest, succeeded only in clinching Caesar's historical immortality. The conspiracy formed the subject of Shakespeare's tragedy, while the hero's adventures in Egypt after Pompey's death inspired George Bernard Shaw's sardonic comedy *Caesar and Cleopatra*. Elsewhere, Caesar has figured as the hero of operas, films and novels, while offering an obvious role model to world leaders as disparate as Napoléon Bonaparte and Benito Mussolini. His laconic summary of the capture of the city of Zela in Asia Minor, '*Veni, vidi, vici*' ('I came, I saw, I conquered'), was to become sufficiently famous in his lifetime to be borne aloft as a slogan in his many triumphal processions through the streets of Rome.

56 BC Returning briefly to Italy, Julius Caesar seals a pact of mutual political support with Crassus and Pompey, known as the **Triumvirate** (from the Latin 'three men'). Eager to curry favour with these powerful figures, the Senate renews their respective military commands and consulships.

55 BC **Crassus** is killed in a disastrous battle against the Parthians at Carrhae (in modern Iraq): **Pompey** and **Caesar** are now rivals for power in Rome. Bringing his **Gallic War** to a close, Caesar leads an army to **Britain**, the earliest known Roman contact with the island. The Gaulish tribal kingdoms become clients of Rome, paying a yearly tribute.

49 BC Caesar leads his victorious army from Gaul into Italy. Pausing at the **River Rubicon** (an unidentified stream somewhere in the present-day region of Romagna), which marks the boundary between the two, he decides to launch all-out war against Pompey – an irrevocable decision that will give rise to the phrase 'crossing the Rubicon'. Pompey escapes to northern Greece, leaving Caesar master of Italy.

48 BC After defeating forces loyal to Pompey in Spain, Caesar pursues him to **Greece** and wins a decisive victory at the battle of **Pharsalus**. Pompey flees to **Egypt**, where he is murdered as he sets foot on land, probably on the orders of the Egyptian king Ptolemy XIII. When Caesar himself arrives, Ptolemy's sister **Cleopatra** seeks his help in her attempts to usurp her brother's throne. Caesar defeats Ptolemy and installs Cleopatra as queen. Her love affair with Caesar results in the birth of a son, **Caesarion**.

46 BC Mopping up the remaining opposition from Pompey's supporters in Africa, Caesar returns to Rome in triumph. His reform of public finances and concession of citizenship to communities in Gaul and Spain increase his popular standing, and a **personality cult** begins: the Senate showers him with honours and titles, and coins are issued bearing his image.

44 BC A senatorial decree confirms Caesar as **dictator of Rome** in perpetuity, though he refuses the title of king. A group of senators, led by **Marcus Brutus** and encouraged by **Cicero**, resolves to murder him and restore republican government. On 15 March, known as the Ides in the Roman calendar (which Caesar has recently revised), he is stabbed to death at the foot of a statue of Pompey. Far from reviving the Roman republic, the assassination sets in motion the chain of events that will lead to its collapse.

> **❝** Twenty-three dagger thrusts went home as he stood there. Caesar did not utter a sound after Casca's blow had drawn a groan from him; though some say that when he saw Marcus Brutus about to deliver the second thrust, he reproached him in Greek with the words, 'You too, my son?' **❞**
>
> Suetonius, *Life of Julius Caesar*

2
The Roman empire
44 BC–476 AD

The Roman empire remains the most successful imperial regime in history. It had already come into being long before **Octavius Caesar** assumed the title of **Augustus** and became the first emperor, in 27 BC. By this time, Rome held sway over large areas of the Mediterranean, including Spain, Greece and the recently conquered kingdom of Egypt. Within Italy itself, peoples of varying ethnic origins, including **Etruscans**, **Sabines**, **Samnites** and **Gauls,** had become Roman subjects, adopting the legal and administrative structures of Rome while retaining many aspects of their ancient culture and religious ritual.

It was this **pluralism** and **tolerance** which to a great extent ensured the empire's survival as a political entity over several centuries and throughout diverse and far-flung areas of Europe, the Near East and Africa. What was more, Rome showed itself willing to acknowledge the rights and claims of local monarchs and chiefs, provided that they in return were prepared to recognize the **emperor** as supreme ruler and to cooperate with Roman governors and generals. Although figures such as these, and especially the **prefects** (provincial administrators) and **procurators** (high-ranking civil servants directly responsible to the emperor), constituted the ultimate authority within any one region, the main emphasis of Roman imperial rule was on effective local government – the most sophisticated of its kind to be seen until the 20th century. **Elected magistrates**, drawn from the bourgeoisie and local landowners, oversaw the administration of justice, the maintenance of roads, civic defences, drainage and policing, as well as the regulation of religious worship and entertainments such as drama or gladiatorial displays. **Provincial councils**, meanwhile, could send representatives to Rome to bring complaints of bad government, or to institute legal action against any procurator who had incurred local resentment.

One of the universal factors that lent stability to imperial power was **Roman civil law**. Another was the use of **Latin** as the common language in official documents and inscriptions, as well as in education. But the most conspicuous symbol of continuity was the great tradition of **Roman architecture**, in the form of roads, walls, triumphal gates, aqueducts and public buildings, the ruins of which impress us even now. From Scotland to the Sahara, and from the Atlantic to the Euphrates, a traveller was never far away from temples, baths, amphitheatres and forums. The **collapse** of this remarkable civilization was a gradual process, due to no one single factor (and certainly not to the rise of Christianity, as expounded by the 18th-century historian Edward Gibbon in *The Decline and Fall of the Roman Empire*).

The failure of successive emperors to deal effectively with the power of a **restive army** during the 3rd century AD certainly played a part in undermining the imperial authority at the apex of the pyramid of government. Far more damaging, however, were the shock waves of **barbarian migration** that now pushed against the frontiers of the empire, which had been over-extended under powerful emperors such as Trajan and **Antoninus** in an earlier and more optimistic age. Warfare on these fronts brought constant interruptions to trade which adversely affected the economy, especially in the cities, while agriculture was hit by inevitable shortages in the supply of slaves to work the land. Though the empire recovered to a degree under **Diocletian** and **Constantine**, the traditional values of established Roman systems and hierarchies were overturned by new and more complex social structures, which challenged the authority not only of senators and high-ranking provincial officials, but also of the emperor. During the late 3rd century, **Rome** itself finally lost its pivotal role as imperial capital. Over the following fifty years it was **sacked** and looted by **barbarian invaders** – a fate that would have been unthinkable in the reign of **Augustus**, the emperor who had done so much to make the city into a fittingly grand metropolis for a prodigious empire.

44 BC The murder of **Julius Caesar** creates a major power vacuum at the heart of the empire. Influential elements in the army and among ordinary Roman citizens lend their support to Caesar's protégé Marcus Antonius (**Mark Antony**). Moves towards a power-sharing arrangement with **Brutus**, **Cassius** and the conservative republican **Cicero** are brought to a halt by the revelation that in his will Caesar has named his great-nephew **Octavius** as his adoptive son and heir.

43 BC Seeking to use the 19-year-old Octavius as a political pawn, Cicero turns on Mark Antony in a series of scorching orations (known as the *Philippics*), urging the Senate to attack him. Mark Antony marches north to Mutina (Modena) to attack forces led by Brutus's brother Decimus and the two consuls Hircius and Pansa. When the consuls are killed, Octavius takes command (in defiance of the Senate) and marches on Rome, gaining popular support. Mark Antony meanwhile forms an alliance with the wealthy **Marcus Aemilius Lepidus**, governor of Transalpine Gaul. Octavius joins them in the **'Second Triumvirate'**, a shared dictatorship established, in the words of its official description, 'to reorder the state'.

42 BC The triumvirs begin a **ruthless purge** of their political opponents. Cicero is murdered while trying to escape to Greece, where Octavius and Mark Antony subsequently defeat Brutus and Cassius at the battle of **Philippi**.

40 BC The empire is divided into three spheres of influence. **Lepidus** is given **Africa**, whilst **Octavius** is to control **Italy**, **Spain** and **Gaul**, and **Mark Antony** takes over in the **eastern Mediterranean**. After a failed campaign against the Parthians to avenge the death of Crassus, Mark Antony retires to Egypt to join Caesar's former mistress, **Cleopatra VII**. Their relationship is later exploited by Octavius in a mounting propaganda war against Mark Antony.

Herod 'the Great', son of Antipater of Idumaea, is named **king of the Jews** by the triumvirs.

39 BC Sextus Pompeius, Pompey's son, is recognized by the triumvirs as overlord of the islands of Sicily, Sardinia and Corsica, and of the Greek Peloponnese.

36 BC Octavius seizes **Sicily** from Sextus Pompeius, who flees to Miletus in Asia Minor, where he dies. **Lepidus** tries to take control of the island, but his troops desert to Octavius, who imprisons him for the next 23 years.

31 BC Having isolated or crushed potential opponents in Italy and beyond, **Octavius** feels free to move against **Mark Antony**, whose fleet is defeated in a battle off the Greek coast at **Actium**. Antony and Cleopatra retreat to Egypt, where further warfare results in Mark Antony's death from battle wounds and **Cleopatra's suicide**. Octavius thus has no serious challengers to his command of the Roman world.

27 BC Octavius, remodelling the Roman state in order to repair the damage of over two decades of civil strife, is endowed with the *imperium*, supreme authority granted by the Senate to generals and magistrates in times of national emergency. As emperor, he is accorded the title of Augustus by the Senate. **'Caesar Augustus'** becomes the official style by which all future emperors will be known.

19 BC The poet **Virgil**, friend and supporter of Augustus, dies after catching a fever on a trip to Greece. His unfinished epic the *Aeneid*, telling the story of Rome's foundation by Aeneas, a fugitive prince of Troy, celebrates ancient heroic virtues and, by analogy, the fulfilment of Roman ideals in the achievements of the emperor. It soon comes to be regarded as the classic example of Latin poetry at its most expressive.

17 BC To mark the dawning of a new age of civic order and prosperity, in which the arts are to flourish and historic Roman values are to be revived, Augustus announces the festival of the **Saeculum**, a ceremony of special sacrifices and games that he declares is to be repeated every 100 years. The poet **Horace**, a protégé of the emperor's friend **Maecenas**, celebrates the occasion in his *Carmen Saeculare*.

> ❝ Conscious that the city of Rome was unworthy of its position as imperial capital, besides being vulnerable to fire and flooding, Augustus so improved its appearance that he could justifiably claim, 'I found Rome built simply out of bricks: I leave her clad in marble.' ❞
>
> Suetonius, *Life of Augustus*, trans. Robert Graves

c.4 BC Jesus Christ is born. Historians cannot agree on an exact date, but the event must have taken place before the death in this year of **Herod the Great**, king of the Jews. The original assignment of the start of the Christian era to a date three years afterwards is based on a miscalculation by a monk in the 6th century AD.

2 BC On his 60th birthday, Augustus receives the title *Pater Patriae* ('Father of the Fatherland') from the entire community of Rome. This confirms his status both as emperor and as the figure chiefly responsible for re-establishing firm government and administrative continuity within the empire.

9 AD While extending the frontiers of the Roman empire between the rivers Rhine and Elbe, three legions under the command of Publius Quintilius Varus are wiped out in a devastating attack by **Germanic tribes** led by the chieftain Arminius (**Hermann**), at the **Teutoburger Wald**, somewhere in north Saxony. No further attempts are made by the Romans to expand their German territories.

14 AD Augustus dies and is succeeded by his stepson **Tiberius**. The Senate declines the new emperor's offer to step down in favour of a re-established republic and hastens to confirm him as sovereign, invested with all the powers of his predecessor. Henceforth the Senate becomes merely a formal assembly, with no governmental authority.

19 AD Tiberius's nephew **Germanicus** dies while on a visit to Syria and Egypt. Tiberius had been forced by Augustus to adopt Germanicus as his successor, and had become wary of the young man's increasing popularity. When Piso, a high-ranking government official, commits suicide after being accused of poisoning Germanicus, Tiberius and his mother **Livia** are widely assumed to have masterminded the supposed murder.

c.30 AD Jesus Christ is crucified by order of **Pontius Pilate**, procurator of the province of Judaea (historians cannot agree on an exact date).

37 AD Tiberius dies, having named two joint successors: his grandson Tiberius Gemellus and his great-nephew Gaius, known by his nickname **Caligula** ('Little Boot'). Caligula soon has his co-emperor murdered.

41 AD After displaying alarming signs of megalomania and possible insanity (according to legend these included declaring his horse Incitatus a consul of Rome), Caligula is assassinated by a group of conspirators. The **Praetorian Guard** (the imperial bodyguard) forestalls the Senate's attempt to re-establish the republic by proclaiming his uncle **Claudius** emperor.

43 AD Caligula's planned **invasion of Britain** now begins, led by the general **Aulus Plautius**.

48 AD Prompted by her numerous infidelities and involvement in various political intrigues, Claudius has his first wife, **Messalina**, executed. Claudius now marries his niece **Agrippina** and adopts her son **Nero** as heir.

54 AD Claudius dies, supposedly poisoned by Agrippina. Nero is acknowledged by the Senate as emperor. His tyrannical rule and extravagant lifestyle will make him many enemies.

59 AD Nero has Agrippina, his mother, murdered.

64 AD Nero sets fire to part of Rome with the object of rebuilding the city. The conflagration is blamed on a new sect of monotheistic followers of Jesus Christ, known as **Christians**, many of whom are rounded up and executed.

65 AD A conspiracy is uncovered to depose Nero and offer the empire to the senator Gaius Calpurnius Piso. Among the conspirators are several erstwhile friends of the emperor, including the satirist **Petronius Arbiter**, the poet **Lucan** and Nero's former tutor **Seneca**. All the plotters are either put to death or forced to kill themselves.

66 AD Revolts in the province of **Judaea** are systematically suppressed by the general Titus Flavius Vespasianus (**Vespasian**) and his son Titus, at the head of three legions.

68 AD Legions in **Gaul** and **Spain** mutiny against **Nero**. The 63-year-old **Servius Sulpicius Galba**, commanding the Spanish legions, is proclaimed emperor. The Senate declares Nero a public enemy and he commits suicide – according to some historians with the words '*Qualis artifex pereo!*' ('What an artist I die!').

69 AD Vespasian and Titus besiege **Jerusalem**. The city falls and the Jewish Temple is destroyed. The Temple treasures

Roman amphitheatres

In the time of the Roman republic, gladiatorial games generally took place in large open spaces such as the **forum** of a city, where spectators could watch from the steps of public buildings. In the early years of the empire such entertainments grew more elaborate, requiring purpose-built structures to accommodate them. The earliest amphitheatres (which took their name from the Greek word *amphitheatron*, meaning a place in which the audience surrounds a central arena) were built during the 1st century in Rome and Pompeii.

One of the largest and most impressive of all amphitheatres was the Roman **Amphitheatrum Flavianum**, dubbed the **Colosseum** in the Middle Ages. Begun as a two-storey building by **Vespasian** in 70 AD, it was given an imposing third level by his son **Titus**. The sanded floor that was a standard feature of amphitheatres (*arena* being the Latin word for sand) was constructed from thick timber planking, beneath which lay cages to hold wild beasts and subterranean chambers for the use of the gladiators and their managers and trainers. **Gladiators** were often captive barbarians or criminals, and this demonstration of their prowess with the traditional weapons of a sword and shield or a trident and a net represented their only chance to escape the death penalty. Although their lives could be spared by thumbs-up signals or the waving of scarves by members of the crowd, the victor in armed combat was frequently expected to finish off his opponent. Gladiators also faced **wild beasts**, which as an alternative diversion were often pitted against each other. Part of the entertainment value of a visit to the amphitheatre, in Europe at least, lay in the opportunity it offered to see exotic species such

are brought to Rome, where they will later be depicted in the relief carvings that decorate the **triumphal arch** dedicated to Titus on the Via Sacra.

Legions in **Germany** contest Galba's nomination as emperor, supporting their commander Aulus Vitellius

as lions, elephants, rhinoceroses and crocodiles. Under the emperors of the late 1st century and 2nd century AD 'the games', as these spectacles were called, became increasingly ambitious and extravagant: the celebrations of Trajan's triumph over the Dacians, for example, featured as many as five thousand pairs of gladiators. Twenty or so years earlier, some **nine thousand animals** reputedly perished to celebrate Titus's completion of the Colosseum. It is hardly any wonder that intensive hunting to supply the amphitheatres of the empire is blamed for the **extinction** of numerous animal species throughout Roman North Africa during the imperial epoch.

View of the remains of the Colosseum in Rome

instead. In Rome, Galba is murdered by **Marcus Salvius Otho**, an ambitious associate of Nero. The Senate recognizes Otho as emperor.

Vitellius's troops arrive in Italy and defeat Otho's army near **Cremona**. Otho commits suicide and the Senate acknowledges **Vitellius** as emperor. However, **Vespasian** is proclaimed emperor by legions in Syria and the province of Pannonia (modern Hungary). He returns to Italy and defeats Vitellius's forces at Cremona. Vitellius is murdered in Rome, and the Senate recognizes Vespasian as emperor.

70 AD Vespasian orders work to begin on a new amphitheatre in Rome. Called the Amphitheatrum Flavianum, after Vespasian's family, it will become better known as the **Colosseum** or Coliseum, one of the largest such structures in the Roman world.

> ❝ I three times gave a show of gladiators in my own name, and five times in the name of my sons and grandsons, in which about 10,000 men contended … I gave the people wild beast hunts, of African animals, in the circus and forum and the amphitheatres 26 times, in which some 3500 animals were killed. ❞
>
> Caesar Augustus, from the Ancyra Inscription, trans. Evelyn Shuckburgh

77 AD **Julius Agricola** extends the Roman conquest of Britain into the island's northernmost area, known as **Caledonia**.

79 AD Vespasian's son **Titus** succeeds his father as emperor.

The southern city of **Pompeii**, probably founded in the 6th century BC, and its surrounding area on the Bay of Naples are engulfed by a massive lava flow, following the cataclysmic eruption of Vesuvius. A pyroclastic blast smothers the neighbouring city of **Herculaneum** in a cloud of ash, which then solidifies. The sites will remain hidden for 1700 years.

© SCALA

The cobblestoned Via Stabiana once connected the Vesuvius Gate to the Stabiae Gate – the highest and lowest parts of Pompeii

> **❝** I cannot describe its appearance and shape better than as resembling an umbrella pine tree, with a very tall trunk rising high into the sky and then spreading out into branches ... At one moment it was white, at another dark and dirty, as if it carried up a load of earth and cinders. **❞**
>
> Pliny the Younger describing the eruption of Vesuvius (in which his uncle Pliny the Elder died) to Tacitus, trans. John Ward-Perkins and Amanda Claridge

81 AD Titus dies and his brother Domitianus (**Domitian**) succeeds as emperor. Domitian's arrogance and ruthlessness antagonize influential Romans, as do his attempts to curry favour with the legions and the Roman mob. Increasingly paranoid about those closest to him, he orders a series of high-profile executions.

96 AD Domitian is murdered in a palace coup. The Senate decrees that his name be removed from public inscriptions and declares all his imperial decrees null and void. **Marcus Cocceius Nerva**, an elderly senator chosen by the conspirators, is proclaimed emperor.

98 AD Nerva dies and his adopted son Marcus Ulpius Trajanus (**Trajan**) becomes emperor. A Spaniard from the southern city of Italica, he is distinguished by his benign and generous rule, which lasts nearly twenty years. His letters to the Roman author and civil servant **Pliny the Younger** on the subject of the treatment of **Christians** demonstrate his characteristically humane approach towards the new religion.

101 AD Trajan begins a series of successful campaigns against the **Dacians**, inhabitants of the area nowadays called Romania. A superb **triumphal column** commemorating these wars will form the centrepiece of the new **Forum** he plans in Rome.

Ravennese mosaic depicting the judgement of Caiaphas, an episode from the life of Christ

105 AD Publius Cornelius **Tacitus** begins work on his *Histories*, an account of events and personalities during the reigns of the early emperors.

Roman historians

The two major historians of Rome from its foundation to the reign of Domitian are **Livy** (Titus Livius) and **Tacitus**. Both significantly influenced the writing of history throughout Europe after the Renaissance when their work was rediscovered and properly evaluated for the first time.

Livy, born in 59 BC in the northern city of Patavium (Padua), was a friend of **Augustus Caesar** and tutor to the young **Claudius**, though he did not necessarily share the emperor's political beliefs. His great work *Ab urbe condita libri* (*Books from the city's foundation*) was intended to trace the history of Rome from Romulus and Remus as far as the year 9 BC. Most of its 142 books have been lost, but the 35 that survive (describing the earliest period and the **Punic Wars** and relying mostly on existing literary sources) are impressive for the clarity of their narrative and their vivid dramatic pace.

Tacitus, born a century after Livy, was a patrician from Cisalpine Gaul who spent most of his life in Rome. His first known work was a life of his father-in-law **Julius Agricola**, governor of Britain, in which he brilliantly combined biography with a fierce attack on the reigning emperor, **Domitian**. *Germania*, his account of the German tribes, provided another excuse for a critique of contemporary Rome, drawing unfavourable comparisons between the decadence of civilized society on the one hand and the bravery and noble simplicity of the barbarians on the other. His two greatest works, the *Histories* and the *Annals*, probably written between 105 AD and his death in 108, embrace the reigns of the Roman emperors from Augustus to Otho. In some of the finest Latin prose ever written, they present a deftly structured historical portrait of an era and its characters. Tacitus was not, and did not pretend to be, an impartial historian and modern scholars have been at pains to qualify a number of his judgements, whether favourable or critical. Our understanding of imperial Rome is nevertheless indelibly shaped by his remarkable narratives.

117 AD Trajan dies in Cilicia (now southeastern Turkey) while campaigning against the Parthians. He is succeeded by his ward and second cousin Publius Aelius Hadrianus (**Hadrian**), who continues his wise rule. As the perfect setting for his studies of Greek literature, art and philosophy, Hadrian builds himself a splendid villa at Tibur (**Tivoli**) north of Rome. His standardization of the 'edict', a proclamation setting out the legal programme to be followed by Roman magistrates and governors, makes an important contribution to what is now known as **Roman law**. He also extends **citizenship rights** both in Italy and throughout the empire.

132 AD Appalled by Hadrian's decision to make **Jerusalem** a Roman colony known as Aelia Capitolina and to build a shrine to **Jupiter** on the site of the former Temple, the **Jews of Judaea** rise in revolt. The rebellion is brutally suppressed, resulting in widespread depopulation of settled areas. Jews are officially forbidden to enter Jerusalem except once a year.

138 AD Hadrian dies and is buried in the colossal mausoleum beside the River Tiber in Rome known since the Middle Ages as **Castel Sant'Angelo**. His successor **Antoninus Pius** enjoys a long and peaceful reign, during which the empire prospers and expands. In *The Decline and Fall of the Roman Empire*, the 18th-century British historian **Edward Gibbon** will cite Antoninus's rule as the era in which the empire was at its most flourishing and peaceable.

161 AD Marcus Aurelius succeeds his uncle Antoninus as emperor. In some ways a model ruler, he combines an interest in philosophy, and particularly **Stoicism** (composing a series of *Meditations* in Greek), with a happy family life and a determination to hold the empire together. For the first time, Italy yields **economic supremacy** to prosperous imperial provinces such as **Egypt**, **Africa** and **Syria**.

> **❝** Does paltry fame disturb you? Look how swift is the forgetting of all things in the chaos of infinite time before and after, how empty is noisy applause, how liable to change and uncritical are those who seem to speak well of us, how narrow the boundaries within which fame is confined. The whole earth is but a point in the universe, and how small a part of the earth is the corner in which you live. And how many are those who there will praise you, and what sort of men are they? **❞**
>
> Marcus Aurelius, *The Meditations*, trans. G.M.A. Grube

171 AD Migrant **Germanic tribes** from Bohemia cross the Julian Alps (now the **Dolomites**) to sack the cities of Opitergium (**Oderzo**) and **Aquileia**, both of which are later rebuilt. Despite Marcus's attempts to police the imperial frontiers, Italy is threatened for the first time in centuries with a **barbarian invasion**.

180 AD Marcus dies at Vindobona (**Vienna**), while campaigning against the Germanic tribes, leaving the empire to his son **Commodus**, who is less interested in military and political leadership than in gladiatorial shows and the amusements of the arena.

192 AD Having betrayed the traditions of benign government established by his father, the profligate and corrupt Commodus is strangled on the orders of his mistress Marcia and the prefect of the Praetorian Guard, Laetus. **Publius Helvius Pertinax** succeeds him as emperor, but is soon murdered by soldiers resentful of his apparent meanness.

193 AD **Septimius Severus**, an aristocrat and army officer of Carthaginian descent, is made emperor by the legions. Purges of his political opponents and vigorous campaigns to defend weak frontiers ensure a period of stability throughout the empire, but quarrels between Severus's sons force him to keep them occupied with continual military expeditions.

211 AD During a successful campaign against native tribes in northern **Britain**, Severus dies at Eboracum (**York**). For the next 24 years the empire will be ruled by members of his family, with the army's support. Severus's son and successor **Caracalla** extends **Roman citizenship** to all free (non-slave) inhabitants of the empire.

217 AD Caracalla is murdered by army officers as he plans a campaign against the Parthians. The African officer Macrinus briefly becomes emperor but is killed by troops angry at a threatened pay cut. They proclaim Caracalla's nephew Elagabalus (or **Heliogabalus**) his successor.

222 AD Elagabalus is murdered by the Praetorian Guard, so bringing to an end a reign of notorious indulgence and excess. His adopted son **Alexander Severus** is declared emperor by a regency committee dominated by the boy's mother, Julia Mamaea.

235 AD Alexander Severus, last of the Severan dynasty, is murdered in a military coup at Moguntia (**Mainz**) in Germany. The fifty-year period of lawlessness and decline that ensues is presided over by no fewer than 22 successive emperors, most of whom are murdered by discontented troops.

Julius Verus Maximinus, a Thracian peasant who had risen through the ranks of the army, is named emperor by the mutinous legions in Germany. The Senate refuses to acknowledge him, substituting the senators **Pupienus Maximus** and **Calvinus Balbinus**. African legions declare the popular proconsul **Marcus Gordianus** and his son, also named **Gordianus**, emperors, but both are put to death by the prefect of the northwest African province of Mauretania (modern **Morocco** and **Algeria**).

Hadrian's Wall

HIBERNIA

BRITANNIA

ATLANTIC OCEAN

GERMANIA

GALLIA

RAETIA

NORICUM

Vienna

Mediolanum

PANNONIA

Po

ILLYRIC

HISPANIA

Massilia

ITALIA

CORSICA

Roma

Cannae

SARDINIA

Neapolis

Tarentum

MAURETANIA

Carthago

Syracuse

Zama

NUMIDIA

MEDITERRANEA

N

AFRICA

| 0 | 400 kms |

THE ROMAN EMPIRE c.200AD

SARMATIA

DACIA

BLACK SEA

UM MOESIA

THRACE   Ephesus

MACEDONIA   BITHYNIA   PONTUS   ARMENIA

ASIA   GALATIA

Actium   CAPPADOCIA

ACHAEA   Ephesus   CILICIA   MESOPOTAMIA

LYCIA   PAMPHYLIA   Antioch   Euphrates

N SEA   CRETE   CYPRUS   SYRIA

JUDEA   ARABIA

CYRENAICA   Alexandria

AEGYPTUS

> ❝ Twenty-two acknowledged concubines, and a library of sixty-two thousand volumes, attested the variety of his inclinations, and from the production which he left behind him, it appears that the former as well as the latter were designed for use rather than ostentation. ❞
>
> Edward Gibbon, *The Decline and Fall of the Roman Empire*,
> Chapter VII, on the emperor Gordian II

238 AD Maximinus, Pupienus and Balbinus are all murdered. Marcus Gordianus's grandson becomes emperor as Gordianus III (**Gordian III**).

244 AD Julius Philippus Verus, known as **Philip the Arab**, prefect of Syria, murders Gordian and assumes his title.

249 AD **Quintus Traianus Decius**, an officer supposedly loyal to Philip, raises an army in revolt against him. Philip is killed in battle near Verona. Decius becomes emperor and, during his brief reign, he orchestrates a widespread **persecution of Christians**.

251 AD Decius is murdered in the frontier province of **Dacia**. **Trebonianus Gallus**, who has connived at the assassination, proclaims himself emperor, but is in turn killed by his soldiers.

253 AD Licinius Valerianus (**Valerian**), legion commander in Germany, becomes emperor. After a series of campaigns designed to halt barbarian incursions across the Rhine and the Alps, he leaves for Syria, where the Persian king **Shapur** has seized **Antioch**. Valerian recaptures Antioch but is subsequently lured to a meeting with the king, who takes him prisoner in perpetuity. In a stone carving at Naksh-i-Rustam (in modern Iran), Shapur is shown stepping on the crouching Valerian in order to mount his horse.

Martyrs in the arena

During periods of Roman persecution in the 3rd and 4th centuries, **Christians** continued to practise their religion in secret, and if discovered would often choose to embrace martyrdom rather than acknowledge the emperor as a god, as was required by law. Martyrs routinely became saints, but over the centuries a number of fictional examples of heroic deaths for the faith crept into the church calendar. The cult of **St Philomena**, for instance, is probably a pious 19th-century fraud founded on a quite unconnected set of bones found in a Roman catacomb, while the impressive 11,000 virgin companions of **St Ursula**, supposedly martyred by the Huns, are as fictitious as the saint herself.

Better documented in early Latin sources is the story of **Perpetua** and **Felicitas**, a housewife and her slave who formed part of a small Christian community in 3rd-century **Carthage**. Arrested with their companions, they were sentenced to death by wild beasts in the arena. Their menfolk were to be torn apart by leopards, while the two women were to be gored by a mad cow. After taking their last communion in prison, they were led into the amphitheatre. Though butted by the cow, Perpetua fell into a religious trance and appeared to feel no pain. She also managed to revive Felicitas – to the fury of the crowd, who demanded their instant execution. With their friend **Saturninus**, who had been half-eaten by a leopard, they were dragged off to be hacked to death. Perpetua, it was said, guided the executioner's sword to her throat. Such extraordinary strength of will was not uncommon among the early Christians, and the story of Perpetua and her companions swiftly became an inspiration for believers during a critical period in the spread of the new faith.

259 AD Valerian's son **Gallienus**, who hitherto has reigned as his fellow emperor, now rules alone. The empire is menaced for the first time by the Germanic tribe known as the **Goths**, originally from the Baltic but by this time long settled around the **Black Sea**.

268 AD Gallienus is murdered by his soldiers in **Milan**. Marcus Aurelius Claudius becomes emperor. Defeating the Goths, he assigns them lands in **Pannonia** and **Dacia** on which to settle.

270 AD Claudius (**Claudius II Gothicus**) dies of the plague during an epidemic and is succeeded by Lucius Domitius Aurelianus (**Aurelian**), who rebuilds the walls of Rome in their entirety in order to repel barbarian invaders.

271 AD Zenobia, widowed queen of the Syrian desert kingdom of **Palmyra**, proclaims her realm's independence from Rome. Aurelian takes her prisoner and destroys the city of Palmyra, before removing her to Rome, where she is paraded in a triumphal procession.

275 AD Aurelian is murdered by some of his officers. The Senate names **Claudius Tacitus** emperor, but he too is killed by his soldiers.

276 AD Aurelian's general **Aurelius Probus** is proclaimed emperor by the legions. He spends the next few years pacifying the barbarians on the imperial frontiers and strengthening the empire's defences.

281 AD Probus is murdered by troops angered at being used for peacetime duties. **Marcus Aurelius Carus**, another of Aurelian's generals, becomes emperor. His sudden death is followed by the murder of his son Numerianus, whose brother Carinus is then killed by his own soldiers during a battle against barbarians in **Pannonia**.

284 AD The cycle of army officers becoming emperors only to be assassinated by their discontented troops is broken at last when Aurelius Valerius Diocletianus (**Diocletian**), a general from **Illyria** (present-day **Slovenia**, **Croatia** and **Bosnia**), is named emperor by the army. He divides the empire into eight **tetrarchies** (meaning 'rule over a fourth part'), four apiece in the west and east, and splits the provinces into smaller administrative units. **Frontier forts** are reinforced and the army's strength is doubled using money raised by a complete reform of the **taxation system**. Diocletian also seeks to revive traditional Roman legal and religious values, and to this end instigates widespread **persecution of Christians** once more throughout the empire.

> ❝ Nothing was more astonishing than the fearless courage of these saints, the unflinching endurance of these young men and women. A youth of 19 spread his arms wide in the form of a cross and calmly murmured prayers to God, not budging an inch as he felt the breath of growling, death-delivering panthers and bears on his face. ❞
>
> Eusebius, *History of the Church*, on Christian martyrs under Diocletian

285 AD Diocletian names his fellow Illyrian Valerius Maximianus (**Maximian**) as co-emperor, with responsibility for the **western empire**. Maximian chooses the Italian city of Mediolanum (**Milan**) as his capital. In the east, Diocletian rules from **Nicomedia** in Asia Minor.

305 AD Diocletian abdicates and retires to his birthplace, the Dalmatian town of Salonae. Outside the walls he builds an immense palace, which later forms the nucleus of the city of **Split**. The empire is now ruled by the four **tetrarchs**.

310 AD A prolonged struggle for overall control of the empire sees **Constantine**, son of tetrarch Constantius Chlorus, emerge as the most powerful contender. Invading Italy, he defeats the usurper Maxentius at the battle of **Pons Mulvius** (the Milvian Bridge), and the Senate proclaims him **senior emperor**. Supposedly as a result of seeing a vision of the cross in the sky before this battle, Constantine becomes a **Christian**. He not only ends the persecution begun by Diocletian, but also promotes Christianity throughout the empire and encourages unity among its quarrelling sects.

> **❝** Nobody whatsoever must be denied the right to follow or choose the Christian form of worship. All must be permitted to dedicate themselves to whatever kind of ritual is adapted to their needs. **❞**
>
> Edict of the Emperor Constantine, 313 AD

314 AD At a council of Christian bishops in Alesia (**Arles**) in Gaul, **Rome** is recognized as the centre of Christian authority, and its bishop acknowledged as **primate** (spiritual leader): an important step towards the creation of the **papacy**.

324 AD Constantine reunites the Roman empire under his sole rule and founds an eastern imperial capital in the strategic city of **Byzantium**, commanding the entrance to the Black Sea. The city is renamed **Constantinople** and quickly becomes a centre of government and religious authority, adorned with splendid churches and public buildings.

325 AD Constantine summons an **ecumenical** (universal) **council** of the Christian church at the city of **Nicaea** in Asia Minor. The purpose of the meeting is to settle once and for all the controversies over heretical beliefs, especially the teachings of the Alexandrian priest Arius, who has denied that Christ was of one substance with God. The council pronounces against the **Arian heresy**.

337 AD Constantine dies. Having murdered their numerous relatives in order to safeguard their succession, his sons **Constantine II**, **Constantius** and **Constans** divide the empire among them.

340 AD **Constantine II** invades Italy and is killed at Aquileia during a battle with Constans's troops.

350 AD Constans is killed in a military coup led by the general **Magnentius**.

354 AD After defeating Magnentius in battle, **Constantius** becomes sole ruler of the empire, appointing his nephew **Julian** as ruler of the **western provinces**.

361 AD Proclaiming himself emperor, Julian marches against Constantius, who dies before civil war can begin. Julian seeks to restore **paganism**, forbidding Christians to teach rhetoric, while at the same time rebuilding temples and encouraging the renewal of ancient ceremonial at sacred sites.

362 AD Julian is killed in a battle against the Persians. Christianity now becomes the empire's dominant religion.

363 AD **Jovianus**, a soldier and a captain of the imperial bodyguard, is elected emperor by the troops.

364 AD Jovianus dies, having succeeded in negotiating peace with the Persians during his short reign. He is succeeded by Flavius Valentinianus (**Valentinian I**), another respected soldier chosen by the legions.

365 AD On all its frontiers the empire faces serious threats from **barbarian invasion**. Particular dangers are posed by the migration of tribes in **eastern and northern Europe**, in search of fresh pastureland for their herds and attracted by the wealth of settled communities under Roman rule.

374 AD Ambrosius (**Ambrose**), a Roman patrician and senior civil servant, becomes **bishop of Milan**. His zealous promotion of Christianity against the claims of paganism and Judaism leads to conflict with the emperor.

375 AD Valentinian I dies and is succeeded by his son Gratianus (**Gratian**), who appoints his half-brother **Valentinian II** as western emperor.

The barbarians

The term 'barbarian' originally meant 'someone who speaks an incomprehensible language', the sound of the Greek word *barbaros* being intended to imitate the babbling of an unfamiliar tongue. The Romans applied it in a fairly loose fashion to all tribes and nations who posed a threat to the empire on its various frontiers. At different times these included the **Germanic peoples** beyond the Rhine whom Rome had failed to subdue during Emperor Augustus's attempts at imperial expansion, the **Celtic tribes** of Britain north of Hadrian's Wall, and the **Goths**, who lived on the shores of the Black Sea. Some of these ethnic groups, such as the Goths and **Longobards**, had developed identifiable **cultures**, producing metalwork and pottery and evolving traditions of oral poetry. Others, such as the **Huns**, were **nomads**, travelling light and at speed, living in tents and relying on their horses for meat and even milk.

Although these peoples accepted **romanization** as a concomitant of **trade contacts**, their leaders – kings, priests and warriors – were frequently hostile to Roman influence, fearing the threat it posed to their basic freedoms and established traditions. As the combined effects of climate change, population growth and the exhaustion of natural resources forced these peoples into large-scale **migration**, so the pressure on **imperial frontiers** grew more intense. Under the Antonine emperors of the 2nd century AD Rome had over-extended its empire, and the army was unable to police the outlying provinces effectively against repeated surges of barbarian attack. Constant warfare devastated agriculture and the urban economy in these areas, from **Britain** to **Africa**, **Syria** and the **Balkans**, and during the late 4th century the empire began a swift process of implosion, culminating in the arrival of the Goths in Italy and the sack of Rome itself.

378 AD After their early success in holding back the advance of the **Goths** (a Germanic tribe migrating from northern

Europe) the Roman army, led by Valentinian's son Valens, is overwhelmed in a major battle at Adrianople (**Edirne** in modern Turkey).

379 AD Theodosius, son of Valentinian's chief general, becomes emperor. After pacifying the Goths by allowing them to settle on territory along the **Danube**, he concentrates on bringing much-needed stability to the empire and creating an established catholic (meaning 'universal' in Latin) church under the leadership of **Pope Damasus**.

390 AD Ambrose excommunicates Theodosius for ordering a massacre at Thessalonica to avenge the death of one of his generals. Theodosius is soon reconciled to the church and, probably under Ambrose's influence, issues an edict in Milan banning **pagan worship** throughout the empire.

395 AD The death of Theodosius marks the beginning of a permanent split between the eastern and western parts of the empire, now awarded to his two sons **Arcadius** and **Honorius**. Neither is fit to rule, and the imperial frontier territories gradually fall into the hands of **barbarian leaders**.

406 AD Alaric, king of the **Visigoths**, invades Italy. Resistance is weak and his barbarian army advances towards Rome.

408 AD Theodosius II, son of Arcadius, becomes emperor of the east while still a boy.

410 AD After a succession of sieges, **Rome** falls to Alaric, whose warriors sack the city. To later ages, Rome's downfall becomes symbolic of wider imperial collapse. In 17th-century Europe the adjective '**Gothic**' will be applied to the architecture of the Middle Ages in order to imply its perceived outlandish barbarity, in contrast to the serene proportions of buildings of the classical era.

> Terrifying news comes to us from the west. Rome has been taken by assault. Men are ransoming their lives with gold. Though despoiled, they are still hounded, so that after their goods they may pay with their very lives. My voice is still, and sobs disturb my every utterance. The city has been conquered which had once subjugated the entire world.
>
> St Jerome. As quoted in *The Fall of the Roman Empire*, Michael Grant

425 AD **Valentinian III**, Honorius's nephew, becomes emperor of the west.

429 AD After sweeping through Spain, the Germanic tribe known as the **Vandals** lays siege to cities in **northern Africa**. Among them is the town of **Hippo** where Augustinus, known to history as **St Augustine**, is bishop.

430 AD Augustine dies during the siege of Hippo. The **Vandals** take control of the **African provinces** of the Roman empire.

450 AD The **Huns**, a Mongolian nomadic tribe who originally pushed the Goths out of their lands along the Danube, invade Italy under their chief **Attila**.

> Toys and trifles, utter vanities had been my mistresses, and now they were holding me back, pulling me by the garment of my flesh and softly murmuring in my ear: 'Are you getting rid of us?' and 'From this moment shall we never be with you for all eternity?' and 'From this moment will you never for all eternity be allowed to do this or to do that?' My God, what was it that they suggested in those words 'this' or 'that' which I have just written?
>
> St Augustine, *Confessions*, trans. Rex Warner

St Augustine

Charismatic and controversial during his lifetime, Augustine was both the last great **philosopher** of classical antiquity and the first major Christian **theologian** after St Paul. Born to a pagan official, Patricius, and his Christian wife Monica at Thagaste (in modern Algeria) in 354 AD, he was educated locally before travelling to **Carthage**. Here he cultivated an interest in philosophy and lived with a mistress, by whom he had a son, although he never married. Moving to Italy he settled in **Milan**, where he taught rhetoric and began investigating various philosophical systems and religious persuasions, before coming under the influence of the city's bishop **Ambrose** (later also canonized), who baptized him into the Christian faith in 386.

Returning to Africa, Augustine became bishop of the African city of **Hippo** and in 395 embarked on his famous *Confessions*, a spiritual autobiography distinguished by the beauty of its Latin style and the intensity of the experiences it records. His other most important work – among nearly a hundred ascribed to him – is *The City of God*, begun in 413, in which he champions Christianity against paganism, neo-Platonism and a variety of heresies. His focus on the **doctrine of grace** is balanced by a preoccupation with **sin and damnation**, prompted in part by his repentance for his early life amid the worldly temptations of Carthage. His last years were reputedly spent as an exemplary spiritual leader of his community, caring for the poor, preaching, teaching and acting as a magistrate. Canonized soon after his death, he was particularly venerated in Italy, the country in which he had spent his formative years, and he was a favourite subject of the painters and sculptors of the Middle Ages and Renaissance.

451 AD After sacking cities in **northeastern Italy**, the Huns fail to achieve any further significant conquests. Already lacking an organizational structure, their kingdom falls apart on Attila's sudden death, supposedly caused by poison administered by his wife Ildico on their wedding night.

455 AD Rome is plundered and sacked once more, this time by the **Vandals**, whose name becomes synonymous with barbarism and desecration.

476 AD The western emperor, **Romulus Augustulus**, is deposed by **Odoacer**, son of one of Attila's Germanic followers, who becomes ruler of Italy. There will be no further western emperors, though the emperors of the east (**Byzantium**) will continue to lay claim to Italy.

3
The early Middle Ages
493–1177

As the western European provinces of the Roman empire fell under the sway of the barbarians, Italy at the close of the 5th century became a coveted prize for **foreign invaders**. Some historians have chosen to see in this period the beginning of a perceived 'victim status' that Italians have tended to invoke ever since in response to any international criticism of their social mores or political culture. The 17th-century poet Vincenzo Filicaja depicted Italy as the historical casualty of her 'fatal gift of beauty', and this enduring (if romantic) notion of a country raped and exploited by foreigners for its wealth and artistic patrimony was later to provide ammunition for the ideologues of the 19th-century Risorgimento, in their quest for national unity.

In fact, while **Gothic rulers** filled the power vacuum left by the final collapse of the western empire's by now flimsy administrative infrastructure, Italy's native-born patrician families continued to hold and administer their landed estates. The survival of a written code of laws and some sort of literary culture were meanwhile guaranteed by the ascendancy of the **Christian Church**, founded on the ruins of paganism – in many cases quite literally: numerous former temples were reused as church buildings, including Rome's **Santa Maria sopra Minerva** and the **temple of Artemis** at Syracuse, which became the city's cathedral. Local **bishops** meanwhile assumed the charismatic leadership formerly expected of generals and civil governors. Now invested with more than merely symbolic importance, the **pope** became a sovereign ruler entitled to intervene and take sides in disputes between temporal powers. Although papal authority was not to reach its apogee until the close of the Middle Ages, by the end of the 6th century the pope was already viewed as a sort of spiritual successor to the **Roman emperors**, a supreme decision-maker and authority in a divided and often lawless Italy.

Rome itself, despite its acknowledged status as the papal capital, fell into a swift decline during the early Middle Ages. Many splendid buildings from the republican and imperial eras were demolished or allowed to deteriorate. Some, such as the 3rd-century **Septizonium**, a grand theatrical façade marking the end of the Appian Way, vanished entirely; others, such as the **Forum** which was henceforth used for grazing cattle, languished under invading vegetation. By contrast, other Italian cities gained significantly in importance. **Verona** became a major stronghold of **Theoderic**, king of the **Ostrogoths**, who ruled most of Italy from his splendid palace in **Ravenna**. When the emperor **Justinian** sought to claw Italy back into the eastern empire during the mid-6th century, Ravenna became a key **Byzantine** administrative centre. The Germanic **Longobards**, who invaded northern Italy in 568, absorbed the more sophisticated social structures of late Roman Italy, making **Milan**, **Pavia**, **Brescia** and towns in Friuli such as **Udine** and **Cividale** the focus of their court and ecclesiastical life.

The balance of power between Longobards and Byzantines was finally overturned in the 8th century by **invasions** from both north and south. In 753, disturbed by Longobard encroachments on his sphere of influence, **Pope Stephen II** invited the Frankish Carolingian king **Pepin** to enter Italy at the head of an army. When the Longobard kingdom was later absorbed by Pepin's son **Charlemagne** in 774, his reward (in return for giving large areas of Italy to the pope) was coronation in 800 as the first Holy Roman Emperor. This was to have incalculable political consequences for centuries to come. The creation of a secular overlord in Italy with as much power, in real terms, as the pope himself led to a prolonged battle for supremacy, over several centuries, between successive holders of each office. In 827, meanwhile, the Byzantine domains in the Italian south were invaded by **Muslim** armies from North Africa. While the Islamic influence on Sicily is well documented, the Arabic-speaking communities that became established in **Apulia**, **Calabria** and **Basilicata** – which left fewer written records and are consequently less well known – constituted an equally powerful element in the cultural make-up of these regions. Raids by these **'Saracens'** penetrated as far as **Rome** and the coast of **Tuscany**, and traces of Islamic settlements can be found as far north as Italy's Alpine border with **France**.

The survival of Italy's eclectic mixture of peoples and powers during the early Middle Ages was dependent on properly maintained trading networks. During the 9th and 10th centuries, maritime cities such as **Bari** and **Amalfi** gained in importance and prosperity by acting as business links between **Christian Europe**, the **Muslim east** and **Byzantium**. Several of these commercial centres, such as **Pisa** at the mouth of the River Arno in Tuscany, were **independent republics**, and by the close of the 11th century two in particular – **Venice** and **Genoa** – dominated trade in the Mediterranean. Governed by republican oligarchies, both these cities cultivated a vigorous political independence, based on a pragmatic approach to advantageous alliances, and on the residual loyalty of their citizens to the **state** as an abstract embodiment of freedom, legality and civil order.

Throughout medieval Italy, the necessity for individual cities to attend to their own government and security in the face of threats from invaders, or from overweening princes, prelates and aristocrats, became of paramount concern. Much of the enduring Italian culture of loyalty to a home town and its essential identity – whether expressed through dialect, food, or football – has its roots in the historically defensive autonomy of these *communi*, which were dependent on **civic solidarity** to ensure their survival in a war-torn and unsettled era.

By the end of the 12th century, the *communi* in northern and central Italy had become important centres of wealth and political power, with some of them, most notably **Florence**, extending their influence over a wide surrounding territory known as a *contado*. This power and prosperity made for an increasingly uneasy relationship with the **Holy Roman Emperors** on the one hand and the **popes** on the other. In the ongoing power struggle between these sovereign authorities, temporal and spiritual, the *communi* had thrown in their lot with one side or the other at various times. Though the empire had passed by inheritance through several dynasties of purely **German** origins, it was among **Italians** that this major papal-imperial conflict was fought out. The cities of northern and central Italy still bear the signs of it in their extensive **medieval fortifications**.

The Italian church in the Middle Ages had no intention of acting merely as the spiritual arm of civil society. As elsewhere in Europe, **religious foundations** such as monasteries, convents and charitable confraternities formed a significant element in community life, whether urban or rural. The popes devoted increasing amounts of energy and resources to extending their influence over European politics, preaching crusades against Islam, settling questions of dynastic succession, instigating armed campaigns against **heretics** and using spiritual blackmail to see off challenges to their overall supremacy within the Christian world.

Italy during the 12th century revealed a gradually fragmenting political landscape, in which the continuing strife between popes and emperors was further complicated by two factors: the refusal of the *communi* to serve either side unconditionally, and the development within the cities themselves of strong factional interests among local clans and dynasties. Moreover, the old feudal aristocracy was now challenged by the rise of wealthy **merchant families**, who owed their prosperity to Italy's central position on the maritime **trade routes** across the Mediterranean from Spain, Africa and the Middle East.

This commercial success had a major impact on cities such as **Venice**, **Genoa**, **Pisa** and **Lucca**, where huge sums were spent on the building and embellishment of **churches** and **public buildings**. Local schools of **sculpture** and **painting** began to evolve in response to the desire of prominent citizens to enhance their status through patronage and special commissions – indicators of the growth of a sophisticated **urban culture**, in which learning and artistic achievement were seen as essential adjuncts to a rounded life. As in ancient Greece, where government and the arts evolved simultaneously with continuing warfare among cities, a settled, socially confident environment developed within Italian *communi* despite ongoing conflict, whether external or internal. Within this environment lay the roots of the Italian civilization of the later Middle Ages and the Renaissance.

493 Following the collapse of the Roman empire, power in Italy now lies in the hands of the remnants of the **Roman army** and the victorious **barbarian kings**. **Theoderic**, king of the Ostrogoths, defeats **Odoacer**, commander-in-chief of the army. He appears ready to make a power-sharing arrangement with Odoacer, but then has him murdered at a banquet. Theoderic now becomes ruler of all Italy. The structures of Roman imperial rule are preserved and upheld, and a period of unaccustomed peace and civic order begins. The Gothic capital is established at **Ravenna**, scene of Theoderic's victory, where he builds himself a marble palace.

Pope Gelasius I refuses to accept the authority of the Byzantine emperor **Anastasius**, who seeks to promote the **Monophysite** doctrine. This maintains that Jesus, despite

The power of the popes

The word 'pope' derives from the Latin *papa*, father, and Holy Father is a name generally given by Catholics to every holder of the office. Another papal title is **Bishop of Rome**, and it was in this capacity that two of the early popes, **Victor I** (189–98) and **Leo I** (440–61), laid claims to exercising authority over the universal church. Victor established the dating of **Easter** according to the full moon following the vernal equinox, and was the first pope to use **excommunication** to enforce his rule over Christian bishops. It was Leo, however, who insisted on the primacy of the **Western Church** over its Eastern (Orthodox) counterpart, and who endowed the office of pope with true prestige at a time when secular law and order in Italy were breaking down. His immediate successors, **Gelasius I** (492–96) in particular, used his example to promote the pope's role as a **spiritual overlord** of Christian sovereigns, serving as a diplomatic influence and power broker.

Both within Italy and throughout western Europe, the pope had come to be regarded as the ultimate **arbitrator** in all important religious or political issues by the end of the first millennium AD. He was dignified by titles such as Supreme Pontiff of the Universal Church, Patriarch of the West, Successor to the Chief of the Apostles (referring to St Peter, traditionally regarded as first bishop of the Christian Church in Rome) and Primate of Italy. The vexed question of the nature and extent of papal authority, rights and privileges, as symbolized in these titles, was to have an enduring impact on Italian history until the present day.

living on earth as a human being, was always divine, rejecting the traditional belief in 'two natures in one person'. In
defying the emperor, Gelasius becomes the first pope to
assert his independent spiritual authority. For this the
church later makes him a saint.

524 Theoderic condemns to death the statesman and scholar
Anicius Manlius Severinus **Boethius** on trumped-up
charges of conspiracy. Boethius is recognized in his own
time as a man of formidable learning, deeply versed in
Greek philosophy and Christian theological argument.
During his imprisonment he composes *De consolatione
philosophiae* (*Consolation of philosophy*), a dialogue between
the writer and the personification of philosophy. It was to
have a profound influence on European intellectual life
throughout the Middle Ages and into the Renaissance.

526 Theoderic dies in Ravenna of dysentery, apparently
caused by eating undercooked fish. His daughter **Amalasuntha** rules as regent for her son **Athalaric**.

527 In Constantinople, **Justinian** becomes eastern emperor
and establishes a commission to investigate all aspects of
Roman law: the resulting *Digest* or *Pandects* will form a
standard legal code for European jurists.

529 After living for some years as a hermit in a mountain
gorge near Subiaco in eastern Lazio, **Benedict** of Nursia
(Norcia) establishes his monastic order at **Montecassino**.
The **Benedictine Rule**, a daily routine of work and
prayer, quickly becomes the most widely followed in the
monastic communities of medieval Europe.

535 Amalasuntha is poisoned by the usurper Theodahad. Justinian uses the resulting succession crisis as an excuse to
invade Italy, in an attempt to recover it for the empire. He
orders the Byzantine general **Belisarius**, who is engaged in
conducting a successful campaign against the Vandals in
North Africa, to occupy **Sicily**.

Montecassino and the Benedictine rule

The word 'monasticism' derives from the Greek *monos*, meaning single or alone, and the earliest *monachoi* or monks, later to be known as the **Desert Fathers**, lived in scattered **hermitages** in the Egyptian desert. The concept of a shared retreat governed by a clearly formulated code of conduct evolved only some two hundred years later in Italy, under the guidance of **St Benedict**. In 529 (led, according to legend, by the croaking of ravens) he founded a religious community at **Montecassino**, where the daily routine was based on a rule of prayer, study, obedience, poverty and chastity. The **Benedictine** order as we know it today developed as a direct result of the workable nature of this rule, which offered a viable combination of spirituality and practical self-sufficiency. Its demands, meanwhile, were less stringent than those of other religious orders, allowing time for talk and relaxation, as well as contact with the outside world.

In some respects, the Benedictine rule reflected its founder's critical view of the late imperial Roman community (where paganism still lingered on) into which he had been born around 490 in the Umbrian town of Nursia (present-day **Norcia**). The rule renounced this hierarchical, property-owning society in favour of

543 Having completed a successful reconquest of Byzantine domains on behalf of Justinian, Belisarius leaves Italy. Taking advantage of his absence, **Totila**, king of the **Ostrogoths**, rallies the scattered Gothic forces and advances on Rome.

546 Totila captures **Rome** but is driven out by Belisarius, who has been sent back to Italy by Justinian. The city becomes almost deserted, its population reduced to barely five hundred. Belisarius begins reconstructing the walls and encouraging resettlement.

548 Under the rule of a Byzantine viceroy, **Ravenna** is endowed with new churches, such as San Apollinare in

shared possessions and a common programme of work, and in a disintegrating world it offered a promise of stability and continuity. The regular 'offices' of prayer and worship, which divided the day into blocks of a few hours each, were conceived in order to cut across the traditional working hours of the world outside the monastery. Work itself was seen as a form of penance for sin, and a means of fending off the assaults of the devil.

Montecassino became the richest, most important Benedictine abbey in medieval Italy, and in the late 11th century it was splendidly rebuilt and enlarged under the direction of **Abbot Desiderius**. The new abbey was revered for its encouragement of scholarship and its production of fine **manuscripts**, including some of the only surviving copies of works by pagan Roman writers such as **Tacitus**, **Seneca** and **Apuleius**, author of the scurrilously entertaining *The Golden Ass.* Through its contacts with the Greek and Islamic worlds, it also obtained valuable scientific and medical works, which the monks translated into Latin. Sadly the abbey, with its Romanesque fresco cycles and priceless examples of medieval religious art, was completely destroyed by Allied bombardment in 1944.

Classe and San Vitale, to denote its enhanced civic status. The **mosaic decoration** of these buildings, in which Christian themes are combined with the glorification of Justinian and his nobles, places these churches among the most important works of Christian monumental art.

568 The **Longobards**, a Germanic tribe originally settled on the Danube, invade northern Italy.

572 The Longobards capture the key city of **Pavia**, which later becomes their capital. The surrounding region north-east of the Po will become known as Longobardia (and later **Lombardia**).

Mosaic from Ravenna

590 The **Franks**, a tribe of Germanic origin settled in the former Roman province of **Gaul**, invade Italy but are bought off by the Longobards. The two peoples will later compete for mastery over Italian territory. In Rome, Gregory, its prefect of Rome, becomes pope as **Gregory I**. His papacy will earn him canonization as St Gregory the Great and inclusion among the theologians of exceptional distinction and holiness known as Doctors of the Church.

> ❝ Where are those who once delighted in Rome's glory? Were not her generals and princes like bloodthirsty lions overrunning the whole earth in search of plunder? Now she sits deserted and destroyed: like an eagle without her feathers is the city without her inhabitants. ❞
>
> Pope Gregory I, on the city of Rome in the year 600

The Longobards and Italy's German heritage

According to early chronicles, the Longobards came originally from Scandinavia and north Germany. By the 5th century AD they had migrated to the lower Danube basin. Pressure on grazing lands and food supplies from surrounding tribes then drove them westwards, and in the mid-6th century they crossed the eastern Alps into the **Friuli** area. Gradually they established Italian power bases further west, in cities such as **Milan** and **Pavia**, which became the capital of the Longobard kingdom. The surrounding area, along the rivers Ticino and Po, became known as Longobardia, and later **Lombardia**.

Longobard means literally 'long beard', and their popular image was initially that of hairy savages or barbarians. They were reputedly given to monstrous practices such as executing criminals by tying them to wild horses, or to cruel refinements in the manner of the early Longobard king Alboin, who made the skull of his wife's lover into a drinking cup before offering it to her as a gift.

In fact, the Longobards soon became a force for **stability** in a troubled Italy following the collapse of Roman imperial rule. Extending their dominion over central regions such as **Tuscany** and **Umbria** and establishing a powerful southern dukedom around the town of **Benevento**, they embraced **Christianity** and influenced local customs and habits in ways which can still be seen to this day. The traditional arrangement of farms, or *cascini*, in this area, with buildings grouped around a courtyard, derives from the defensive stockades of the original Longobard settlers, and many place names in northern Italy have Longobard roots, as indicated by the endings 'ago', 'igo' and 'engo'. A large number of Longobard words (their language was related to English and German) live on in modern Italian, and one of the foundations of medieval Italian law was the legal code issued by the Longobard king Rothari. All in all, recent archaeology and scholarship tend to offer a positive reappraisal of the Longobard contribution to early medieval Italy.

592 Pope Gregory begins successful peace negotiations with the Longobards, so asserting the papacy's diplomatic independence from the Byzantine imperial government.

598 Agilulf, king of the **Longobards**, consolidates his people's hold on most of northern Italy, forcing the Byzantine governors to acknowledge his conquests in a series of treaties.

> " By these Longobard warlords the churches were despoiled, the throats of their priests were cut, cities were pillaged and the inhabitants, packed close together like grains of corn in an ear of wheat, were destroyed. "
>
> Paul the Deacon, *History of the Longobards*, 787

604 Pope Gregory I dies, having consolidated his temporal authority over Rome's surrounding territory. His other achievements include the promotion of **monasticism**, the encouragement of liturgical music (**Gregorian chant** takes its name from him) and the development of the doctrine of **purgatory**, a halfway house between heaven and hell where certain souls may expiate their sins and earn remission (through the prayers of those on earth), before finally being allowed to enter paradise.

643 Rothari, king of the Longobards, issues the first **Latin legal code** for the Lombard realm.

652 Rothari's successor **Aribert** becomes a Catholic, forsaking the **Arian heresy**. Propagated by Arius of Alexandria during the early 4th century, this heresy asserts the uniqueness of God by declaring Christ to be a purely human being.

653 Pope Martin I is arrested by the Byzantine governor of southern Italy for daring to denounce **Emperor Constans**

II as a heretic. First taken to Constantinople and sentenced to death, he is subsequently reprieved and banished to the Crimean peninsula on the Black Sea, where he perishes of cold and hunger. The Church names him a martyr.

697 The city of **Venice**, originally founded as a group of huts on mud banks in an Adriatic lagoon by refugees from the Huns, becomes powerful enough to elect its first leader. Orso Ipato is given the title of **doge** ('duke', from the Latin *dux*). The powers of the early doges are considerable, but will be gradually reduced during the later Middle Ages.

> " Their strange situation made them prosperous and rich when the rest of Europe was plunged in poverty and darkness. Water was their street, their square, their promenade. The Venetians were forced to become new creatures, and Venice could be compared with nothing except itself. "
>
> Johann Wolfgang von Goethe on the founding of Venice

712 Following a palace revolution, the strong-willed and ambitious **Liutprand** becomes king of the Longobards. In alliance with the Byzantine governor of Ravenna, Liutprand invades the independent Longobard duchy of **Spoleto** and threatens to attack Rome.

739 Liutprand seizes more and more papal territories. **Pope Gregory III** appeals for support to **Charles Martel**, king of the Franks.

742 Pope Zacharias, Gregory III's successor, manages to stem Liutprand's advance, persuading him to restore property and estates seized from the Church.

751 Liutprand's son **Aistulf** captures **Ravenna** from the Byzantines.

756 The Frankish king **Pepin III** thwarts Aistulf in his bid to attack and conquer **Rome**. **Pope Stephen II** now submits to Frankish protection, aligning the papacy with a western ruler for the first time and abandoning its traditional links with the eastern empire.

772 The Longobards, under their king **Desiderius**, make a further assault on papal domains. **Pope Hadrian I** summons help from the Frankish king **Charlemagne**.

774 Charlemagne invades and conquers the Longobard kingdom.

800 In Rome, **Pope Leo III** crowns Charlemagne **Holy Roman Emperor**. Henceforward his imperial successors will become heavily involved in the affairs of Italy.

810 **Venice** asserts its independence by supporting the Byzantine emperor Michael against Frankish claims to overlordship, driving off Charlemagne's son Pepin in his attempt to blockade the city.

827 **Euphemius**, Byzantine governor of **Sicily**, is dismissed from his post after conducting an affair with a nun. Rising in revolt, he summons help from Muslim rulers in North Africa. The **Saracens**, as the Muslim invaders become known in Italy, soon seize the whole island for Islam, though they allow Christian and Jewish communities **freedom of worship** on payment of an annual *jizya* (poll tax).

846 A Saracen force, landing from pirate ships, attacks **Rome** and destroys a section of the city.

902 **Taormina**, the last Byzantine stronghold in Sicily, yields to Saracen attack.

922 **Berengar** of Friuli, the last of Charlemagne's descendants to rule as **Holy Roman Emperor**, is defeated at **Piacenza** by King Rudolf of Burgundy, who challenges his claim to the title.

The Muslims in southern Italy

During the 9th century, Muslim forces began to carry out raids on southern Italy from ports in **Sicily**, **Morocco** and **Tunisia**. In early attacks on **Brindisi** and **Taranto**, they succeed in destroying the former and occupying the latter. Venetian ships attempting to drive off the raiders were pursued almost as far as **Venice** itself, and the emboldened **Saracen** force now prepared for further Italian conquests. **Bari** was seized in 841 and remained under the rule of Moroccan emirs for thirty years. **Rome** was attacked in 846, when the basilicas of St Peter and St Paul (San Paolo fuori le Mura) were looted and desecrated. Further raids on the city prompted **Pope John VIII** (872–82) to make frantic appeals for help to **Frankish** and **Byzantine** rulers, declaring that 'they [the Saracens] cover the earth like locusts and merely to describe their outrages would need more tongues than there are leaves on the trees'. The Byzantine military presence was strengthened throughout southern Italy in response, and by the end of the following century had succeeded in dislodging the Islamic invaders altogether.

Muslim civilization nevertheless left an enduring mark on southern Italy, and can still be traced in certain fundamental features. One is the widespread cultivation of **citrus fruits**, introduced from North Africa and the East by the Saracen conquerors. The most conspicuous is the distinctive layout of the **old quarters** of many towns, with their 'honeycomb' accretions of houses – all with flat roofs, white walls and courtyards – clustered haphazardly along narrow, tunnel-like alleys.

923 Berengar is murdered by one of his followers. The title of Holy Roman Emperor lapses for the following 39 years.

935 The **Saracens** launch assaults on the ports and inland towns in northwestern Italy, among them the maritime republic of **Genoa**.

962 **Otto I**, king of Germany, is crowned **Holy Roman Emperor** in Rome by **Pope John XXII**, to whom he has offered military support. Otto's **despotic rule** antagonizes his Italian subjects and marks the beginning of uneasy relations between the *communi* and the empire which will continue for several centuries.

982 Otto's son **Otto II** is defeated by a Saracen army summoned to help the Byzantines in southern Italy.

1004 Following street fighting in **Pavia** between citizens and German soldiers at the coronation of Emperor Henry II, much of the city is destroyed by fire.

1032 An attempt by a group of Venetian nobles to make the office of **doge** hereditary is defeated. **Venice** is now ruled by elected senators forming a grand council.

1043 Building starts on the **Basilica of St Mark** in Venice, a fusion of Byzantine and Romanesque architectural styles celebrated as one of the grandest Italian buildings of the early Middle Ages.

1046 Matilda, countess of Tuscany, is born at Lucca.

1053 Pope Leo IX leads an army against locally hired **Norman mercenaries** who have seized power in **Apulia**. From the ramparts of the town of Civitate he watches his numerically superior force being routed by the skilful Norman commander **Robert Guiscard**. Taken prisoner, Leo is forced to negotiate with the Normans, eventually confirming their rights of conquest in the south.

1053 Papal support for the Norman conquests in southern Italy leads to a definitive rift with the **Greek Orthodox Church** in Constantinople, whose patriarch **Michael** has disputed Pope Leo's authority in the south. No further attempt at reconciliation between the two churches is made for the following four centuries.

1061 The **Normans**, under Roger de Hauteville, invade **Sicily** at the request of Emir Ibn-al-Timmah, who is feuding with his fellow ruler Ibn-al-Hawas.

1072 Robert Guiscard, now duke of Apulia, completes the Norman conquest of Sicily by taking Palermo from the Saracens.

1073 Hildebrand of Sovana becomes pope as Gregory VII. Robert Guiscard attacks and captures the maritime republic of Amalfi.

1075 At the **Synod of Rome**, Gregory VII issues the *Dictatus Papae* (*Dictates of IIildebrand*), setting out the popes' absolute power over earthly sovereigns and their unchallenged supremacy within the Church hierarchy. This will bring popes into conflict with secular rulers on many occasions during the centuries to come; the issue of **papal privilege** and authority will also become the most contentious element in the dialogue between Catholicism and other Christian communions.

1077 Following the death of her mother, Beatrice of Tuscany, **Matilda** returns to Italy from Lorraine to govern her Italian estates. At her castle of **Canossa**, Pope Gregory VII makes the emperor, Henry IV, wait three days in the snow before granting him an interview. The episode is seen as a major **propaganda coup** for the papacy in its power struggle with the empire.

> ❝ I have received from God the power to bind and set free, both in heaven and on earth. Relying on this power, I forbid Henry, a rebel against the Holy Church, to govern his empire. I absolve all Christians from their oaths to him and command that none shall obey him. ❞
>
> Pope Gregory VII excommunicates the Holy Roman Emperor, Henry IV, in 1077

1094 The Venetians consecrate the completed **Basilica of St Mark**. The saint's body has been smuggled out of **Alexandria** (where he was martyred in the 1st century AD) by enterprising merchants, who wrap it in pieces of pork to deter Muslim customs inspectors. Venice's earlier patron saint, Theodore, is now demoted in favour of the Evangelist,

Matilda of Canossa

The Middle Ages are often thought of as a period when women were held firmly under the thumb of their domineering menfolk. In fact there are numerous outstanding female figures who challenge this stereotypical view, and few better than Matilda of Canossa (1046–1115), known as 'La Gran Contessa', or Great Countess. One of the most powerful personalities of her day, she achieved almost legendary status in her lifetime, and after her death – though she was never canonized – she was viewed by many as an **unofficial saint** of the Catholic Church.

Born in the rich Tuscan city of **Lucca** in 1046, Matilda entered the political arena at an early age, when her father's assassination and the deaths of her brother and sister left her heiress to great estates in Tuscany, Emilia and southern Lombardy. In 1069 she married **Godfrey, duke of Lorraine**, but after spending eight years as a wife and mother in her husband's eastern French duchy, she returned to Italy to rule over her estates as **countess of Tuscany**. Since Godfrey's family had quarrelled with the emperor, she took the side of **Pope Gregory VII** in the ongoing power struggle between papal and imperial interests in Italy. Her castle of **Canossa**, in the Appennines above Parma, was the scene of Emperor Henry IV's symbolic submission of authority to Gregory in 1077. The two rulers soon resumed their fight, however, and Matilda not only gave money and weapons to the papal army, but also sometimes took the highly unorthodox step of joining the campaign herself, dressed in specially designed armour.

A spirited, strong-willed character, Matilda was also admired for her generosity, especially towards the builders of churches. The great Romanesque abbey at **Nonantola**, near Modena, for example, was partly raised under her patronage. In a life which trod a careful tightrope between **Christian piety** and shrewd **political calculation**, she made two major errors. The first was

whose symbolic lion becomes the Venetian badge, carrying a book between its paws bearing an inscription that reads: *Pax tibi Marce Evangelista* (Peace to you, Mark the Evangelist).

her second marriage, at the advanced age of 43, to **Welf of Bavaria**, a youth of 17 whose parting from her six years later occasioned a further quarrel with the emperor. Her second mistake was to make more than one will, with the result that estates that she had initially left to the **pope** turned out, in another document, to have been bequeathed to **Emperor Henry V**, with whom she had made peace before her death at Bondeno, near Ferrara, in 1115. This disputed legacy was to widen the rift between emperors and popes in Italy. The pope nevertheless blessed Matilda as a friend to the Church, and in 1634 her remains were solemnly reburied at St Peter's in Rome. The honour accorded to her in her native Tuscany finds echoes today in the girl's name 'Tessa', a shortened form of her title 'Contessa', which remains popular throughout the region.

Countess Matilda (centre) shown donating all her possessions to the Holy See of Pope Urban II (left)

1095 At Clermont Ferrand, Pope Urban II proclaims the **First Crusade**. This expedition to recover the Christian holy places from the Muslims has an important commercial impact on Italy: **Genoa**, **Amalfi**, **Pisa** and **Venice** will all

Pope Gregory VII

The most dynamic and determined of the 11th-century popes, Gregory VII (r.1083–1085) was admired or feared by European rulers from the English king William the Conqueror to the Holy Roman Emperor Henry IV. A Tuscan educated in Rome, he rose rapidly through the ranks of the Church hierarchy, becoming a kind of *éminence grise* to the popes who preceded him, before himself being raised to the papacy at the age of 53.

A **committed reformer** who had already been involved in revising the regulations governing monastic orders, Gregory now tackled such vexed issues as **clerical marriages**, **simony** (the buying and selling of official positions in the Church) and the development of an adequate sense of status among the various ranks of the clergy by clarifying the duties of **bishops** and **priests**. He also strove to ensure that the appointment of local bishops and archbishops should be a matter for the Church alone, and not a privilege enjoyed by secular rulers. Arguments with the emperor Henry IV over this issue reached such a pitch of intensity that in 1075 Gregory was briefly kidnapped by nobles loyal to the emperor. When Henry called the pope 'a false monk' Gregory promptly excommunicated him, and as the emperor's supporters fell away he found himself begging Gregory's forgiveness at **Canossa**, where the pontiff had sought refuge with **Matilda of Tuscany**. Although this event was regarded from that point on as a landmark in the establishment of **papal authority**, Henry nevertheless challenged Gregory once again, and once again was excommunicated. He succeeded in driving him out of Rome and installing an **anti-pope**, however, and it was in **Salerno** that Gregory died in 1085, under the protection of Robert Guiscard's Norman army. Soon afterwards he was declared a saint.

benefit from trade with ports in the new crusader kingdoms along the coast of **Palestine** (modern Israel, Syria and Lebanon).

1128 Roger II becomes king of Sicily. His reign marks a period of unparalleled splendour and prosperity on the island.

1155 Frederick Barbarossa is crowned emperor in Rome by **Hadrian IV** (Nicholas Brakspear, the only English pope). The occasion is marred by the trading of insults between pope and emperor; in the ensuing riot, Frederick's troops kill at least one thousand of the city's population.

1158 The university of **Bologna**, the first such institution in Europe, is officially established by Frederick Barbarossa. Meanwhile he embarks on a campaign in northern Italy to check the power of wealthy *communi* seeking self-government.

1160 Alexander III becomes pope. Seeking to free the papacy from imperial influence, he excommunicates Frederick and canvasses support for his initiative among the cities of **Lombardy**. Frederick retaliates by besieging the prosperous town of **Crema**, slaughtering its inhabitants and ordering its total destruction.

1167 The northern Italian cities, led by Milan, establish the **Lombard League** in opposition to Frederick.

1176 The Lombard League defeats Frederick at **Legnano**. He is forced to make peace with Pope Alexander III.

1177 Having failed to enthrone an alternative papal candidate, Frederick is forced to accept Alexander's authority. In a ceremony held in the portico of St Mark's basilica in Venice, Frederick kneels to Alexander as his overlord. The **act of submission** heralds a century of almost unchecked power for the papacy over the secular rulers of Europe.

Sicily under Roger II

It is all too easy for historians to romanticize the Sicily of Roger II (1095–1154) as an ideal world in which races and religions mixed freely under a benign and tolerant monarch. Yet it seems that during his reign the island really did sustain a successful **multi-ethnic, multi-faith culture**, of a type virtually unknown elsewhere in Christian Europe at the time. The king's own background was that of a Norman French warrior clan, but one whose perspectives had been significantly widened by contact with the **flourishing Muslim cities** he and his army overcame during their invasion of the island.

Medieval Islamic society was an inclusive one, lacking the bigotry and dogmatism that limited the Christian world at the same period. Under this influence, Roger's Catholic court absorbed and reflected aspects of all the various religions and lifestyles which had mingled freely in Palermo before Sicily's Norman conquest. There was a strong **Byzantine** influence, for example, visible in court dress and the elaborate mosaic decoration of palaces and churches. But the royal robes would be bordered with inscriptions in **Kufic**, the Muslim script which sanctifies everything from vases to mosque doorways with praises of Allah and the Prophet. From their Islamic predecessors the Norman rulers of Sicily also inherited a well-trained **civil service**, whose officials continued to write in Arabic under their new masters. A prominent **Jewish community**, meanwhile, enjoyed many more civil rights than its counterparts elsewhere in medieval Christendom.

Roger's passion for **scholarship** and thirst for information ensured that savants and travellers from all nations were welcome at his court, and the cosmopolitan nature of the island was further enhanced by the presence of **merchants** from northern Italy, France, Spain, Greece and Egypt. Under Roger's grandson **William II**, key positions in the Church hierarchy were occupied by senior clerics from England. With its fair but firm administration of justice, its tolerant and ecumenical religious climate, and its fine churches and palaces, the 120-year Norman kingdom represented a golden age which Sicily had not known since the days of the ancient Greeks.

4
The later Middle Ages

1179–1434

The later Middle Ages saw a widening of the social and political rifts which had characterized the history of Italy during the 11th and early 12th centuries. Conflicts between the empire and the papacy reached a crisis during the long reign of the emperor **Frederick II** (1194–1250), an outstanding soldier, scholar, statesman, polymath, poet and linguist who in his dazzling accomplishments embodied the ideal qualities of the 17th-century 'Renaissance Man'. But this towering figure, known to his contemporaries as the 'Wonder of the World', suffered from one major flaw as a ruler. Persisting in upholding the feudal power of his barons against the growing freedom of the northern *communi*, he failed to understand how the cities of the **Lombard League**, such as Milan, Bologna, Mantua and Verona, might be won over by any other means save open warfare – of the kind they had successfully resisted in the previous century when menaced by Frederick Barbarossa. His lack of magnanimity, especially towards **Milan**, antagonized them still further when he might have turned them into useful allies.

Though broadly supportive of the pope, the ever more prosperous *communi* now began to take matters into their own hands. The late 13th century saw a tussle for commercial supremacy in the Mediterranean among the **maritime republics**, with the **Genoese** effectively robbing **Pisa** of its trading interests in the western seas forever, and securing trade links with the East through the crusader port of **Acre**. **Venice,** meanwhile, wary of Genoese encroachments in the Adriatic, proved quite capable of seeing off a naval challenge from its longstanding rival in the **War of Chioggia** (1378–81). With this threat removed, the Venetians now embarked on a more or less unbroken period of over two hundred years of prosperity and territorial expansion, which would see their 'Most Serene Republic' grow into a state that was envied, imitated and feared throughout Europe.

Just as a new kind of **merchant aristocracy** had evolved among Venice's wealthiest families, so too, in the cities of northern and central Italy, an upper echelon based on urban prosperity emerged to challenge the old feudal baronage. Buying up property in both town and country, these merchants and bankers gradually assumed the trappings, pretensions and aspirations of traditional aristocrats, often complete with fraudulent pedigrees tracing their ancestry back to Charlemagne or even Julius Caesar. The merchant's counting house was now abandoned for, or absorbed into, the status-conferring **palazzo**. While they retained defensive features, these sumptuous buildings were designed increasingly to reflect their occupants' enjoyment of their wealth and leisure, with frescoed salons and handsome furnishings surrounded by ostentatious amounts of space, given the dense population of Italian cities at the time.

Overcrowding was indeed becoming a serious problem in late medieval Italy. From the Alps to Sicily, the peninsula was Europe's most densely populated area. As elsewhere in Europe, the **Black Death** of 1348 cut a swathe through populations, trade and agriculture, and upset the balance of regional and civic economies throughout Italy. Yet most towns and cities quickly recovered and continued to grow and flourish, their citizens becoming ever more aggressive in their pursuit of influence and privilege. Traditional rivalries and **hostilities** between cities such as **Florence**, **Siena** and **Pisa** often erupted into war, with local governments frequently relying on *condottieri* – soldiers of fortune – at the head of mercenary forces to conduct their campaigns.

Increased prosperity brought with it a desire among proud, loyal citizens to honour their cities with fine new buildings, and to enlarge or embellish their existing churches. **Florence** offers several superb testimonies to this civic pride, in the shape of the **Orsanmichele** (a church created from a granary), the **Loggia dei Lanzi** and the **Palazzo Vecchio**, all begun or completed during the 14th century. Alongside this characteristically Italian attention to the visual as a vital, ennobling aspect of urban living, there grew a parallel desire to promote **learning** and the **arts**. By the beginning of the 15th century, Italy had the largest number of **universities** of any country in Europe, and the distinguished reputations of **Bologna**, **Padua**, **Naples** and **Pavia** persuaded large numbers of foreign students to undertake hazardous journeys by land or sea, in search of a curriculum that was broader and deeper than anything offered by scholastic institutions in their own countries.

The spread of **education** and rising levels of **literacy**, however, posed a problem for the Church authorities, whose determination to control access to knowledge was driven by an overriding need to restrict the spread of **heresy**, or indeed of anything likely to challenge official dogma, papal authority or the traditional hierarchy. Eager to promote **Catholic orthodoxy** among sections of the population who were often inadequately ministered to by the parochial clergy, the early 13th-century popes had encouraged the development of the two most prominent orders of friars, the **Franciscans** and the **Dominicans**. By the end of the following century, the ideals of poverty, chastity and preaching the gospel, to which both orders were committed, had become widely abused by the friars. The Church in general, meanwhile, was beginning to attract open criticism for its **worldliness** and **cupidity**, and it suffered from an absence of a pope with firm leadership or charisma. At the same time, a gradual rediscovery of the **classical past** through the study of Roman history and literature, and the **non-Christian values** and **secular themes** they offered to painting and sculpture, was beginning to undermine the whole structure of Catholic spiritual authority under which the medieval world had operated up to this point.

> **"** O servile Italy, inn of sorrows, rudderless ship in a raging storm, once a mistress ruling over many provinces, but now nothing better than a brothel! **"**
>
> Dante Alighieri on Italy c.1300, *Purgatorio*, Canto VII

1179 **William II of Sicily** begins to build the abbey of **Monreale**, outside Palermo, as a burial place for his dynasty.

1189 The **Third Crusade** is proclaimed, led by Frederick Barbarossa, Richard Coeur de Lion, king of England, and Philip Augustus, king of France.

William II of Sicily dies, leaving the throne to his aunt Constance, who is married to Barbarossa's son Henry. Her claim is challenged by her nephew Tancred of Lecce who, although illegitimate, declares himself rightful king. In Cilicia (part of modern Turkey), **Frederick Barbarossa** drowns while fording a river.

1190 Barbarossa's son is crowned Emperor **Henry VI** by Pope Celestine III.

1194 Tancred of Lecce falls ill and dies. Henry invades **Sicily** and is crowned king in Palermo cathedral. The island is now officially part of the **Holy Roman Empire**. In a tent in the marketplace at Jesi, near Ancona, the 40-year-old Constance gives birth to a son, the future Emperor Frederick II.

1197 Henry VI dies at Messina. Rival claimants to the imperial succession emerge in Germany, but his widow Constance successfully marshals Italian support for Frederick as the rightful heir.

1202 Lotario de' Conti, nephew of Clement III, becomes **Pope Innocent III**. His relatively long papacy will become noted for its consolidation of papal rights and privileges, the punishment of heretics and the ruthless exercise of pontifical authority over European sovereigns.

1204 Pope Innocent proclaims the **Fourth Crusade**. Profiting from a contract to ship the crusaders to Palestine, the Venetians convince them to divert their attentions to **Constantinople**, where they loot the city and divide the **Byzantine empire** among western rulers. St Mark's and other churches in Venice are enriched with Byzantine artworks and holy relics, and a **Venetian empire** is established in the Aegean islands, Euboea and the Peloponnese.

> ❝ His garments were soiled and torn, his person thin, his face pale, but God gave his words unheard-of power. Love and veneration for him were universal; men and women thronged about him, and happy were those who could so much as touch the hem of his robe. ❞
>
> A Croatian student in Bologna describes St Francis's visit to the city

1210 Innocent III gives his blessing to an order of 'Friars Minor' founded by **Francis of Assisi** and devoted to good works among the poor. The friars will become known as the **Franciscans**.

1212 **Frederick of Hohenstaufen**, son of Henry VI and Constance, is crowned king of Germany at the petition of a number of German princes who support his claims.

1215 Pope Innocent III opens the **Fourth Lateran Council**, a congress of Church dignitaries at the Lateran basilica in

Francis of Assisi

Among Christians, Francis of Assisi (1181–1226) ranks only slightly below Jesus Christ and the Virgin Mary as an example of perfect holiness. He was the son of a rich merchant of Assisi, and received the name Francesco in reference to his mother's French origins. A story about Francis in his early years tells of his dramatic renunciation of his affluent background. As a symbol of his acceptance of a life of poverty and self-denial, he stripped himself of all his clothes and gave them to his father, refusing to acknowledge any father but God.

Gathering like-minded followers, he established a small religious community in **Assisi**, dedicated to charitable missionary work among beggars, lepers and other outcasts of society. A journey to **Palestine** in 1212 to preach Christianity to the Muslims was a failure, although the Mameluke Sultan of Egypt was impressed by Francis's fervour. Returning to Italy, he sought approval for his order from the papal court in Rome and, in 1223, Pope Honorius gave his assent to the Franciscan rule of **poverty, chastity and obedience** to the Church. Francis's later life inspired further tales of his saintliness. He tamed a savage wolf, which had menaced the citizens of Gubbio but grew docile under his influence and followed him around like a dog; he, famously, preached a sermon to the birds; and he received the stigmata (the wounds of the crucified Christ).

Francis died in 1226, was canonized only two years later, and the Franciscan order he established grew steadily to become a significant force in medieval European society. **Mendicant friars** lived on alms, preached in churches specially designed to receive the large congregations they attracted, and travelled long

Rome. This lays the foundations of **modern Catholicism** by affirming the miracle of 'real presence' (the communion wafer becoming Christ's body), the duties of confession and attendance at Mass, the sin of heresy and the inferior status of Jews.

St Francis' renunciation of worldly goods, from a Giotto fresco at Assisi

distances, venturing as far as Asia and Genghis Khan's **Mongol empire**. Francis's message was founded on Christ's teaching in St Matthew's gospel, 'As ye go, preach, saying, The kingdom of heaven is at hand. Heal the sick, cleanse the lepers,' and many were convinced of his saintliness from the very start of his mission. So charismatic was he that mothers are said to have hidden their sons in cupboards on his approach, for fear that they would hear him preaching and seek to follow him. From Cimabue and Giotto onwards, Italian artists created memorable images inspired by episodes of his life, and he became the most celebrated of Italy's many saints, venerated for his simplicity, self-discipline and unfailing charity towards the weak and disadvantaged.

1217 Innocent III recognizes the Friars Preacher, an order founded by the Spanish priest **Dominic of Caleruega**, who will later be canonized. Zealous prosecutors of heretics, the **Dominicans** will soon adopt a competitive attitude towards the activities of the **Franciscans**. A Tuscan legend describes a meeting of reconciliation between St Francis and St Dominic at a place known as l'Incontro, south of Florence, though this encounter has no known foundation in fact.

1220 Frederick of Hohenstaufen is crowned Emperor **Frederick II** by Innocent's successor **Honorius II**.

> " He had loyal admirers, but very few friends. The world in general regarded him with suspicion. His fellow monarchs were repelled by his amorality and blasphemy. To his enemies, horrified by the richness of his intellect and the fearlessness of his irreverence, he was the embodiment of Antichrist. "
>
> Sir Steven Runciman on Emperor Frederick II, *The Sicilian Vespers*

1221 Frederick II founds a university at **Padua**, which soon becomes noted for its medical and legal faculties.

1223 Pope Honorius III gives the Church's approval to the rule of St Francis and the establishment of the **Franciscan order**.

1224 Frederick II founds the university of **Naples**, to train candidates for his civil service.

1226 The **Diet of Cremona**, Frederick II's attempt to secure allegiance from the cities of the Lombard League, ends in failure.

1228 Pope Gregory IX (Ugolino da Segni, nephew of Innocent III) excommunicates Frederick II.

1233 Gregory IX founds the Holy Office, better known as the **Inquisition**, to eradicate heresy.

1234 The **Lombard League** allies itself with Frederick's son **Henry**, so aiding his (ultimately unsuccessful) revolt against his father.

1237 At Cortenuova, near Cremona, Frederick successfully crushes the **Lombard League**.

1245 At the first Council of Lyon, **Pope Innocent IV** accuses Frederick of **heresy** and demands a crusade against him. The council strips the emperor of his title and finds him guilty of crimes against the Church.

1250 Frederick dies at Castel Fiorentino in Puglia.

1260 Taking advantage of the political meltdown in Italy that follows the sudden death of Frederick II, **Charles of Anjou**, brother of King Louis X of France, invades the northern duchy of **Savoy**.

© SCALA

Palazzo della Signoria, Florence

Frederick II

Frederick II (1194–1250) was born in a tent in the marketplace of a small Italian town. To prove his legitimacy to the world, respectable matrons were summoned to observe his mother, **Constance de Hauteville**, in the throes of labour: they could then act as witnesses against any future rival challenges to the boy's claims to the imperial estates in southern Italy. Frederick was destined to be crowned three times, first as **king of the Romans and Sicily** at the age of four, then as **king of Germany** in 1212 (when he was 18), and finally, eight years later, as **Holy Roman Emperor**.

His long reign was also a turbulent one, in which agencies ranging from popes and kings to local vested interests sought to challenge and undermine his authority. Through sheer force of **personality** and **intellect**, however, Frederick emerged as one of the most dynamic figures on the late medieval Italian stage. He worked tirelessly to create a stable and unified realm stretching from Sicily to the Alps, resisting the strong-arm tactics of the papacy (which was determined to thwart him) and devising a sturdy secular legal code, the *Liber Augustalis*, which combined elements of Norman, Byzantine and Longobard law. Like England's Edward I at the century's end, Frederick was fascinated by state-of-the-art **castle-building**: his most sensational

With assistance from the army of Frederick II's illegitimate son Manfred, Siena, traditionally hostile to the territorial ambitions of Florence, wins a decisive victory over the Florentines at Montaperti.

1261 **Urban IV** (Jacques Pantaléon) becomes pope. The first Frenchman to hold the office, he encourages Charles of Anjou to push further into Italy, and offers material support to the Tuscan **Guelfs** (supporters of the **papacy**) against the **Ghibellines** (supporters of the **empire**).

commission, **Castel del Monte** in Apulia, boasted an unorthodox design and classical features which anticipated the architectural ideas of the Renaissance. An accomplished **author** and **poet** in his own right – with a treatise on falconry and a number of appealing love lyrics to his name – Frederick was passionate in his encouragement of the **arts** and founded **universities** at Naples and Padua. It was under his rule that **Italian** first began to be used in a literary context in southern Italy and Sicily, in preference to Provençal, the French *langue d'Oc*, which until then had been the language of poetry in chivalric Europe. He was fluent in **Arabic**, and while in Jerusalem had successfully negotiated with the Sultan of Egypt to ensure safeguards for Christian travellers in Muslim lands.

Frederick's prodigious energies, talents and wide-ranging interests, combined with his eclectic lifestyle in which he urbanely mixed elements from both **Christian** and **Muslim** cultures, ensured him the envy and loathing of successive popes, who condemned him as a **heretic** and exploited every opportunity to undermine his authority. Less partial contemporaries admired him – with justice – as a remarkable man who was almost better than medieval Italy deserved, and fully worthy of his Latin soubriquet '*Stupor Mundi*' ('Wonder of the World').

1266 In a major battle against the forces of **Charles of Anjou** at **Benevento**, Frederick II's son Manfred is defeated and killed. **Pope Clement IV** confers the crown of Sicily on Charles, who angers the Sicilians by transferring his capital to **Naples**.

1274 **Thomas Aquinas** dies in France, on his way to the second Council of Lyon, at which **Pope Gregory X** will attempt, unsuccessfully, to unite the Roman Catholic and Greek Orthodox churches.

Guelfs and Ghibellines

The Guelfs and Ghibellines were the two rival factions who supported the **pope** and the **Holy Roman Emperor** respectively during their bitter and seemingly endless struggle for supremacy in medieval Italy. Each name was derived from a war cry or rallying call of two rival German houses: Guelf from the Welf dynasty of northern Saxony, some of whose members sought the imperial crown; Ghibelline from the name of a castle, Waiblingen, that belonged to the lords of **Hohenstaufen**, Frederick II's family. The two factions first took hold in **Florence**, where Guelf and Ghibelline rivalry was at its fiercest during the 13th century, and quickly spread to other cities, many of which declared a blanket allegiance to one side or another. **Bologna**, for example, was predominantly Guelf, whereas **Siena** and **Arezzo** supported the Ghibellines.

After Frederick's death, the Guelfs took their political direction from the papacy and lent their support to **Charles of Anjou**. When the later emperors lost interest in trying to recover former imperial lands in Italy, the Ghibellines, lacking a political focus, fell into decline. Subsequently, the Guelfs split along family alignments into '**Black**' and '**White**' factions, with the former emerging triumphant and showing very little mercy to their enemies. **Dante**, the most distinguished of the White Guelfs, devoted much of his *Divine Comedy* to lamenting the various errors, failures and sins that had brought down his cause, kept him in exile and allowed a power-hungry, domineering and nepotistic papacy to triumph. For Dante's native **Florence** the feuding had important social consequences. By the end of the 13th century, the city's Ghibelline families were bereft of money and influence, their feudal power broken by the new, ambitious and energetic merchant class, as well as by the growing influence of the city's trade guilds and banking families. Although both factions eventually died out altogether in the changing political climate, the term 'Guelf' was briefly revived in the 19th century to describe **liberal Catholics** who saw Pope Pius IX as a potential leader of a united Italy.

> For with no other quarrel of land or seigneury, they have only to say, 'You are Guelf and I am Ghibelline; we must hate each other,' and for this reason only and knowing no other, they kill and wound each other every day like dogs, the sons like the fathers, and so year by year the malice continues and there is no justice to remedy it.

Maréchal de Boucicaut, governor of Genoa, quoted in *A Distant Mirror*, Barbara W. Tuchman

1282 In an uprising known as the **Sicilian Vespers**, the citizens of Palermo massacre the troops of the tyrannical Charles of Anjou. The island's nobles offer the crown to **King Peter of Aragon**, who is married to one of Manfred's daughters. Aragonese rule over the island will ensure the dominance of a feudal nobility, as trade and cultural life in its towns and cities begin a slow decline.

1284 The Genoese admiral **Benedetto Zaccaria** leads a fleet of thirty galleys to blockade ports on the Tuscan coast belonging to its longstanding rival **Pisa**. On 5 August, at **La Torre della Meloria**, Zaccaria attacks the Pisan fleet, sinking seven large galleys and taking 9000 prisoners.

1285 After making an alliance with Genoa to destroy Pisa, **Florence** and **Lucca** suddenly change sides, thwarting Genoese ambitions to control Tuscany.

Charles of Anjou dies, embittered by his failure to become ruler of all Italy.

1288 Pisa is forced to make peace with **Genoa**, ceding control of **Elba** and **Corsica**. When Pisa fails to honour the agreement, the Genoese destroy its harbour at **Porto Pisano**, which never re-establishes itself as a port. With Pisa effectively finished as a maritime republic, Genoa now becomes the major economic power in the Mediterranean,

Thomas Aquinas

Known to the medieval Church as 'the Angelic doctor', in part because of his speculations on the nature and purpose of angels, Thomas Aquinas (1225–74) was the most important and influential Christian theologian of the Middle Ages.

Born the son of a nobleman in the southern Italian town of Aquino, Thomas studied at the university of **Naples** before deciding to join the newly founded order of Friars Preacher or **Dominicans** – a decision to which his family was passionately opposed. Having studied under **Albertus Magnus** in Cologne, he took his vows and became a teacher, going first to **Paris**, where he became famed for his eloquence and wrote a defence of Christianity against heretics, Muslims and Jews. His reputation spread, and he was summoned to Rome by **Pope Urban IV**. It was in Italy, in around 1260, that he embarked on his greatest work, the *Summa Theologica* (*Complete Theology*), a series of closely reasoned considerations of Christian doctrine which was to become one of the central pillars of Catholic dogma. By now his international reputation was formidable, and while still continuing to work on the *Summa* he also produced a prodigious opus of **theological commentary**, **biblical studies** and works on **philosophy** centred on the writings of **Aristotle**.

The works of Aristotle had recently been rediscovered, firstly via Arabic translations and subsequently – following the establishment of the universities – through **Latin translations** from the original Greek. Aquinas applied the colossal weight of his intellect, reason, learning and faith to seeking to reconcile the principles of **Aristotelianism** and of **Christianity**.

The **saintliness** of Aquinas's character was noted during his lifetime: although offered an archbishopric, he preferred the modest life of a monk and preacher and was signally lacking in the arrogance and condescension of many distinguished scholars of the time. He viewed his achievements as simply the expression of a duty to interpret God's purpose, as manifested in the sacraments and mysteries of the Church. In 1274 he died in France and was buried in Toulouse. He was canonized in 1323.

controlling markets in not only **Seville** and other Spanish cities, but also in **Constantinople**.

1289 The debauched **Matteo Visconti** is given the title of Imperial Vicar of Milan by the emperor. His extravagant, decadent family – who will become the wealthiest dynasty in Europe – will dominate the city's politics for the next 150 years.

1294 In an unprecedented step, the saintly **Pope Celestine V** abdicates after only five months in office, preferring to return to a life of self-mortification and prayer. He is succeeded by the worldly and ambitious **Boniface VIII**.

1297 Election to the **Venetian Grand Council** is now closed to all except those who have been members during the past four years and their male heirs, with other names added only by a commission of nobles. This restricted franchise is to become a permanent feature of the government of Venice.

1302 Boniface summons the French prince **Charles of Valois** to support the reactionary and extremist **Black Guelfs** in their struggle with the more moderate **White Guelfs** for control of Florence. The Whites are defeated and expelled. Among them is the poet **Dante Alighieri**, who spends the rest of his life in exile.

The treaty of Caltabellotta ends the **War of the Vespers** between Frederick, Aragonese king of Sicily, and the pope. The result of the conflict is a stalemate, with Frederick allowed to retain Sicily until his death, when the Angevin rulers of Naples expect to regain control of the island.

1303 In a move that will have fateful consequences, **Philip IV** ('*le Bel*'), king of France, escalates the power struggle between temporal and ecclesiastical authorities by taking prisoner **Boniface VIII** – who had excommunicated him for arresting a bishop – by force. The 86-year-old pope dies only weeks later.

> **❝** It is necessary to salvation that every human creature be subject to the Roman pontiff. **❞**
>
> Pope Boniface VIII, *Unam Sanctam*, 1302

1305 King Philip of France manipulates the election of Bertrand de Got, archbishop of Bordeaux, as **Pope Clement V**.

1308 In protest against the oligarchy created by restricting membership of the **Grand Council**, **Bajamonte Tiepolo**, member of a noble Venetian family, attempts a coup d'état against the government of **Venice**. Leading his supporters down a narrow lane into Piazza San Marco, he is hit on the head by a pot thrown out of a window by an old woman, and dies. The rebels flee and the government tightens its grip on the city by creating a series of executive committees, centred on the **Council of Ten**, which effectively concentrate political power in the hands of a aristocratic oligarchy.

1309 Fearing reprisals for the death of Boniface VIII, **Clement V** moves the papal court from Rome to **Avignon**, where it remains for nearly seventy years. Since the papacy is now under the thumb of the French monarchy, the move becomes known as the **Babylonian Captivity**.

Robert, son of Charles of Anjou, inherits the **kingdom of Naples**. Though much time and energy will be devoted during his 34-year reign to fighting Ghibelline armies in northern Italy, his prudent rule brings stability and prosperity to both Naples and the surrounding realm. The city itself develops a rich international culture during this period, with a distinct French influence in its art and architecture.

1321 **Dante Alighieri** dies at Ravenna on 14 September. His recently completed masterwork, *La Divina Commedia*

> 66 In both commerce and culture, the kingdom of Naples flourished during the reign of King Robert, the 'new Solomon' whose literary approval Petrarch came to seek. Boccaccio followed because he preferred life in the 'happy, peaceful, generous and magnificent Naples with its one monarch' to his native republican Florence 'devoured by innumerable cares'. Robert built his palace, Castel Nuovo, on the water's edge facing Naples' incomparable bay, where ships of Genoa, Spain and Provence came to trade. Nobles and merchants added their palazzos alongside, commissioning Tuscan artists to fill them with frescoes and sculpture. Under just laws and a stable currency, with security of roads, hostels for travelling merchants, festivities, tournaments, music and poetry, Robert's reign, which ended in 1343, was said to be 'something like Paradise'. 99
>
> Barbara W. Tuchman, *A Distant Mirror*

(*The Divine Comedy*), fuses religious allegory, narrative fantasy, personal record and contemporary history. Composed in **vernacular Italian** rather than Latin, the language of scholarship, the work quickly establishes itself as a classic of Italian literature.

> 66 [Dante] was born in the country and at the time which furnished the most stern opposition of horror and beauty and permitted it to be written in the clearest lines ... and therefore I think that the 21st and 22nd book of the 'Inferno' are the most perfect portraitures of the fiendish nature which we possess. 99
>
> John Ruskin, *Stones of Venice*

Dante

Dante Alighieri (1265–1321), Italy's greatest poet, spent much of his life as an **exile** or a wanderer, banished from his beloved native city of **Florence** by politics and war. He was born in 1265, the son of moderately prosperous parents who gave him a good education in the context of the medieval city's sophisticated cultural life. One of his teachers was **Brunetto Latini**, who fostered his loyalty to Florence and encouraged him to read widely in both ancient and modern languages. At the age of about 18, he had already started writing poetry, Dante married Gemma Donati; his real love, however, was for the girl he referred to as **Beatrice** (her identity remains uncertain), daughter of an aristocratic family, whose early death left him emotionally devastated. He commemorated his passion in **La Vita Nuova**, a verse and prose composition containing poems written over a ten-year period, and completed around 1293.

In 1300 he entered Florentine politics, siding with the **Ghibellines**, whom he had formerly opposed, against the **Guelfs** who supported Pope Boniface VIII and Charles of Valois. When the Guelfs seized power in Florence in 1302, Dante went into exile, living in various northern Italian towns before settling in **Ravenna**, where he died in 1321.

To this last period belongs *La Divina Commedia*, an epic poem in three parts describing the writer's imaginary journey through hell, purgatory and paradise. In the first part his guide is the Roman poet **Virgil**, in the last he is welcomed by the spirit of **Beatrice**, and throughout his journey he meets figures from

---

1337 The painter **Giotto di Bondone** dies in Florence. His work, and particularly his **fresco cycles** at Padua and Assisi, has revolutionized the art of painting in Italy.

1346 Having borrowed heavily from **Florentine banking houses** to finance his war with France, **King Edward III** of England defaults on his debts and imprisons their London

Dante stands before a tableau incorporating hell, heaven, and the Duomo of his native Florence

history, mythology and recent Italian politics. For the poet himself the experience is one of spiritual rebirth; the reader, meanwhile, becomes aware that he is testing and ultimately proving the worth of Italian as an expressive medium – as opposed to Latin, the language of intellectual discourse in the Middle Ages. Breathtaking in its scope and expression, *La Divina Commedia* places Dante alongside Shakespeare as one of world literature's truly universal writers.

agents. Several leading Florentine families are declared bankrupt, with devastating effect on the city's economy.

1347 Inspired by idealistic notions of returning to the republicanism of ancient Rome, Nicola di Lorenzo, better known as **Cola di Rienzo** leads a **popular revolt**, and rules the city for six months before being overthrown.

Giotto

Giotto di Bondone (1266–1337) is generally acknowledged as the most important and influential painter of the Italian Middle Ages who, in breaking away from the Byzantine tradition, changed the course of European art. Born in 1266, he spent much of his working life in Florence, possibly beginning as a pupil of Cimabue before developing his markedly individual manner, which involved a break with medieval figurative traditions in favour of a more dramatic and realistic style of religious painting. Major commissions took him to **Assisi**, where scholars have sometimes disputed his contribution to the frescoes of the Upper Church; **Padua**, where he decorated the Scrovegni Chapel with three astonishingly vivid and compelling fresco cycles; and **Naples**, although none of his work from there has survived. His last commission was the design of the *campanile* (bell tower) of the **Duomo** in Florence.

Giotto's achievement in creating a new kind of religious art, whose images related directly to the medieval Italy in which he flourished, was widely admired in his own lifetime. Later Italian artists, from the Renaissance onwards, saw him as a founding father of a national school of painting, placing an emphasis on colour, form and originality of composition.

That Giotto's contemporaries, Dante among them, readily acknowledged his work's significance is suggested by the wealth of imitators who surrounded him in Florence and its neighbouring towns. His greatest achievement was to lend a convincingly three-dimensional quality to figures, backgrounds and compositions as a whole, instilling works such as the *Arrest of Christ in the Garden of Gethsemane*, part of his fresco cycle in Padua's Scrovegni Chapel, with a profound sense of drama and movement. In rendering the emotional intensity of religious scenes, he thus brought them closer to the ordinary lives of the worshippers they surrounded.

Assuming dictatorial powers, he reforms Rome's civic government, proclaiming a confederation of Italian cities which, he intends, will elect their emperor rather than hav-

> **In my opinion painters owe to Giotto, the Florentine painter, exactly the same debt they owe to nature, which constantly serves them as a model and whose finest and most beautiful aspects they are always striving to imitate and reproduce ... There is a story that when Giotto was still a young man in Cimabue's workshop, he once painted on the nose of one of the figures Cimabue had executed a fly that was so lifelike that when Cimabue returned to carry on with his work he tried several times to brush it off with his hand, under the impression that it was real, before he realized his mistake.**
>
> Giorgio Vasari, *Lives of the Artists*, trans. George Bull

ing one thrust upon them. Noble Roman families conspire to crush Rienzo, and the pope excommunicates him as a heretic. Fleeing the city, he seeks refuge in Prague. To later ages he becomes a hero of popular protest, and is championed by Richard Wagner in his opera *Rienzi, Last of the Tribunes* (1840).

1348 The **Black Death** – a combination of bubonic and pneumonic plagues – rages throughout Italy, cutting a swathe through the populations of **Florence**, **Venice**, **Pisa**, **Naples** and innumerable other towns, cities and villages. Trade and agriculture are devastated in its wake. Many

> **One man shunned another ... kinsfolk held aloof, brother was forsaken by brother, oftentimes husband by wife; nay, what is more, and scarcely to be believed, fathers and mothers were found to abandon their children to their fate, untended, unvisited as if they had been strangers.**
>
> Giovanni Boccaccio on the plague in Florence, *The Decameron*

interpret the epidemic as God's punishment for sin and overindulgence.

1354 Marin Falier becomes doge of Venice. Seeking to limit the power of the city's unruly patricians, he is found guilty of plotting to overthrow the state and is beheaded, by order of the Senate, on the spot where he had been invested as doge. Henceforth in any representation of the Venetian doges his portrait is blacked out: in **Tintoretto's frieze** in the Palazzo Ducale he is represented by a painted black veil.

Cola di Rienzo returns to Rome in triumph, but his brief second dictatorship ends when the mob, encouraged by the Roman nobles, turn against him. In the rioting that ensues he is killed.

1374 Francesco Petrarca – better known as **Petrarch** – dies at Arqua, near Padua. Italy's leading poet, he has devoted much of his long life to reconciling **Christian** and **classical cultures** through a wealth of writings in Latin, together with poems in Italian collected in a volume entitled *Il Canzoniere* (*The Songbook*). They include several hundred sonnets, in which Petrarch perfected a form originally created by Italian poets of the previous century. Many of these are addressed to a mistress named **Laura**, and Petrarch is subsequently admired as the creator of the **love sonnet**, a poetic form which will become popular throughout Europe during the Renaissance. His Italian contemporaries revere him as a sage and consult him on matters of **philosophy** and **diplomacy** as well as literature. The **humanist** aspects of his works anticipate the ideas of the Renaissance, as does his famous ascent of **Mont Ventoux** in Provence, in its spirit of enquiry for its own sake. It is also the first known example of mountain climbing (and perhaps even the appreciation of sweeping, panoramic views) solely for pleasure.

> **❝** To the west we have a wide view over a solitary region, very quiet and pleasant. I do not remember ever seeing from so slight an elevation such a noble spectacle of far-spreading lands. By turning about one can see Pavia, Piacenza, Cremona and many other famous cities besides ... To our rear are the Alps separating us from Germany, their snow-clad peaks rising into the clouds, into heaven; before us stand the Apennines and innumerable cities. **❞**
>
> Petrarch, letter from San Colombano, trans. M. Bishop

1375 **Giovanni Boccaccio** dies in Florence. Famous as a poet and diplomat, he is best known as author of *Il Decamerone* (*The Decameron*), a collection of linked stories in the manner of the *Arabian Nights*, in which serious and romantic tales are interspersed with bawdy anecdotes of Italian low life. The stories will provide inspiration for many other authors, including **Geoffrey Chaucer** and **William Shakespeare**.

Following an uprising against the **Guelfs,** which spreads throughout Tuscany, **Pope Gregory XI** places **Florence** under an interdict. He orders the expulsion of all Florentines from foreign countries.

1378 A mob burns down the palaces of the **Florentine Guelf** leaders. On 22 July thousands of the city's workers march on the Palazzo Vecchio to drive out the civic government (**Signoria**). For six weeks Florence is governed by guild representatives and artisans, led by the **Ciompi** (cloth-workers) and their spokesman **Michele di Lando**. Commercial rivalries lead to the break-up of this alliance, however, and on 31 August the Ciompi are overcome in a battle in Piazza della Signoria. A number of historians in the 19th and 20th centuries have interpreted the revolt of the Ciompi as a precursor of modern struggles between capital and labour. Others see it merely as an attempt by the proletariat to secure a bigger share of Florence's renewed prosperity following the Black Death.

Supporters of the Italian pope **Urban VI** and a rival French candidate for the papacy, elected as **Clement VII**, create a radical division within the Catholic Church, known as the **Great Schism**.

1380 At a battle off the Adriatic coast near **Chioggia**, Venice defeats the **Genoese navy**, so gaining the upper hand in the two cities' longstanding commercial rivalry. Peace is concluded at Turin the following year.

1385 Giangaleazzo Visconti seizes power from his ruthlessly despotic uncle Bernabo and becomes ruler of **Milan**.

1389 Florence sends an army, under the English *condottiere* **Sir John Hawkwood**, to drive out the **Milanese** forces of **Giangaleazzo Visconti**, who aims to extend his power from northern Italy into Tuscany.

> ❝ I know Gian Galeazzo. Neither honour nor pity nor sworn faith ever yet inclined him to do a disinterested deed. If he ever seeks what is good, it is because his interest requires it, for he is without moral sense. Goodness, like hate or anger, is for him a matter of calculation. ❞
>
> Francesco Carrara of Padua, quoted in *A Distant Mirror*, Barbara W. Tuchman

1402 Giangaleazzo Visconti seizes control of **Siena**, **Pisa**, **Perugia** and **Bologna**. Having defeated the Florentines at Casalecchio, his army lays siege to **Florence**. The siege is broken after news arrives of his death, on 3 September, during a plague epidemic in Milan.

1405 Giovanni Maria Visconti, Giangaleazzo's heir, sells

Pisa to the **Florentines** for 200,000 florins (the Florentine gold coin which replaced the English sterling as Europe's strongest currency). When the Pisans resist, Florence mounts a siege. With Pisa's eventual surrender, Florence secures a maritime outlet for its trade.

1420 **Cosimo de' Medici**, 'the Elder', becomes manager of his family's Florentine banking firm.

1423 **Filippo Maria Visconti** invades Florentine territory in an effort to recover his father's lost conquests.

> ❝ What might have become of his [Giangaleazzo's] sons Giovanni Maria and Filippo Maria, had they lived in a different country and among other traditions, cannot be said. But, as heirs of their house, they inherited that monstrous capital of cruelty and cowardice which had been accumulated from generation to generation. ❞
>
> Jacob Burckhardt, *The Civilization of the Renaissance in Italy*,
> trans. S.G.C. Middlemore

1424 **Masaccio** and his assistant Masolino begin work on the frescoes of the **Brancacci Chapel** in the church of Santa Maria del Carmine in Florence. In its emphasis on the human drama at the heart of each episode, its handling of perspective and its subtle use of colour, the fresco cycle – depicting scenes from the Acts of the Apostles and also the *Expulsion from Paradise* and the *Tribute Money* – marks a profoundly important development in the history of art. Masaccio's work is seen by many art historians as the earliest major example of Florentine Renaissance painting.

1428 The war between **Florence** and **Milan** ends in stalemate. Filippo Maria Visconti cedes control of Milanese affairs to his son-in-law, the *condottiere* **Francesco Sforza**.

1433 After a prolonged power struggle between Florence's noble families, Cosimo de' Medici is banished from the city. Welcomed in Padua and Venice and supported by **Pope Eugenius IV**, Cosimo plots to overturn the Florentine government.

1434 Cosimo de' Medici makes a triumphant return to Florence. With one brief interval his family will rule over the city for the next three hundred years.

5
The Renaissance

1436–1527

The later Middle Ages had witnessed a number of important changes in the **political map** of Italy (such as the capture of Pisa by the Florentines and the growth of a mainland Venetian empire), resulting in the growth of bigger and richer **city states** and the extinction of many independent *communi*. During the 15th century this process of expansion began to quicken with the help of improved **military technology** (especially the use of gunpowder), better training of armed forces, and the employment by various rulers of *condottieri*, professional soldiers of fortune, as strategists and war leaders. Thus the mid–century saw the republic of **Venice** pushing its mainland frontiers almost to the gates of **Milan**, as well as acquiring towns and territories along the River Po. In Tuscany, meanwhile, **Florence** and **Siena** became the principal contestants for supremacy, in a struggle which ended only in the mid-16th century, with the absorption of the Sienese domains by the **Medici grand dukes**.

The Medici, lords of Florence, offer the most flagrant example of the way in which the fortunes of Italian states were controlled more and more by powerful family interests. Ruling dynasties such as the **Este** in Ferrara, the **Sforza** in Milan and later the Gonzaga of Mantua were all well established by 1500. In the south, the ongoing strife between partisans of the **Aragonese** kings of Sicily and the **Angevin** rulers of Naples was brought to an end by the union of the two crowns in the person of **Alfonso V** of Sicily, whom the Neapolitan queen Giovanna II had named as her heir. Even – and, arguably, especially – the **papacy** was guided by dynastic imperatives. **Pope Alexander VI**, for example, shamelessly promoted the interests of his children **Cesare** and **Lucrezia Borgia**, while **Leo X** ensured that his own Medici family would benefit as much as the Holy Church from his energetic reign as pope.

This consolidation of power in the courts of various rival states induced a greater emphasis on **diplomatic skills** and manoeuvrings, which were deployed increasingly in the cause of the **dynastic marriages** that now became a significant feature of the Italian political scene, and they would remain so at least until the end of the 18th century. In order to govern efficiently, rulers required the services of properly trained **bureaucrats**. Simultaneously, the diffusion of **Renaissance values**, encouraging the acquisition of secular learning, meant that these princes became preoccupied with **learning**, **scholarship** and **artistic accomplishment** as indicators of a civilized society. But the greatest gift of the Italian Renaissance to European culture was **humanism**: a concentration on the achievements of human beings as opposed to those of God and the saints, and the idea of mankind as providing its own measurable standards of conduct and morality. As well as freeing the domains of academic study and scientific enquiry from the restrictions of religious dogma, humanists such as **Leon Battista Alberti**, **Lorenzo Valla**, **Marsilio Ficino** and **Giovanni Pico della Mirandola** recovered the wisdom of the ancients from texts that had long been believed lost. In doing so they awoke popular consciousness to the beauty and fascination of the **pagan** and **classical worlds**. Nor was this an exclusively scholarly exercise: classical authors also offered examples – whether of military prowess, philosophical sophistication or artistic excellence – that could by association be turned to purposes that were more **political** and **pragmatic**, and used to present contemporary achievements in a more positive or even heroic light.

Not surprisingly, it is the visual arts of **painting** and **sculpture** that offer us our most familiar images of Italy during the High Renaissance, in works such as **Botticelli's** *Primavera* or the sculptures of **Donatello**. This was an age of murder, corruption and nepotism on a grand scale, the age of the notorious **Borgias** and the exquisitely cynical **Niccolò Machiavelli**, but it was also the era of **Michelangelo**, **Raphael** and **Leonardo da Vinci**, in which figurative art in Italy attained hitherto unparalleled levels of expressiveness, humanity and technical expertise. The work of these and other masters also raised the status of artists. No longer mere craftsmen among many, the most successful of them were now international celebrities. Their very presence enhanced the image of the rulers who commissioned their works, so publicly confirming them as judicious and discerning **patrons**.

The cultural achievements of the Italian Renaissance in all their richness and diversity developed against a volatile background of chaos and strife. Humanism, the visual arts and architecture, poetry and music all flourished within a political context of virtually unremitting **instability**. **Violence** in appalling variety, including family feuding, political assassinations and sporadic warfare between rival states, dogged rulers and their subjects alike. Armies marched incessantly back and forth across Italy in campaigns that achieved little except short-term advantage for this or that state and its sovereign duke.

Then, during the early 16th century, the struggle for supremacy took on an international dimension once more, as **France** and the **Holy Roman Empire** turned northern Italy into a continuous battleground on which the **popes**, now at the zenith of their power as secular rulers, routinely shifted their alliances. By 1530, republicanism and the communal autonomy of the city states had been more or less consigned to history. With the exception of **Venice**, **Lucca** and the tiny republic of **San Marino**, Italy was now divided into sovereign **duchies** sandwiched between the domains of the **emperor** and the **pope**.

> ❝ If we are to call any age golden, it is beyond doubt that age which brings forth golden talent in different places. For this century, like a golden age, has restored to light the liberal arts, which were almost extinct, the arts of grammar, poetry, rhetoric, painting, sculpture, architecture and the ancient singing of songs. ❞
>
> Marsilio Ficino on the achievements of the Renaissance, 1492

1436 The dome of Florence's cathedral, the **Duomo**, is consecrated following its completion by architect **Filippo Brunelleschi**. The first large-scale dome erected in Christian Europe since Roman times, it will later provide a model for structures such as St Peter's Basilica in Rome and London's St Paul's Cathedral.

1438 **Fra Angelico** (Guido di Pietro) begins his great series of some fifty frescoes, intended to serve as devotional aids in the friars' cells and other rooms of the Dominican friary of **San Marco** in Florence.

1439 Pope **Eugenius IV** convenes the **Council of Florence**, an ecumenical council between the Catholic and Greek Orthodox churches, in the Franciscan church of **Santa Croce**. **John Palaeologos**, the Byzantine emperor, accedes to union between **Greek** and **Roman Christendom**. The Greeks retain their religious rites but acknowledge the **pope's supremacy**. In return, the pope agrees to provide the emperor with archers and galleys against the **Muslim Turks** now preparing to attack **Constantinople**.

Under **Doge Francesco Foscari**, the new **Palazzo Ducale** (Doge's Palace) in **Venice** is completed after fifteen years of rebuilding work. A masterpiece of **Venetian Gothic** style, mixing French and Italian elements with features from Byzantine and oriental architecture, it will influence the design of many buildings in the city.

1440 **Lorenzo Valla**, a professor at the university of **Pavia**, completes a treatise entitled *De falso credita et ementita Constanini donatione* (*Concerning the falsely believed and lying Donation of Constantine*). This proves to be a wholesale demolition of the forged 8th-century document of unknown authorship known as the *Donation of Constantine*, which maintained that the Roman emperor Constantine had given the pope sovereignty over Italy and the whole of western Europe and its rulers, temporal and spiritual. Though Valla is a devout Catholic and his work is intended to strengthen the Church's spiritual authority, its publication represents the first significant criticism of the popes as temporal rulers.

1441 **Filippo Brunelleschi** designs a new palace for the immensely wealthy and ostentatious Florentine merchant Luca Pitti. In the following century the **Palazzo Pitti**, acquired by the **Medici family**, will become the official palace of Tuscany's grand dukes.

1442 With help from **Filippo Maria Visconti**, duke of Milan, **Alfonso of Aragon**, king of Sicily, seizes **Naples** from the Angevin **king René**, driving him into exile. **Pope Eugenius IV**, having supported the Angevins as their overlord, withholds his assent to Alfonso's investiture for a year. After providing armed assistance to the pope in various campaigns, Alfonso is eventually formally acknowledged by Eugenius as king. Under its cultivated and enlightened new ruler, the city of Naples becomes a haven for **scholars**, **artists** and **men of letters**, and the mainland part of the new kingdom enjoys its first real **stability** for a hundred years.

1444 **Cosimo de' Medici** opens Europe's first **public library**, at the monastery of **San Marco** in Florence.

Bernardino Albizzeschi dies at L'Aquila. A Franciscan friar born in Siena, he had spent his life wandering through Italy with a message of reconciliation between warring states, attempting to reform the lax morals of his fellow Italians and preaching a series of memorable sermons along the way. He is soon canonized as St Bernardino da Siena.

1450 **Leon Battista Alberti**, already established as an important theorist of **classical principles** in architecture and **perspective** in painting, designs the **Tempio Malatestiano** at **Rimini** for its rulers Sigismondo Malatesta and Isotta degli Atti. Though never completed, the Tempio (and the **decorative scheme** designed for its interior by **Agostino di Duccio**) will become celebrated as embodying the Renaissance ideal of **harmony** and **proportion** in all things.

Francesco Sforza becomes **duke of Milan**, founding a new ruling dynasty in the city's history.

> " In everything suited to a man born free and liberally educated, he was considered the best among the youth of his time. Skilful in the practice of arms, riding horses and playing musical instruments, as well as in the pursuit of letters and the fine arts, he was dedicated to finding out the most difficult things and eagerly embracing whatever might bring him fame. "
>
> Leon Battista Alberti describes the ideal Renaissance man

West facade of Alberti's Tempio Malatestiano, Rimini

1451 The sculptors **Domenico Gagini** and **Francesco Laurana** begin work on a **triumphal arch** to celebrate the achievements of **King Alfonso I of Naples**. Placed between two medieval bastions of the Castelnuovo, it is the first major example of Renaissance art in Naples.

1452 **Lorenzo Ghiberti** completes more than twenty years of work on the bronze relief panels of the doors for the **baptistry** of the Duomo in Florence.

1453 The city of **Constantinople** falls to the Turks under Sultan **Mehmet II**. **Venetian** and **Genoese colonies** in the eastern Mediterranean are now under serious threat. **Greek scholars** from the conquered city flee to Italy, bringing with them many ancient manuscript texts of **classical authors**, including some hitherto unknown in the west.

The governance of Venice

During the 14th and early 15th centuries, most of the Italian states were **republics**, in which leading citizens from the most powerful families assumed various civil and military responsibilities. The first of these to be established – the Most Serene Republic of Venice – was also destined to be the most resilient, owing to its sophisticated administrative structure and to the loyalty that its political ethos fostered among those in government.

By 1300 the republic of Venice had established itself as a state ruled by a **merchant aristocracy**. For members of this aristocracy, the highest honour was to receive one of the many official positions that lay at the disposal of the regulatory authorities; these governed everything from weights and measures, street crime and dress codes, to the administration of the various ports and islands which formed part of Venice's growing empire. In 1297, a law had been passed restricting admission to the **Great Council** of the republic to all but members of families whose names were inscribed in the *Libro d'Oro* (*Golden Book*), and from that point on the lives of adult males within this oligarchy were in theory dedicated to the state.

At the pinnacle of government sat the **doge**, elected by a laboriously complex system involving the dropping into an urn, at various stages, of small balls (*ballotti*, giving rise to the word

Donatello completes his statue of the *condottiere* **Gattame-lata** in Padua. Cast in bronze, it is the first life-size equestrian statue to be created since Roman times.

1454 Via a treaty signed between them at Lodi, Cosimo de' Medici and Pope Nicholas V seek to unite **Florence**, **Venice** and **Milan** in a defensive alliance. Venice gains possession of Treviso, Bergamo, Brescia and Padua.

1455 The painter and Dominican monk **Fra Angelico** dies in Rome and is buried in the church of **Santa Maria sopra Minerva**. His vivid yet eloquently simple religious

ballot). It is commonly believed that the doge was a powerless figurehead. While it is true that doges were invariably old and the office was hedged about with restrictions, these were measures aimed at reducing the otherwise unrivalled powers of the dogeship. Beneath the doge lay a series of committees, elected from among the patricians, including the **Senate**, the **Tribune of the Forty** and the influential **Council of Ten**, with responsibility for matters of internal security. Members of these and other committees were distinguished by a panoply of different robes with variations in their colour, sleeve-length and borders, derived in both style and purpose from the Chinese imperial court by way of medieval **Byzantium**. Collective obedience was offered to the abstract concept of the **Republic of St Mark**: corporate, indivisible and, as far as Venetian pride could make it, indestructible.

The endurance of Venice as a political construct, long after it ceased to enjoy any real say in the affairs of the rest of Italy, was undoubtedly due to this binding confidence in its system of government, symbolic as it was of the uniqueness of the state. The influence of this kind of rule by **elected executive** (however limited in Venice's case) may be seen in the tenets of the political theorists of 17th-century England under Oliver Cromwell and by their immediate heirs, the American colonists of the 1770s.

scenes, especially the frescoes decorating the Florentine monastery of **San Marco**, are already much admired by his contemporaries. Famed for his saintliness, he will nevertheless have to wait until 1984 to be beatified by the Catholic Church.

1457 After 34 years as doge of Venice and successful leader of wars against the Milanese, **Francesco Foscari** is forced to resign his office on 23 October. The ailing and elderly doge's enemies accuse him of plotting the murder of Admiral Pietro Loredan, and he is further discredited by the banishment and death in exile of his son, found guilty on trumped-up charges of treason against the state. Eight days after his resignation Foscari dies, reputedly of a broken heart. Lord Byron will later base a play (*The Two Foscari*) and Giuseppe Verdi an opera (*I Due Foscari*) on this poignant tale.

1458 On the death of **Alfonso I**, the Neapolitan barons reject his brother John II of Aragon as their king, preferring to support the claims of Alfonso's illegitimate son **Ferrante**.

1459 **Benozzo Gozzoli** decorates the chapel of the **Palazzo Medici Riccardi** in Florence. His fresco depicting the arrival of the Magi combines fantasy, elegance and vivid colouring in its depiction of what is essentially a group of contemporary aristocrats and their pages in gala costume. In memory of a brother of King Alfonso V of Portugal, Bishop Alviano of Florence orders the building of a new chapel in the church of **San Miniato al Monte**. Housing an effigy of the dead man by **Antonio Rossellino**, a fresco by **Antonio Pollaiuolo** and ceramic medallions by **Luca della Robbia** and **Antonio Manetti**, the **chapel of the Cardinal of Portugal** is an ideal ensemble of Florentine Renaissance art.

Commissioned by Cosimo de' Medici, **Marsilio Ficino**, a medical student and Greek scholar, begins the task of translating the complete works of **Plato** into Latin. Ficino's synthesis of Platonic ideals and Christian doctrine will become known as '**Neoplatonism**', and will deeply influence thought and culture throughout Europe.

c.1460 **Giovanni Bellini** begins his long and influential career as a painter in **Venice**. His evolving style makes use of a rich and subtle palette, and his incorporation of romantic mountainous landscapes into religious scenes is a feature imitated by his pupils and younger contemporaries in Venice, including **Titian**, **Giorgione** and **Cima da Conegliano**.

1464 **Cosimo de' Medici** dies after thirty years' ascendancy over the affairs of **Florence**. He is posthumously accorded the title *Pater Patriae* ('Father of his Country'), in tribute to his wise government. Under his rule Florence has become one of the wealthiest and most splendid of all Italian cities.

1465 Italy's first **printing press** is set up at Subiaco by the German printers Sweynheim and Panartz.

1468 **Lorenzo de' Medici**, Cosimo's grandson, becomes ruler of Florence with his brother **Giuliano**. **Siena**, long-standing enemy of **Florence**, welcomes **Alfonso, duke of Calabria**, son of King Ferrante of Naples, to command its armies. From here, with the assistance of **Pope Sixtus IV**, he will plan a war against Florence that will last for the next twelve years.

1470 **Lodovico II Gonzaga**, marquis of Mantua, commissions the magnificent church of **Sant'Andrea** from the architect and theorist **Leon Battista Alberti**.

The Venetians lose the Greek island of Negroponte – modern Evvia – to the **Ottoman Turks**, who then send raiding parties as far as the northern Adriatic to attack towns in the area around **Venice**.

1471 **Brunelleschi** creates a new design for the church of **Santo Spirito** in **Florence**, after his first building has been destroyed by fire. Using Corinthian columns, the wondrously simple plan breathes new life into the ancient form of the Christian basilica. The architect does not live to witness its completion.

Ercole I d'Este inherits the duchy of **Ferrara** from his brother Borso. The scion of a restless, art-loving and politically astute clan which has ruled Ferrara since the 13th century, he concentrates on developing his capital city as a bulwark against further territorial expansion by the republic of **Venice**.

1472 Caterina Cornaro, daughter of a Venetian noble family, marries Jacques II de Lusignan, king of **Cyprus**, who dies soon after the wedding, leaving her regent and ward of their infant son.

1474 Andrea Mantegna, brother-in-law of Giovanni Bellini, completes his decoration of the **Camera degli Sposi** in the palace at Mantua of Marquis **Lodovico II Gonzaga** and his wife, **Barbara of Brandenburg**. His

Italy and the birth of the printed book

Brought to Italy during the 15th century from its European birthplace in the **Rhineland**, the art of printing was by 1500 established in a number of different centres, mostly in **Lombardy**, **Tuscany** and the **Veneto**. Calligraphic styles based on the study of Roman monumental inscriptions and the decorative features of ancient architecture influenced the development of the 'roman' and 'italic' typefaces that have since remained standard typographical fonts throughout the world. Paper was already an important Italian export product, from an industry based largely in Pioraco and Fabriano on the eastern spurs of the Apennines, which provided the fast-flowing streams essential for the manufacture of paper-pulp. In response to increased demands from the new printing technology, workers from these towns now carried their skills further afield.

By 1500, Italy's major centre of **book production** lay in **Venice**, where long traditions of shrewd business practice mixed easily with the more idealistic aspects of **humanism** and the new fields of learning it opened up. The city's leading printer was Tebaldo Manuzio, known to us by his Latin trade name of **Aldus Manutius**, a Roman born in 1450 who had been educated in Ferrara and spent some time under the tutelage of the humanist **Giovanni**

depiction of intimate family groupings and household pets, and above all the bold use of trompe-l'oeil and perspective effects, are a new and highly influential departure in fresco painting.

1475 The *condottiere* **Bartolomeo Colleoni** dies in **Venice**, leaving his immense fortune to the republic he has served faithfully as commander of its mainland army, mostly fighting the Milanese. A statue is raised in his honour outside the church of **Santi Giovanni e Paolo**. The work of the Florentine sculptor **Andrea Verrocchio**, the monument is widely acknowledged, then and since, as the finest **equestrian statue** in the world.

Pico della Mirandola. Aldus set up his first press in **Venice** in 1494, devising his own italic typeface, developing a sun-resistant ink and using only the finest Fabriano paper. Passionately devoted to the **classics**, he produced many of the first modern editions of ancient texts in Greek and Latin, as well as launching the earliest-known cheap 'pocket series', beginning with the works of **Virgil** in 1501. 'Aldine' editions were a key factor in the spread of Renaissance learning, and, during the period 1490–1520, Italy became a leader in European printing.

The potential of print for **political propaganda** had quickly been grasped by Italian rulers. King Ferrante I of Naples, for instance, had published the confession statements of rebellious nobles for general circulation. Conversely, the Catholic Church realized that printing represented the most dangerous threat to its traditional hold over intellectual freedom and education. Thus it was that Pope Alexander VI introduced the first **press censorship**, and Leo X's Lateran Council forbade the printing of books without **ecclesiastical approval**. By the early 16th century, Church and state were cooperating in the suppression of dangerous publications of all kinds, and the introduction of the notorious **Papal Index of Prohibited Books** was not far distant.

Ferrara and the Estense

The city of Ferrara during the late 15th and early 16th centuries offers a classic example of a small Renaissance princely state developing its cultural activities on the most lavish and sophisticated scale. Under dukes Borso and Ercole d'Este the **university**, in addition to its usual courses in medicine, philosophy and law, encouraged the study of Greek literature and thought, and offered lessons in oratory, music and the writing of verse in Italian and Latin. One envious satirist from nearby Modena declared that there were as many Ferrarese poets as there were frogs croaking in the fields. It was here that a new kind of Italian epic was developed by the courtier **Matteo Boiardo**, whose *Orlando Innamorato* mixed the old French chivalric story of Roland with aspects of Arthurian legend, classical mythology and touches of comedy and fantasy. Duke Ercole also encouraged translations of the classics and the writing of history. No fewer than seventy painters were employed by the court, including **Piero della Francesca**, **Cosimo Tura** and **Francesco Cossa**, who was responsible for the lyrical fresco sequence adorning the **Palazzo Schifanoia**, rebuilt by Duke Borso in 1469.

  Though Ercole failed to hold off Venice's predatory assault on his northernmost territories along the Po, he reaffirmed his brother

1476 Venice makes a costly peace with the **Turks**. The republic is forced to yield its conquests in Albania and territory in the Peloponnese to the sultan.

1478 **Girolamo Riario**, encouraged by his so-called uncle (almost certainly his father) **Pope Sixtus IV**, plans to snatch the town of Imola from the Milanese and use it as a base for papal expansion. But his plans are thwarted by the Medici, who, although the pope has approached them in person, refuse to bankroll the affair. Enraged by this rebuff, and by Lorenzo's refusal to recognize the unilateral papal appointment of **Francesco Salviati** as archbishop of Pisa, Sixtus

Borso's ambition to make Ferrara a **cultural capital**. The first **plays** to be written in Italy since Roman times were produced here in a purpose-built theatre, and what we now know as **ballet** had at least some of its roots in Ferrarese court entertainment. While Ercole's son **Alfonso** was more interested in pottery than poetry (the city was famous during the 1500s for its **majolica**, some of it made by the duke himself), his wife **Lucrezia Borgia** welcomed writers of all kinds to the court, where she reigned as duchess for fourteen years before dying in childbirth.

Even if he was forced to devote most of his energies to fine-tuning the subtle **diplomatic intrigues** of the popes, the Medici family, the Venetians and Emperor Charles V, Alfonso nevertheless sought to maintain Ferrara's reputation as a centre of learning and art. The ducal family, the Estense, imposed constant **tax rises** upon their subjects in order to finance it all, and when, in 1597, the duchy was brought to an end for lack of a legitimate heir, the Ferrarese did not mourn its passing as much as they might have. However, under its new overlord, the Church, the city quickly declined and despite a brief 20th-century economic revival during the Fascist era, Ferrara was never to recover its former splendour and importance.

turns to the Pazzi, chief commercial rivals of the Medici in Rome. Thus is born the **Pazzi Conspiracy**, one of the more brutal acts of treachery in Florentine history. Two disaffected priests are hired to murder **Lorenzo** and **Giuliano de' Medici** while at Mass in the **Duomo** of Florence. While Giuliano is killed in a frenzied attack, Lorenzo breaks free and rallies his supporters. A furious mob dispenses summary justice to the conspirators and their troops.

Lorenzo now rules Florence as an **enlightened despot**, noted for his patronage of artists such as **Botticelli**, **Ghirlandaio** and the young **Michelangelo**.

Lodovico Gonzaga and his son, Cardinal Francesco, and retinue from Mantegna's *Camera degli Sposi* series

Sandro Botticelli (Alessandro Mariano Filipepi) paints the mythological allegory known as *La Primavera*, depicting the season of spring personified in the form of a graceful young woman. His patron is Lorenzo de' Medici's cousin **Lorenzo di Pierfrancesco de' Medici**, who also commissions *The Birth of Venus* at about this time. Both works embody a new concept in European art, that of large-scale pictures based on subjects drawn from pagan mythology.

During a severe outbreak of **plague** in Mantua, Marquis **Lodovico II Gonzaga** dies, having tried to escape the epidemic by fleeing to his country villa at Goito, north of the city. Mantua mourns its most visionary and enterprising ruler.

1479 **Lorenzo de' Medici** goes to **Naples** to negotiate a treaty with **King Ferrante**. He seeks to end the war **Pope Sixtus IV** has been waging against **Florence**, in which Ferrante's son the **duke of Calabria** has been leading the papal army. After two months' hesitation Ferrante accedes, and Sixtus is forced to make peace with the Florentines.

Following the death of his two brothers, **Lodovico Sforza**, known as *il Moro* ('the Swarthy' or 'the Moor'), foils attempts by other members of the family to cut him out of the succession and so gains the duchy of **Milan**. His rule is tyrannical and oppressive, yet during his reign Milan becomes an important centre of culture and ideas.

1480 A **Turkish fleet**, with assistance from the Venetians, attacks **Otranto** and slaughters its inhabitants. Eight hundred survivors are offered their lives in return for converting to Islam, but they refuse and are put to death. Moved by their example, the chief executioner himself converts to Christianity and is also martyred.

1481 Otranto is recaptured from the Turks by **King Alfonso VI** of Aragon.

The *condottieri*

Condottiere in Italian means literally 'leader', but the term is now used specifically to refer to the **soldiers of fortune** who commanded the armies of Italian city states during the wars of the late Middle Ages and Renaissance. Demand for their services arose from the simple fact that the citizens of great commercial centres such as **Florence** and **Venice** were more interested in business than in warfare. As long as the money was available to pay mercenaries (sometimes entire armies of them), this often turned out to be a more profitable short-term investment than the recruiting and drilling of local militias. Unfettered by political loyalties or ties of blood, the **condottieri** took their professional skills wherever they could find a buyer.

Sir John Hawkwood, for example, leader of the infamous White Company, was an Englishman from Essex who ended his life in wealth and honour among the Florentines, and was given a splendid funeral in the Duomo in 1394. **Niccolò da Tolentino**, who won a victory for the Florentines over the Sienese at San Romano in 1432, originally came from the Marche district, under papal rule. By the end of Florence's war against Lucca in the following year, he had cost the city the vast sum of 50,000 florins. Both Hawkwood (also known as Giovanni Acuto) and Niccolò were commemorated by their grateful employers in fresco paintings by **Paolo Uccello**

In **Venice**, the architect and sculptor **Pietro Lombardo** begins work on the church of **Santa Maria dei Miracoli** to house an image of the Virgin Mary. With its use of variegated marble and its decorated portals, the church is a masterpiece of High Renaissance Venetian architecture.

1482 **Leonardo da Vinci** arrives in **Milan** from Tuscany, at the invitation of its duke, **Lodovico Sforza**. Under Lodovico's patronage he will work as painter, scientist, town planner, architect and organizer of court entertainments, as well as decorating the refectory of **Santa Maria**

and **Andrea del Castagno**. The **republic of Venice**, meanwhile, commissioned equestrian statues for two of its greatest *condottieri*. That of Erasmo da Narni, known as **Gattamelata** (tortoiseshell cat) was cast in bronze by **Donatello** at Padua, while in Venice the arrogance and ruthlessness of **Bartolomeo Colleoni** were superbly portrayed in **Andrea Verrocchio's** figure of him.

Colleoni died peacefully enough at his Lombard castle of Malpaga. A sadder fate befell Francesco Bussone, the poor swineherd whose military prowess as *condottiere* for the duke of Milan earned him the title of **conte di Carmagnola**. After a bitter quarrel with the duke, Carmagnola transferred his services to Venice in 1426. A Venetian war against the Milanese offered him a chance for revenge, but after a series of fruitless campaigns his new masters lost patience and had him arrested and tried, by a secret court, for 'injury wrought by him to our affairs and against the honour and wellbeing of our state'. Although Doge **Francesco Foscari** tried to intervene on his behalf, Carmagnola was beheaded between the two columns of the Piazzetta of San Marco. The crimson velvet cape he wore to his execution set a fashion among modish Venetians for capes alla Carmagnola. Four centuries later, the poet and novelist Alessandro Manzoni used his story as the inspiration for a tragedy.

delle Grazie with a fresco representing the *Last Supper*. In the centuries that follow, and even today, it remains one of the most admired of all Italian works of art.

1485 Giuliano da San Gallo completes work on the villa of **Poggio a Caiano** for Lorenzo de' Medici. The first country villa to be built since Roman times, this effectively introduces the status symbol of the 'country house' as a mark of civilized living to Europe.

1489 The rule of **Cyprus** passes from its queen, **Caterina Cornaro**, to the republic of Venice.

Leonardo da Vinci

> ❝ ...Leonardo da Vinci, an artist of outstanding physical beauty who displayed infinite grace in everything he did and who cultivated his genius so brilliantly that all problems he studied he solved with ease. He possessed great strength and dexterity; he was a man of regal spirit and tremendous breadth of mind; and his name became so famous that not only was he esteemed during his lifetime but his reputation endured and became even greater after his death. ❞

Giorgio Vasari, *Lives of the Artists*, trans. George Bull

The Leonardo (1452–1519) revered by his contemporaries and admired by later generations is not just the acknowledged master of tone, expression and composition in painting, but also the **restless genius** of his notebooks and sketchbooks. Crammed with drawings and descriptions, these manifest an unquenchable interest in everything from human and animal movement to **engineering** and **flight**, and from **anatomy** and **botany** to **physics** and **optics**. Though he left few works behind him – a mere seventeen documented paintings (including the *Madonna of the Rocks* and the *Mona Lisa* as well as a number of unfinished works), and some outstanding drawings – we continue to celebrate Leonardo da Vinci not just as a remarkable painter and

Benedetto da Maiano designs a new palace in Florence for the merchant Filippo Strozzi. In its austere monumentality, the **Palazzo Strozzi** provides a model for a new kind of Italian noble residence: considerations of status and elegance now take precedence over the defensive features of aristocratic town houses in earlier ages.

1492 Lorenzo de' Medici dies of chronic gout, aged 43. His son **Piero** inherits the government of Florence, but

sculptor, but also as an intellectual and artistic giant, the epitome of **Renaissance man**.

The son of a craftsman and – as revealed by recent research – a female slave of Middle Eastern origin in the Tuscan village of Vinci, he was apprenticed to the Florentine sculptor and painter **Andrea Verrocchio**, before leaving for **Milan**. There he spent seventeen years at the **Sforza court** as painter and technical adviser. During this period, his major projects included an equestrian statue of Francesco Sforza and the *Last Supper* fresco at the monastery of Santa Maria delle Grazie. The first of these was never fully completed. The second used an experimental paint medium that da Vinci had devised, employing a mixture of paint and wax, which caused its surface to decay almost at once (although it remains indisputably a masterpiece).

After a brief return to Florence, Leonardo entered the service of **Cesare Borgia** as a surveyor and military engineer. A second stay in Milan led to further unfinished projects and, after a visit to **Rome** in 1513 proved scarcely more fruitful, he readily accepted an invitation from the French king, **François I**, to become his chief painter. In 1516 he went to live at the royal palace of **Amboise** on the Loire where he died three years later, showered with honours by the king. Leonardo's lifelong struggle to pin down the teeming fertility of his imagination, the power of his intellect and his extraordinary artistic vision and skills are summed up in his own uncompromising words: 'I wish to work miracles, though I may die a poor man.'

without his father's political acumen he begins to lose support both within the city and among its allies and neighbours. The historian **Niccolò Machiavelli** will later identify Lorenzo's death and Piero's misjudgements as the moment when 'those evil plants began to sprout which in a short time ruined Italy'.

The Genoese mariner Cristoforo Colombo – **Christopher Columbus** – lands on one of the **Bahama** islands, which

Caterina Cornaro

When she was married to **Jacques de Lusignan**, king of Cyprus, in 1472, Caterina Cornaro (1452–1510) was 18 years old. Though it was made for reasons of state, the match offered her a perfect escape route from the domestic seclusion that awaited a Venetian senator's bride. A year later, however, Jacques died, leaving Queen Caterina pregnant and surrounded by enemies. The **Cypriot nobility**, led by the island's **Catholic clergy**, rose in revolt, imprisoned Caterina, murdered her relatives and kidnapped her newborn son. This gave **Venice** the perfect excuse to intervene, offering the queen protection in return for suppressing the revolt. Caterina's son had sickened and died, probably poisoned, in captivity. Without a legitimate heir, she had no choice but to hand Cyprus over to the Venetian state. In 1489, after a sequence of elaborately staged abdication ceremonies throughout the island, she was forced to return to Venice.

Her native city compensated her with the hill town of **Asolo**, north of Venice, where she was allowed to rule as sovereign and make her own laws. Here Caterina came into her own as queen and **patron**, welcoming poets, painters and musicians to her court. Several of them are reputed to have become her lovers, and she certainly revelled in her new-found freedom. **Pietro Bembo**, the most gifted Italian poet of his time, was a frequent visitor who coined the verb *asolare*, meaning literally 'to behave in the Asolo fashion', or in other words to relax and enjoy the civilized pleasures of life in the company of an intelligent and attractive woman. Having returned to Venice during the war of the League of Cambrai, Caterina died aged 56 and was buried in the church of **Santi Apostoli**.

he believes to be not far from the Chinese coast, and identifies the nearby island of **Cuba** as Japan. This, and his subsequent expeditions, fuel expectations throughout Italy of new and profitable **trade routes** to the east.

> ❝ The city was in a state of perfect peace, the citizens united and the government powerful beyond all opposition. Food was plentiful, business flourished, men of talent were rewarded through the recognition given to art and letters – but finally, when all here was tranquil within and glorious without, a terrible calamity destroyed everything, both for Florence and for Italy. ❞
>
> Francesco Guicciardini on the death of Lorenzo de' Medici, 1509

1493 **King Charles VIII** of France invades Italy. His aim is to restore French political ascendancy over Italian affairs and to recover domains that formerly belonged to his family, the royal house of **Anjou**.

1494 King Ferrante of Naples dies, leaving the throne to his brother, **Alfonso II**.

Piero de' Medici is driven out of Florence, having tried to shift its traditionally pro-French alignment by putting out diplomatic feelers to the kingdom of **Naples**. A **republican movement** gathers strength among the Florentines, led by the Ferrarese monk **Girolamo Savonarola**.

Aldus Manutius (Tebaldo Manuzio) sets up his first printing press in Venice.

1495 At the head of an immense army, **King Charles VIII** of France seizes **Naples**. King Alfonso abdicates in favour of his son, **Ferrante II**, and retreats for safety to Ischia.

Venice, **Milan** and **Spain**, with papal support, form the 'Holy League' to drive the French out of Italy. As King Charles's army returns northwards, it is defeated by the League's forces at **Fornovo**.

Savonarola

> ❝ What are You doing, O God? Why do you sleep? Arise and come to deliver your Church from devils' hands, from tyrants' hands, from the hands of wicked churchmen! The only hope remaining for us is that God's sword will soon strike at the whole earth. ❞
>
> Girolamo Savonarola, from an Advent sermon, 1493

As the political situation in Italy grew ever more insecure during the last years of the 16th century, the sensual, pluralist atmosphere of High Renaissance culture found itself challenged by a Christian **religious revival**, appealing to popular doubts and fears as to the destiny of sinful mankind. At the forefront of this reaction was the extraordinary figure of Fra Girolamo Savonarola, a **Dominican friar** born in Ferrara in 1452. Arriving in Florence during the last years of Lorenzo de' Medici's rule, he immediately attracted attention with his coruscating sermons, in which he inveighed against the worldliness and corruption of princes, churchmen and ordinary citizens.

The apocalyptic, fundamentalist vision he described seemed to be borne out by the incursions of Charles VIII's French army in 1494. For the next four years Florence became a **theocracy**, with Savonarola as its moral arbiter. One of the most bizarre features of his ascendancy over the Florentines was the fact that a number of

1497 The worldly and corrupt Pope Alexander VI excommunicates **Savonarola**, who has denounced him as **Antichrist** and praised Charles VIII as God's instrument of purification.

1498 Florence becomes bitterly divided between the *frateschi* (adherents of Savonarola) and the *arrabbiati* (those whom he has antagonized). After one of his followers fails to undergo the challenge Savonarola had initially accepted himself, of

leading humanists and artists took his ideas to heart. The painter **Sandro Botticelli**, for instance, was rumoured to have repented of his earlier works, based on profane or pagan themes, though art historians have since tended to play down Savonarola's influence on his later paintings. **Machiavelli**, meanwhile, was clearly intrigued by the friar as the incarnation of a new type of ruler, able to dominate the community through sheer **force of personality**.

After the French defeat at the battle of Fornovo, in 1495, **Pope Alexander VI** was at last able to undermine Savonarola's power, and eventually pronounced his **excommunication**. It seems that this goaded Savonarola on to yet further extremes, replacing the traditional **carnival** celebrations of 1497 with his notorious 'Bonfires of the Vanities'. At these fervent occasions, Florentines heaped their more ostentatious consumer goods and artworks on specially constructed pyres and watched them burn, a symbolic rejection of worldliness. A year later, however, it was Savonarola himself who was committed to the flames. Political uncertainty, Medici intrigues and Florentine disillusion with the zealot's unfulfilled prophecies of doom had fatally weakened his authority. His enemies had challenged him to submit to a **trial by fire**, which one of his fellow Dominicans volunteered to undertake in his place. When the trial did not take place, the city turned against him. Arrested and tried by a papal commission, he was found guilty of heresy and schism, and condemned to be hanged and burned.

an ordeal by fire, he is arrested by a papal commission, tried for heresy and schism, and executed.

1499 **Venice** backs the claim of Charles VIII's successor **Louis XII** to the duchy of **Milan**. The duke, **Lodovico Sforza**, is forced to quit the city as a French army arrives at the gates.

The painter **Luca Signorelli** journeys from Florence to **Orvieto** in order to embark on his monumental fresco of the *Last Judgement* for its Gothic cathedral.

1500 **Leonardo da Vinci** returns to Florence, where he starts work on the cartoons (sketches on paper) for his *Virgin and Child with St Anne* and on the portrait of a woman known as the *Mona Lisa*.

1503 Giuliano della Rovere is elected pope as **Julius II**. Vigorous and aggressive, he epitomizes the ambition, magnificence and ruthlessness of the Renaissance popes, once again major players on the Italian political stage.

ITALY c.1500

SWISS CONFEDERATION

KINGDOM OF HUNGARY

Trent

Bassano

SAVOY

Milan

MONFERRAT

Padua

Venice

ISTRIA

Turin

MILAN

MANTUA

SALUZZO

FERRARA

MODENA

OTTOMAN EMPIRE

GENOA

Genoa

Pisa

Rimini

FLORENCE

LIGURIAN SEA

SIENA

PAPAL KINGDOM

ADRIATIC SEA

ELBA

CORSICA

Pescara

Rome

KINGDOM OF NAPLES

Bari

Naples

Salerno

KINGDOM OF SARDINIA

Otranto

Messina

SICILY

Syracuse

N

Duchy
Republic
Republic of Venice
Marquisate

0   100 kms

On 13 February, while the French are besieging Barletta in the kingdom of Naples, a group of thirteen Italian knights issues a challenge to an equal number of their French counterparts. In the ensuing combat, decided by generals from the two armies, the Italians emerge victorious. The incident, known as the **Challenge of Barletta**, will become a famous example of national heroism for the Italians of the Risorgimento, the 19th-century struggle to achieve national unity. The defenders of the city, led by **Gonzalo de Cordoba**, drive off the French, pursuing them to nearby Cerignola where they are decisively defeated. Naples and Sicily are invaded by **King Ferdinand of Spain**, heir to the crown of **Aragon**.

1504 The artist **Michelangelo Buonarroti** unveils his statue of **David**, carved from a single block of marble, in Florence's **Piazza della Signoria**.

Leonardo and **Michelangelo** are commissioned to adorn the walls of Florence's **Palazzo Vecchio** with frescoes representing important Florentine victories. Neither artist completes his project, but the implicit rivalry is probably responsible for Leonardo's ultimate decision, two years later, to return to Milan.

Mundus Novus (*New World*) by the Florentine explorer **Amerigo Vespucci** is published. An extended letter to a member of the Medici family, it offers the earliest detailed ethnographical description of any part of **South America**. After its use on a German map, a version of Vespucci's baptismal name, '**America**', becomes current as a name for the whole continent.

1505 **Pope Julius II** lays the foundation stone of a new **Basilica of St Peter** in Rome. His chosen architect, **Donato Bramante**, proposes a revolutionary new design based on a Greek cross surmounted by a dome, which will influence church architecture throughout Europe.

Michelangelo

With the completion of his frescoes for the ceiling and west wall of the Sistine Chapel in 1512 Michelangelo (1475–1564) was hailed as the greatest artist of his day. In his own view he was first and foremost a sculptor, while to posterity he was also a painter, draughtsman, a remarkable architect and poet, whose pre-eminent place in the history of European art is secure. During the 19th century his stature was enhanced by scholarly interest in his **sonnets**, published for the first time in their original form in 1863, which revealed him as one of the most eloquent and polished writers of Italian verse. In the 20th century great emphasis was placed on his genius as a **colourist**, revealed by restoration work on the frescoes of the Sistine Chapel.

The crowds who admire the *David* in its lofty hall within Florence's Accademia may be less familiar with Michelangelo's fierce loyalty to his native **Florence**. As well as offering a classic expression of the nude form in Renaissance art, the mighty figure of *David* – commissioned by the commune of Florence to occupy a key position in Piazza della Signoria – was intended to symbolize the Florentine republic's relentless struggle against tyrants and foreign oppressors. Furthermore, Michelangelo gladly accepted a commission to paint the *Battle of Cascina*, to complement or rival Leonardo's *Battle of Anghiari* in the hall of **Palazzo Vecchio**. Sadly, he completed only an initial cartoon before going to Rome to work on a vast tomb for **Pope Julius II**.

But the most powerful political statement ever made by Michelangelo as an artist must surely lie in one magnificent late work, the bust of **Marcus Brutus**, now in Florence's Bargello Museum. Created for Cardinal Niccolo Ridolfi, the leader of the exiled Florentine faction in Rome, this stern, heroic image of Caesar's killer has often been interpreted as an excited response to the **assassination of Alessandro de'Medici** in 1537, an event which seemed to promise a revival of **Florentine independence**.

Michelangelo's hopes were doomed to disappointment, however. Indeed, his great fresco of the *Last Judgement* in the Sistine Chapel, unveiled 29 years to the day after his ceiling, could be perhaps interpreted on one level as a gloomy response to the **triumph of despotisms**, both large and small, throughout 16th-century Italy.

© SCALA

Michelangelo's *Brutus*

1508 **Michelangelo** begins work on the frescoes of the ceiling and west wall of the **Sistine Chapel** in Rome. Completed in 1481, under the patronage of **Pope Sixtus IV**, the chapel already contains frescoes by **Sandro Botticelli**, **Pietro Perugino** and **Luca Signorelli** on its northern and southern walls. Michelangelo's ceiling features episodes from the book of Genesis, the most famous among them being the *Story of the Creation*, bordered by figures of prophets and sibyls.

Eager to curb the power of **Venice**, Julius II helps to form the **League of Cambrai** with Spain, France and the Holy Roman Empire, in order to seize possession of all the republic's territories on the Italian mainland. He also places the city under a blanket **excommunication**.

1509 Aged only 26, the artist **Raphael** begins work on the frescoes for the *stanze* (reception rooms) of the **Vatican palace** in Rome.

The **French** inflict a crippling defeat on the Venetians at **Agnadello**. **Venice** is forced to yield its conquests in **Romagna**, south of the Po, to the **papacy**.

1510 Fearing that **France** has become too powerful in Italy, **Julius II** lifts his excommunication from Venice and seeks its support in an anti-French alliance under the rallying cry '*Fuori I barbari!*' ('Out with the barbarians!').

The painter **Sandro Botticelli** dies in Florence.

1512 **Julius II** supports the return of the **Medici** to **Florence**, backed by the Spanish and Neapolitan forces of the anti-French alliance. Piero de' Medici's son **Lorenzo** and brother **Giuliano** re-impose their family's rule on the city.

1513 The French forces are routed at **Novara** by a papal force composed mainly of Swiss mercenaries.

Niccolò Machiavelli publishes *Il Principe* (*The Prince*), a classic study of power politics based on his analysis of contemporary rulers, their respective bids for power, and their ability to maintain it once gained.

> **❝** When evening comes, I return home and go into my study. On the threshold I strip off my muddy, sweaty, workaday clothes, and put on the robes of court and palace, and in this graver dress I enter the courts of the ancients and am welcomed by them, and there I ... make bold to speak to them and ask the motives of their actions, and they, in their humanity, reply to me. And for the space of four hours I forget the world, remember no vexation, fear poverty no more, tremble no more at death; I pass indeed into their world. **❞**
>
> Niccolò Machiavelli, 1513

Julius II dies on 20 February and is succeeded as pope by Giuliano de' Medici, as **Leo X**. He announces, notoriously: 'God has given us the papacy, let us enjoy it!'

> **❝** Because the Florentines are devoted to trading and the pursuit of gain, all were thinking of the need to profit from the pontificate. **❞**
>
> Francesco Vettori, c.1513, quoted in *The Civilization of Europe in the Renaissance*, John Hale

The birth of modern history

It was in Renaissance Italy during the late 15th century that our modern concept of history – a study of events, their causes and effects, and of human responses to them – began to develop. As the **classical past**, in particular the annals of ancient Rome, was being rediscovered and examined, the tendency had been to view great men (and very occasionally women) in terms of their exploits and achievements, as examples to contemporary leaders or to those aiming high in politics or warfare. By 1500, in their attempts to grasp the causes of the instability of Italy's political situation, writers started to develop more complex notions of the nature of history and the uses to which it could be put.

At the forefront of this crucial change stood two great **Florentine historians**. Neither could be described as a professional historian or chronicler, though each drew on a broad experience of contemporary politics. **Francesco Guicciardini** (1483–1540) was a lawyer and diplomat who became an administrator and legal adviser in the service of the Medici popes Leo X and Clement VII. His *Istorie fiorentine* ('*History of Florence*'), begun in 1508, and *Storia d'Italia* ('*History of Italy*'), written some twenty years later, examined the recent governance of the Florentine state, under **Cosimo** and **Lorenzo de' Medici**, in terms of the sheer

1514 **François I** leads a French army into Italy to avenge the defeat of Novara, defeating the Swiss mercenaries in turn at **Marignano**.

1516 The painter **Giovanni Bellini** dies in Venice, aged 86. Among his last pupils are **Giorgione** (who dies before him) and **Titian**. The great tradition of Venetian painting he has begun will be continued into the next generation by **Veronese** and **Tintoretto**.

1519 Carlos I, king of Spain, is elected Holy Roman Emperor as **Charles V**. He will soon become the most significant figure in European politics, making a major impact on Italian affairs.

unpredictability of human actions. Guicciardini adopted a fundamentally pessimistic attitude towards historical development as something inevitable and irresistible, anticipating in some respects the view adopted much later by the German philosopher Hegel.

Niccolò Machiavelli (1469–1527), on the other hand, used the past to develop a critique of the present. Like Guicciardini, he was a learned and distinguished diplomat. Firmly convinced that Florence should strive to remain a republic, he took a dim view of the Medici rule, and reproached his fellow countrymen for their failure to live up to the traditions established by their **Roman ancestors**. In his historical writings, especially *Il Principe* (*The Prince*, 1513) and the *Discorsi* (*Discourses on Livy*, 1513–21), he strove to unmask the realities of power as an essential field of study among those responsible for or aspiring to government. However, like Guicciardini, he emphasized the importance of the **human aspect** of the historical process, setting this against such external forces as **destiny and time**. His ideas on these subjects, together with his reflections on **military discipline**, **constitutional reform** and the nature of **freedom**, were to exert a profound influence on western thought during the early modern period.

Lucrezia Borgia dies, aged 39, at **Ferrara**, where she has reigned as duchess of **Alfonso d'Este**. The daughter of Pope Alexander VI, her sensational and unhappy life (with the first of her three husbands divorced and the second murdered) fascinates later historians, dramatists and composers, for whom she becomes an archetype of murderous beauty.

Leonardo da Vinci dies at Cloux, near the French town of **Amboise**.

1520 **Raphael**, generally acknowledged as the greatest painter in Europe, dies in Rome at the age of 37. Pope Leo X plunges the papal court into mourning.

The triumph of Raphael

The career of Raphael Sanzio (1483–1520) confounds in magnificent fashion the notion that an artist has to suffer in order to achieve greatness. Though his was not a long life – he died of a fever on his 37th birthday – it was a staggeringly successful and rewarding one. By the time of his death he had changed the face of western painting, through the sheer force, brilliance and suppleness of his technique and the grandeur and drama at the heart of his compositions.

Born in **Urbino**, the son of a local painter, he eagerly absorbed the **humanist culture** fostered at the court of the **Montefeltro** dukes. His precocious artistic talent was consolidated at **Perugia** as a pupil of **Pietro Perugino**, to whom he was apprenticed at the age of twelve, and whose sinuous, accomplished manner remained an abiding influence on his work. By 1504 Raphael had arrived in **Florence**, where the styles of **Leonardo da Vinci** and **Michelangelo** made a profound impression on him. In a series of works distinguished by a tension between their sumptuous colouring and the relative simplicity and intimacy of their presentation, he gained a reputation as a painter of Madonnas.

He was summoned to Rome by **Pope Julius II** in 1509, where he embarked upon the most significant phase of his career. As well as his grandiose and ambitious **decorative scheme** for the **Vatican** *stanze* (reception rooms), and a series of **Madonnas** that were more visionary and timeless than his earlier treatments of the same theme, he also created his famous sequence of large **cartoons** for tapestries to hang in the **Sistine Chapel**. As well as working on these commissions, Raphael also practised as an architect, designing the **Villa Madama** for Cardinal Giulio de' Medici as a 'country house' within the confines of the city.

Raphael's popularity and success as a **portrait painter** was due in part to the relaxed approach he adopted towards his sitters, many of whom were personal friends. His good looks, intellectual curiosity and charm of manner were widely celebrated, as was his success with women. One of his finest portraits, *La Fornarina*, is of one of his mistresses, and early sources suggested that 'worldly excesses' might have led to his early death. Whatever the truth of the matter, his influence and reputation have endured. Not for nothing was it that, when the Napoleonic armies undertook their wholesale looting of Italian artworks, the spoils they coveted most eagerly were the altarpieces and portraits of Raphael.

Raphael's portrait of Pope Julius II, painted in either 1511 or 1512

1520 Leo X condemns the 95 theses of the renegade German monk **Martin Luther**, in which he attacks papal supremacy, ecclesiastical privileges and the doctrine of transubstantiation.

> " [Rome] is more corrupt than any Babylon or Sodom ever was, ... characterized by a totally depraved, hopeless and notorious wickedness. "
>
> Martin Luther to Pope Leo X, 1520

1521 Emperor Charles V successfully challenges French military supremacy in northern Italy, seizing **Milan** and forcing the election of a pro-imperial doge in **Genoa**.

1523 Leo X's successor, the Dutch pope Adrian VI, dies and is succeeded by Giulio de' Medici as **Clement VII**. For the next 450 years no non-Italian will be elected to the throne of St Peter.

Michelangelo begins work on the architecture and monuments for the new sacristy at **San Lorenzo** in Florence, a mortuary chapel for members of the **Medici family**, as well as planning the adjacent **Laurentian Library** (Biblioteca Laurenziana) to house the collection of precious books left to the city by Lorenzo de' Medici.

1524 The hedonistic **Duke Federico II Gonzaga** of Mantua summons **Giulio Romano** from Rome to his court, and instructs him to build him a new palace on the edge of the city. The decorative scheme he devises for the **Palazzo del Te** combines allegorical elements and humanist symbolism with allusions to the duke's tastes in pretty women and fine horses. The style of Romano's ambitious and dramatic frescoes, with their bold use of **illusion**, is admired and copied all over Italy.

1525 **Charles V** inflicts a crushing defeat on the army of **François I** at **Pavia**. Six thousand French are killed, and François himself is captured, declaring: '*Tout est perdu fors l'honneur*' ('All is lost save honour'). Though François and his successor **Henri II** will make several attempts to avenge the disaster, French power in Italy is effectively at an end. Pope Clement VII hastily organizes a new **Holy League**, involving Rome, Venice and France, to continue the struggle with Charles V.

1527 Charles V's army of 15,000 **German mercenaries**, the *Landsknechte*, marches on **Rome**. The city is sacked and looted, and the troops stable their horses in the Vatican. Charles, whose domains as king of Spain and Holy Roman Emperor are so extensive that he boasts that the sun never sets on them, is now the most powerful monarch in the world and de facto ruler of Italy.

6
The later 16th and 17th centuries

1528–1713

The **sack of Rome** by Charles V's army in 1527 was viewed by many in Europe as God's judgement on the corruption and wickedness of the Italians and their rulers, and most of all on the manifest shortcomings of the Church. The pope and his cardinals, however, needed to hold on to their authority: by the standards of the time, it would clearly have been too much to expect them publicly to acknowledge that the ecclesiastical hierarchy, at every level, was incapable of leading by example.

In the eyes of many Catholics, the papacy's greatest failure lay in its inability to engage constructively with the **Protestants**, in the hope of reconciling them to the communion they had abandoned. While there was no charismatic Protestant leader in Italy, no equivalent of **Martin Luther** or **John Calvin**, a movement towards a more thoughtful, less ostentatious type of Christianity began to develop during the 1530s. At the same time it became increasingly unlikely, as the decade wore on, that Clement VII's successors, more traditional than the worldly **Medici** and **Borgia** popes, would favour anything that smacked of Lutheran reform. The **Council of Trent** (1542–64), convened by the papacy to address the challenge of Protestant dissent, could conceivably have offered an opportunity for **reconciliation**. It soon became clear, however, that the **zealots** of the Church, eager to harry sinful apostasy and stamp out freedom of expression in the form of **printed books**, had won the day.

The Council's deliberations thus became a desperate holding operation against the growth of a more **pluralist society**, favoured as this was by the climate of peace and relative prosperity that prevailed in Italy during the second half of the 16th century. From around 1560, most Italian states experienced some degree of economic recovery from the long-term effects of the sporadic warfare in which they had been engaged since 1300. For example, although **Venice** had already begun to decline in wealth and mercantile influence (its **Mediterranean empire** had been almost totally abandoned to the **Turks** by 1700), the development of the mainland textile industries helped to stem its worst financial losses. Its old rival **Genoa** seemed to fare rather better in terms of material resources, becoming Europe's principal **banking centre** during the 1570s. As late as 1610, by which time the boom was over, visiting artists such as **Rubens** and **Van Dyck** were still able to find profitable employment from the city's ruling oligarchy.

During the 17th century, the political map of northern Italy was redrawn, partly as a result of the pan-European **Thirty Years' War**. The new duchy of **Modena**, created by Pope Clement VIII for the dispossessed **Este** family, formed a significant buffer state between papal and imperial territories. **Mantua**, however, quickly lost its power and importance, becoming a Franco-imperial political football, while **Tuscany** was able to survive only through the commercial success of **Livorno** (Leghorn), proclaimed a free port in 1577 by Grand Duke Ferdinando. The real success story was that of the duchy of **Savoy**, occupying the northwestern Alps and **Piedmont**, the area immediately below them. Though feudalism remained stronger here than elsewhere in the north and urban life was relatively underdeveloped, dukes **Emanuele Filiberto** and **Carlo Emanuele** earned widespread respect through their determination to preserve the duchy's autonomy. As a result, Savoy took on the role of Italy's saviour, protecting it from overweening foreign invaders and laying the foundations for its success as a military power in the **War of the Spanish Succession** (1702–14).

In the south, the economic and social stagnation that had afflicted northern Italy in the mid-17th century was rendered all the more traumatic by neglect and misgovernment under the Spanish crown. Spain saw its kingdoms of **Naples** and **Sicily** as merely a source of **tax revenue**, showing little interest in improving conditions within the cities, whilst upholding feudalism in rural areas, and treating the local aristocracy with disdain. After 1650 when – in the wake of a lull in war-torn Europe – foreign travellers began to visit Italy again, the disparity between conditions in north and south was impossible to ignore. By now, **resignation** was the keynote throughout the peninsula. Even if the **arts** continued to thrive, especially in the **musical life** of **Rome**, **Naples** and **Venice**, rulers and people alike felt powerless in the face of the new power-games being played by **France**, **Austria** and **Spain**. A contemporary aphorism says it all: '*O Francia, o Spagna, pur che si magna?*' ('France? Spain? Who cares so long as we eat?').

> ❝ Rome was a salon for worldly cardinals and a marketplace of international diplomacy as well as a magnet for pilgrims; it was *Caput Mundi*, head of the world, for its admirers, *Coda Mundi*, the world's anus, for those who deplored the mercenariness of its clergy and the numbers of its prostitutes. All these historically induced anomalies and opinions were taken by most in their stride. ❞
>
> John Hale, *The Civilization of Europe in the Renaissance*

1528 **Admiral Andrea Doria** becomes **doge of Genoa** after driving the French out of the city. The new constitution he devises for the republic will remain in force for 250 years.

1529 The **Treaty of Cambrai** is signed between France and the empire. It becomes known as *La Paix des Dames*, as the French king **François I** and the emperor **Charles V** are both absent from the signing, where they are represented by a sister and an aunt respectively. Under the agreement, François renounces all his claims in Italy. Charles V, during lengthy negotiations, uses his newfound power in Italy to put pressure on the pope, **Clement VII**, to refuse to sanction the divorce between his niece, **Catherine of Aragon**, and **Henry VIII** of England.

Baldassare Castiglione, a nobleman of **Urbino**, publishes *Il Cortegiano* (*The Book of the Courtier*). A manual of courtly conduct and ideals, it is also noteworthy for its praise of **learned women**.

In response to the re-establishment of republican government in **Florence** and the banishment of the **Medici**, Charles V sends an army to besiege the city. **Michelangelo**, whose art has often reflected his republican political views, plays a key role in the strengthening of its defences.

> ❝ The conversation of every courtier is always imperfect if the society of ladies does not lend it that share of grace which gives to courtiership its utmost beauty and perfection. ❞
>
> Baldassare Castiglione, *The Book of the Courtier*, trans. R. Samber

1530 On 12 August, Florence surrenders to the imperial troops. The Medici rule is reimposed by **Alessandro**, cousin of **Lorenzo de' Medici**. As duke, he quickly succeeds in antagonizing the aristocracy, who had initially been favourable to his cause.

1531 Charles V lends his support to Alessandro de' Medici, who marries the emperor's daughter **Margherita**.

1533 Ludovico Ariosto dies in **Ferrara**. A civil servant working for Duke Alfonso, he has made his name as the greatest Italian poet of the age with his romantic epic *Orlando Furioso*.

1534 Pope Clement VII dies and is succeeded by Cardinal Alessandro Farnese, as **Paul III**. The **Farnese** clan soon becomes one of the most influential in Italy, and the wealth and artistic taste of its various members are reflected in the villas, churches and sometimes entire towns that they build in the region of **Lazio**, north of Rome.

Michelangelo forsakes Florence to return to Rome, leaving the **Medici Chapel** at **San Lorenzo**, one of his most ambitious projects, unfinished.

Charles V raises **Federico Gonzaga**, marquis of Mantua, to the status of duke in recognition of his loyalty as a commander of the imperial armies. **Mantua** becomes a client state of the empire.

1535 Francesco Sforza, last duke of Milan, dies childless. **Milan** and its surrounding territory pass to his uncle by marriage, Charles V.

1536 François I of France attempts to seize **Piedmont** and is driven off by an imperial army.

Francesco Guicciardini, a politician and writer, publishes his *Storia d'Italia*, an account of Italian politics and warfare during recent troubled decades.

1537 Andreas Vesalius begins his practical anatomy lectures at the university of **Padua**.

Andreas Vesalius and the human body

Born Andries van Wesel in Brussels, Vesalius (1514–64) attended the medical schools of **Louvain** and **Paris** before going to **Padua**, where he became lecturer in surgery at the university. Here, and at **Bologna**, he developed his own techniques of anatomy and dissection, using human bodies (Galen had used monkeys) and working in public. In **Basel** in 1543 he published his meticulous observations, illustrated with astonishingly exact and beautiful woodcuts, probably prepared with assistance from Titian's pupil Stephen Calcar, in his anatomical textbook *De humani corporis fabrica* (*On the fabric of the human body*). This groundbreaking work challenged the tenets of the Roman and Islamic medical theorists, including those of **Galen**, which until then had been an essential part of the training of doctors throughout Europe. So enthralled was **Emperor Charles V** by Vesalius's research that he made him his personal physician, and thereafter this pioneer of anatomical science followed a successful career path at the Spanish courts of Charles and his son **Philip II**.

Vesalius's achievement, crystallized with such precision in his book, was to make **anatomy** an essential part of medical study, and to render medicine itself more precise and accountable as a science. The strong influence of **Italian humanism** during his years in Padua had played an essential part in the development of his work, while the draughtsmanship of **Venetian artists**, with their fluent lines and keen physicality, is powerfully evident in the images of the *Fabrica*. Vesalius died on the Greek island of Zakynthos, while on a pilgrimage to the Holy Land.

Alessandro de' Medici is assassinated in Florence. A hastily assembled council of citizens offers leadership to his relative **Cosimo**, descendant of a brother of Cosimo '*il Vecchio*'('the Elder').

1539 Having quashed various factions opposed to him, Cosimo de' Medici becomes **duke of Florence**, a title recognized by the pope and later by the emperor.

1540 Pope Paul III sanctions the official institution of the **Society of Jesus**, an order of missionary priests founded by the Spanish ex-soldier **Ignatius Loyola**. The **Jesuits**, as they are known, will become the most effective agents of reform within the Roman Catholic Church, noted for their zeal in promoting the faith, their intellectual rigour as educationalists, and the opulence of their churches.

1542 Pope Paul III summons the **Council of Trent**, with the object of reinvigorating the Catholic Church, consolidating religious dogma and fighting the influence of **Protestantism**. At the same time he reinforces the power of the **Inquisition** to deal with all forms of heresy.

1545 Paul III appoints his son **Pier Luigi Farnese** the first duke of the newly created state of **Parma and Piacenza**.

© SCALA

The Council of Trent, as depicted by an anonymous Venetian painter

The Council of Trent

The Council of Trent was both a symbolic acknowledgement of a profound change in the intellectual climate of Europe, created by the Renaissance, and a successful attempt to instigate a **Counter-Reformation** and to restore the authority of the Catholic Church at a point when it seemed in grave danger. Although the conference was originally convened in the Alpine city of Trento by Pope Paul III it was his successor, the puritanical and anti-Semitic **Paul IV**, who established the overall tone of the Council's sessions. It was he who confirmed its final decrees, heralding the triumph of **obscurantism** and the **repression** of **intellectual freedom** throughout Christendom.

A zealous opponent of heresy, Paul IV targeted **printing** and the dissemination of learning through **books** as the real enemies of ecclesiastical dominion, since they provided secular, widespread access to **knowledge**. The Council decreed that all works of a religious nature should be rigorously **censored**, and that printed matter of any kind should be examined by bishops and local inquisitors before publication. Just as significant was the Council's position on aspects of Church doctrine that had been challenged and undermined by **Protestantism**. The truth of Christian revelation, it claimed, was not guaranteed by Holy Scripture alone, but also derived its authority from the strength of **tradition** within the Church. But the Council's most effective moral challenge to Protestantism lay in its championship of the absolute necessity for priestly intercession, and of **good works** as validation of the Christian soul in the sight of God, as opposed to the **affirmation of faith** which Protestants believed could alone justify claims to devoutness. This stance on the part of the Catholic Church undoubtedly led to a greater engagement among the clergy and their congregations with **social issues** such as poverty, hunger and unemployment in both urban and rural areas. The Counter-Reformation promoted by the Council also inspired a new mood of Catholic **evangelism**, not just in Europe but in the **new lands** whose discovery by merchant adventurers was currently enlarging the map of the world.

The Florentine sculptor and metalworker **Benvenuto Cellini** completes his bronze statue of *Perseus*. Displayed in Florence's Loggia dei Lanzi, it is regarded as his greatest work.

1547 Gian Luigi Fieschi, encouraged by the French and the duke of Parma, conspires to depose **Andrea Doria**, doge of Genoa. Doria's son Giannettino, supposedly the lover of Fieschi's wife, is killed, and Fieschi is drowned while attempting to seize a galley in the harbour. Doria escapes, and returns to Genoa to hand out savage punishments to their co-conspirators.

1550 Giorgio Vasari publishes his *Le vite de' piu eccellenti architettori, pittori e scultori italiani*, which will become known in English as *Lives of the Artists*. It is the first major account of Italian art from its medieval origins to the present time.

> ❝ Though a fairly pious Catholic and a fierce patriot, Vasari was not the slightest bit interested in the religious and political issues of his time: the faintest whiff of gunpowder or heresy was enough to send him running for cover. Like Uccello, murmuring about the beauties of perspective as his wife nagged him to come to bed, like his contemporary Benvenuto Cellini, a braver but not a better man, Vasari was obsessed by art: the pictures and plans he was pouring out himself, the products and performance of his fellow artists. ❞
>
> George Bull, Introduction to Vasiri's *Lives of the Artists*

1551 The **Council of Trent** convenes its second session, under the aegis of **Pope Julius III**.

1554 The Neapolitan cardinal Gian Pietro Caraffa becomes pope as **Paul IV**. Stern and puritanical, he launches a full-scale assault on **heresy** throughout Catholic Europe, adopts punitive measures against **Jews** in his domains and creates an index of **prohibited books**.

As he gradually renounces his temporal sovereignty and prepares to retire to a Spanish monastery, Emperor Charles V gives his son, Prince **Philip of Spain**, the kingdoms of **Naples** and **Sicily** and the duchy of **Milan**.

> ❝ Heresy must be rigorously crushed like the plague, because in fact it is the plague of the soul. If we burn infected houses and clothes, with the same severity we must extirpate, annihilate and drive out heresy. ❞
>
> Pope Paul IV to the Venetian ambassador, quoted in
> *The Flowering of the Renaissance*, Vincent Cronin

Cosimo de' Medici sends a **Florentine army** under the marquis of Marignano to seize **Siena**, the only remaining city republic in Tuscany to retain its independence. The citizens prepare for a prolonged **siege**.

1555 After eighteen months of resistance, Siena surrenders to Marignano's army. Seven hundred families leave the city and establish a republic in the nearby town of **Montalcino**.

1556 Charles V entrusts the **Holy Roman Empire** to his brother **Ferdinand** and makes **Philip** king of Spain. The **Spanish presence** will dominate the Italian political scene for another hundred years, and Spanish customs and attitudes will profoundly influence Italian society.

1559 The **Treaty of Cateau–Cambrésis** ends almost two centuries of French intervention in Italian affairs. France withdraws from **Piedmont** and **Savoy**, while Spain gains control of the island of **Sardinia** and of key fortresses along the **Tuscan coast**. **Montalcino** finally yields to **Tuscany**, which now possesses all former Sienese territories.

1560 The saintly and charismatic **Carlo Borromeo** becomes **archbishop of Milan**. An apostle of the Counter-Reformation, he transforms his diocese, establishing seminaries for the training of priests and promoting education for the city's poor children.

Grand Duke Cosimo I in Armour, by Agnolo Bronzino c.1545

1564 The **Council of Trent** publishes its decrees, essentially reaffirming the traditional teachings of Catholicism in all areas and bolstering papal authority.

Michelangelo dies in Rome, aged 89.

1569 Cosimo de' Medici is crowned **Grand Duke of Tuscany** by Pope Pius IV.

1570 Andrea Palladio publishes his *Quattro libri di architettura* (*Four Books of Architecture*), a treatise inspired by the writings of the Roman theorist **Vitruvius**, but also based on his practical experience as a builder of villas and churches in **Venice** and the **Veneto**.

1571 At the battle of **Lepanto**, off the coast of Greece, a massed navy of Venetian, Spanish and papal galleys massacres the navy of **Sultan Selim II** of Turkey.

1576 Titian (Tiziano Vecellio) dies in Venice on 27 August, aged 90.

1580 Torquato Tasso publishes his epic poem *Gerusalemme liberata* (*Jerusalem Delivered*), in which the poet, a gloomy, introverted loner who has led a stormy life in the Italian courts, combines the story of the First Crusade with romantic episodes and tales of sorcery and adventure. Partly inspired by Ariosto's *Orlando Furioso* and written in the same eight-line stanzas, *Gerusalemme Liberata* gains international acclaim both for the beauty of its verse style and for its message of moral integrity at any cost.

1584 Carlo Borromeo dies in Milan. During his twenty years as the city's archbishop, he has worked tirelessly on behalf of the poor, organizing famine relief and medical assistance. He has also promoted better education among the clergy and reformed his diocese according to the decrees of the Council of Trent. A cult begins almost immediately after his death, leading to his canonization.

1585 Felice Peretti becomes pope as **Sixtus V**. **Pasquale Cicogna** becomes **doge of Venice**. During Cicogna's ten years in office, Antonio da Ponte's magnificent **Rialto Bridge**, incorporating shops on both sides, is built to span the Grand Canal.

1588 Jacopo Robusti, a painter known as **Tintoretto**, completes his vast cycle of paintings adorning the upper and

Lepanto

The battle of Lepanto has the dubious distinction of being possibly the most over-hyped event in 16th-century history. At the time **Venetian propaganda** claimed it as a positively apocalyptic turning point in the continuing struggle between **Christendom** and **Islam**, brought about by the Turkish seizure of **Constantinople** in 1453. In 1570, Ottoman forces attacked **Cyprus**, capturing **Famagusta** (the last Venetian stronghold in the island) the following year. Venice now realized how ill equipped its navy was to cope with the Turkish threat to its remaining possessions in **Crete** and the **Adriatic**, and assembled a vast navy including Spanish, French and papal galleys. This force encountered the sultan's fleet at Lepanto in the western Peloponnese on 7 October, 1571.

Under the command of Charles V's illegitimate son **Don Juan of Austria**, the Christian ships rammed the Turkish vessels, sinking 230 Ottoman ships. In the hand-to-hand fighting that ensued, the Turks lost 30,000 men to their enemies' 15,000, and over 10,000 Christian galley slaves were set free. The Venetians, who had borne the brunt of the fighting, proclaimed 7 October the feast of St Justina, a solemn holiday. Scenes from the battle decorated the Palazzo Ducale, and captured Turkish flags and armour were displayed in its state apartments. The importance of the victory was nevertheless wildly exaggerated. Though Turkey refrained, for the time being, from launching an assault on Crete, the Ottoman empire was far from beaten as a naval or military power: in 1573, as part of a humiliating peace deal with the sultan, Venice was forced to concede defeat over **Cyprus**.

Paolo Veronese's *The Battle of Lepanto*, c.1571

lower halls of the **Scuola di San Rocco**, one of Venice's major charitable institutions.

1590 Soon after witnessing the completion of the dome of St Peter's, to a design originally proposed by Michelangelo, **Sixtus V** dies in Rome.

The changing style of Titian

By the time of his death, Titian was recognized as the greatest painter in Europe. The emperor **Charles V** may have boasted that the sun never set on his empire, but he was not above picking up a paintbrush that Titian had dropped onto his studio floor whilst sitting for one of several portraits. One of Titian's most admired qualities was his versatility. As well as painting compelling **portraits** of his contemporaries, he could also depict rapturous **spiritual themes** such as the huge *Assumption of the Blessed Virgin* in the Venice's Frari basilica, **sensuous nudes** such as the famous *Venus of Urbino* (the 16th century's most famous erotic icon), and **humanist allegories** such as *Sacred and Profane Love*, painted for a wedding in 1515.

Titian's artistic style was constantly evolving. The lyrical freedom of his early works, such as the mythological scenes painted for the duke of Ferrara between 1518 and 1523, became more subdued and restrained following the death of his wife in 1530. Luminous, shimmering planes of colour gave way to a darker palette, dominated by brown, white and black. The brushwork on these canvases was energetic, almost tortured, and the whole artistic language assumed a kind of intensity which seems almost to anticipate the manner of the 19th-century French Impressionists. The earlier of his two versions of *The Martyrdom of St Lawrence*, in the Venetian church of the Gesuiti, illustrates this shift perfectly, with its vivid contrasts between shadow and torchlight, the thrilling vagueness of the figures watching the hideous scene as the saint is roasted alive, and the fantasy classicism of the architectural backdrop. Titian continued working until the very end of his life, honoured by popes and princes, and his reputation as the last great painter of the Italian Renaissance remained unchallenged amid changing tastes and styles.

1594 **Giovanni Pierluigi da Palestrina** dies in Rome, after forty years as director of the Papal chapel.

1597 Alfonso III, duke of Ferrara, dies without issue, leaving his titles to his bastard cousin, **Cesare d'Este**. Intent on

Sixtus V and the rebuilding of Rome

Born to humble parents in a village near Ancona, Felice Peretti (as he began life) was already a Franciscan friar by the age of 12, but – fired by his father's dream foretelling that a son of his would be made pope – was determined to become a cardinal. When he was duly elected as Sixtus V (1585–90), his fellow cardinals took his mild manner at face value. They were in for a rude awakening. Sixtus immediately instituted a clampdown on **crime**, with zero tolerance of brigandage and the riotous behaviour of Roman nobles. 'We intend to be obeyed here by all,' he declared, making no exceptions even for cardinals, several of whom he fined and imprisoned. He overhauled **papal finances**, cutting expenditure, raising taxes and instituting an early form of national debt. Perhaps inspired by the example of Venice, he appointed a series of committees to deal with particular areas of government. Known as the **Congregations**, some of these still exist. He left his most visible mark, however, on the fabric of Rome itself. During his five-year papacy, Sixtus totally altered Rome's character, lending it a **grandeur** which was to influence other European capital cities, especially Paris and London, and creating a model **urban landscape** of boulevards, squares, monumental staircases and extensive vistas, dominated by grand buildings.

Although the Renaissance rediscovery of the classical world had

seizing **Ferrara** for the papacy, **Pope Clement VIII** forces Cesare to renounce his claims to the duchy. A new dukedom is established for Cesare around the nearby city of **Modena**.

1600 The philosopher **Giordano Bruno** is burned as a heretic. An ex-Dominican, he had sought to reconcile Catholic and Protestant teachings through the study of science and his intellectual contacts in other European countries.

1604 **Galileo Galilei** begins his experiments to establish the causes of gravitation.

generally increased the respect shown to Italy's surviving antiquities, Sixtus had no qualms in tearing down ancient monuments when they got in the way of his **street-building** projects. A major casualty was the **Septizonium**, the massive shell of a 3rd-century palace, whose appearance is now known only through Renaissance drawings. At the same time, he was a prolific builder of monuments: to Sixtus we owe the spectacular **Spanish Steps**, the **Fontana dell'Acqua Felice** and the completion of the long-delayed work on the **dome of St Peter's**.

In front of the basilica, the pope ordered a tall **Egyptian obelisk** which had lain nearby, half-buried since Roman times, to be topped with a fragment of the true cross and hauled upright. Its domineering presence in front of Catholic Christendom's mother church was intended as a symbol of Christ's victory over **paganism**. 'I am in Rome, after an absence of ten years,' wrote a priest at the end of the 16th century, 'and do not recognize it, so new does all appear to me to be: monuments, streets, piazzas, fountains, aqueducts, obelisks and other wonders, all the work of Sixtus V.' This was no exaggeration. Little wonder, then, that his contemporary Queen Elizabeth I, against whom he had blessed the Spanish Armada in 1588, declared that he was the only man she would contemplate marrying.

1606 **Pope Paul V** places **Venice** under a year's **interdict** for daring to defy his authority in the appointment of clergy. The traditionally strained relations between the republic and the Holy See now descend into mutual hostility which will last for another twenty years. The popes condemn

> Perhaps you who bring this sentence against me are more afraid than I who receive it.
>
> Giordano Bruno to his inquisitors

Venice as a nest of heretics, while the Venetians, despite their fervent Catholicism, increasingly view the papacy as greedy and domineering.

1609 Duke Charles Emmanuel of Savoy routs the Spanish garrisons which have been ensconced in the Alpine valleys by Milan's energetic viceroy, the Conde de Fuentes.

The 19-year-old **Cosimo II** inherits the title of **Grand Duke of Tuscany**. The spectacular festivities he organizes are the most extravagant the Medici court has seen: at his wedding, the legend of Jason and the Argonauts is performed on the River **Arno**, replete with immense statues of dolphins, lobsters and fire-breathing sea monsters.

> ❝ [Many] painters, architects and sculptors have been in Italy; some in order to learn, others to see works of ancient art and to make the acquaintance of people who excel in their profession, others to seek adventure and make themselves known. After having satisfied their desires, they return in most cases to their native country with new experience, ability and honour; and from there they spread, having become masters, to England, all over Germany … and other northern countries, not to speak of France, Spain and Portugal. ❞
>
> Lodovico Guicciardini, *Description of the Low Countries*, quoted in *Northern Renaissance Art 1400–1600*, Wolfgang Stechow

1610 The painter Michelangelo Merisi, known as **Caravaggio** after his north Italian birthplace, dies of a fever at Porto Ercole on the coast of Tuscany, on his way back to Rome, having earlier fled after killing a man in a brawl. His work will have a crucial impact on European art.

1609 Galileo uses his improved telescopes to observe the moons of Jupiter and the motions of the planets.

Typhoeus Beneath the Mountains of Ischia, part of a *veglia* (evening entertainment) of the Medici court in 1616

Charles Emmanuel of Savoy makes a defensive pact with **France** against **Spain**.

1612 The death of Duke **Francesco IV of Mantua** precipitates a succession crisis. Though his brother **Ferdinando**

Caravaggio: image and influence

The works of Caravaggio (1571–1610) were widely imitated by other European artists both during his lifetime and after his death. **Rome**, where he made his name at the end of the 16th century, was to remain a major centre of artistic study and apprenticeship for the next 250 years. The city was especially popular with non-Italian painters, who could live there cheaply, obtain commissions from cardinals, aristocrats and wealthy visitors, and take advantage of the inspiration to be had from its cornucopia of ancient buildings and collections of antiquities. So it was that, during the 1620s or even earlier, the 'Caravaggesque' style flourished, finding favour with outstanding talents such as those of the Frenchman **Simon Vouet**, the Dutch painter **Gerrit van Honthorst** and **Nicolas Regnier**, a Flemish artist who eventually moved to Venice. Their canvases made effective use of Caravaggio's dramatic light effects; his carefully restricted palette; his concentration on the intensity of the event portrayed without excessive, distracting detail; and his realistic depiction of figures from contemporary **street life**, including petty crooks, prostitutes, rent boys, beggars and bravos (cloak-and-dagger hitmen, as Caravaggio was in his youth). It is this aspect of his life that has coloured modern perceptions of Caravaggio as a lowlife genius, living and dying in a climate charged with homoeroticism and

succeeds, Charles Emmanuel of Savoy, father-in-law of the late duke, lays claim to the duchy and invades Mantuan territory. The new duke calls on **Spain** for military support.

1614 **Savoy** gains the upper hand in the Mantuan war. With support from the **duke of Modena**, Charles Emmanuel promotes himself as an Italian champion against foreign oppressors.

1615 France negotiates peace between Spain and Savoy, ending the Mantuan war. Savoy emerges as both moral and material victor, the first sign of Spain's growing political weakness in Italian affairs.

violence, as exemplified in Derek Jarman's film biography and Peter Robb's sensational biography *M*. Belligerent, paranoid and fervently devout, he produced a body of work that will always, it seems, be a focus of passionate controversy. Rejecting the Renaissance quest for the ideal in art, he chose to paint from life, provoking the arch-classicist, Nicolas Poussin, to splutter that he had come into the world in order to destroy painting, while lighting his subjects with highly artificial yet startlingly arresting *chiaroscuro* effects.

In his *St Catherine of Alexandria*, painted around 1598, Caravaggio counterpoints the saint's beauty and her finely embroidered dress with the looming, massive spiked wheel upon which she was martyred and the ominous shadow on one side of her face. An equally imaginative use of simple pictorial elements to create a dramatic effect is seen in the famous *Calling of St Matthew* (1600) in which the nobility of Christ's summoning the tax-collector to follow him illuminates the seedy *demi-monde* of taverns and gambling in which Matthew has been content to dwell. Pictures like these inspired countless imitators, for whom Caravaggio himself was accounted in the words of a contemporary, 'the marvel of art and the wonder of nature'.

1616 **Galileo** is arrested by the Inquisition for his espousal of **Copernicus's** theory that the earth moves around the sun.

1618 The Protestant nobility of Bohemia choose **Frederick, Elector Palatine**, as king of Bohemia, arousing the hostility of the Holy Roman Emperor, **Ferdinand II of Austria**. Ferdinand and his ally **Maximilian of Bavaria** form a **Catholic League** against **Bohemia**. The conflict, eventually involving most of the European states, will become known as the **Thirty Years' War**. **Northern Italian** powers, as well as the **papacy**, are later drawn into the struggle.

Galileo

A truly universal scientist, with an interest in poetry and music as well as mathematics, physics and astronomy, Galileo Galilei (1564–1642) was born in **Pisa**, where he studied **medicine** at the university before graduating as a **mathematician**. His research into the **theory of motion**, with which he initially made his name as a scientist, took place while he was professor of mathematics at **Padua**. There he also published treatises on mechanics and military architecture, besides developing ideas on gravity and building his first telescope. In 1609 he became mathematician to Grand Duke Ferdinand I of Tuscany, whose successor, **Cosimo II**, continued the Medici patronage of him. His international fame was sealed by the publication in 1610 of *Nuncius siderus* (*The Starry Messenger*). Over the next five years he attempted to prove that the Polish scientist **Nicolaus Copernicus** had been correct in asserting that the planets moved around the sun. Catholic teaching maintained exactly the opposite, and in 1616 Galileo was forbidden to defend or even maintain his theory.

Returning to Florence, he began work on *Il saggiatore* (*The assayer*), a book which proposed a new approach to science based on rational enquiry, declaring that 'the book of nature is written in mathematical characters'. When his friend and fellow Tuscan Maffeo Barberini became pope as **Urban VIII** in 1623 (the year of *Il saggiatore*'s publication) Galileo was allowed to go ahead with his *Dialogue on the Two Chief World Systems*, vindicating Copernicus's ideas and completed in 1632. Although the book had been passed by the papal censor and received international acclaim, the pope nevertheless yielded to pressure to try Galileo for **heresy**, and in 1633 he was again summoned to Rome. Made to recant his scientific ideas and sentenced to **house arrest** at his Florentine estate of Arcetri, he was protected by the Grand Duke and allowed to continue with his studies and experiments. Going blind in 1637, he published his last great work, the *Dialogues concerning the new sciences*, the following year. Galileo's experimental methods had laid the

Galileo Galilei by Sustermans, a Flemish painter at the Medici court, c.1636

© SCALA

foundations of the '**scientific revolution**' which swept across
17th-century Europe, and it was clear that the Church had failed
to destroy his achievements or to defeat the spirit of rational
enquiry in which he worked. His basic intellectual principle was
expressed in his words to one of his inquisitors: 'Who can set
bounds to the minds of men? Who dares assert that he already
knows all that in this universe is knowable?'

> **❝** I went to see the marvellous and singular effects of Galileo's spyglass ... placing one eye to it and closing the other, each of us saw distinctly ... to Chioggia, Treviso and as far as Conegliano. We saw the campanile, cupolas and façade of the church of Santa Giustina in Padua; we could distinguish people entering and leaving the church of San Giacomo in Murano; visible also were persons embarking and disembarking from the ferry gondola by the column at the beginning of Rio de' Veneri, as well as many other truly admirable details in the lagoon and the city. **❞**
>
> Antonio Priuli, diary entry for 21 August, 1609, quoted in
> *The Flowering of the Renaissance*, Vincent Cronin

The government of **Venice** uncovers a plot to overthrow the republic, masterminded by the Spanish ambassador, the **marques de Bedmar**. He is ordered to leave the city, the other conspirators (including various senators he has bribed) are executed or imprisoned, and the Grand Council turns the episode into a successful **propaganda coup**, intended to undermine **Spanish diplomatic influence** in northern Italy.

1622 **Pope Gregory XV** founds the *Propaganda Fidei* (Congregation for Propagating the Faith), with the object of encouraging Catholic missionary work in parts of the world newly opened up to European trade.

1623 Maffeo Barberini, son of a minor Tuscan aristocrat, becomes pope as **Urban VIII**. He will use his long papacy to advance his family's power and to increase its wealth. Following the example of Sixtus V, he will also be a major **patron** of sculptors and architects, adorning Rome with their works.

The outstanding historian, theologian, scientist (a colleague of Galileo) and intellectual **Pietro Paolo Sarpi** dies in

Venice. Since the papal interdict of 1606, he has been the Serene Republic's theological adviser, becoming a thorn in the side of the Catholic establishment, which has even tried to have him assassinated. Sarpi's extensive **polemical writings** on the relationship between Church and state are widely read throughout Europe. His sustained (and successful) attacks on the Church's misuse of its powers makes him an intellectual hero among Protestant writers of the period, though he never renounces his vocation as a Servite priest.

> **"** The Church must obey the State in things temporal and the latter the former in things spiritual, each maintaining its proper rights. **"**
>
> Fra Pietro Paolo Sarpi

1624 Venice, France and Savoy agree to occupy the **Valtelline**, a key pass dividing Austria from the Swiss cantons, Venetian territory and the Spanish-held duchy of Milan.

1626 The **French** are forced to withdraw troops from the Valtelline in order to deal with a Huguenot revolt in northwestern France. **Spain** now snatches control of the pass.

1627 **Duke Vincenzo II of Mantua** sells the fabulous **Gonzaga collection** of paintings to **King Charles I** of England. Most of these will be dispersed by Oliver Cromwell during the 1650s.

1628 Vincenzo, duke of Mantua, dies, leaving his distant cousin **Charles, duke of Nevers**, as heir. The duchy also includes the county of **Monferrato**, west of Milan. Rival claims to this territory spark off a war between **France**, supporting Nevers, and **Spain**, eager to keep the French out of Italy and backed by Emperor Ferdinand. Occupying Monferrato, the Spaniards support an alternative Gonzaga candidate, the **duke of Guastalla**. **Pope Urban VIII** gives his backing to Spain rather than France and Austria, the first time in a hundred years that a pope has failed to support the imperial interest.

1631 On the death of the last **duke of Urbino**, Pope Urban VIII annexes the duchy to the Papal States.

1632 Galileo publishes his *Dialogue on the Two Chief World Systems*.

1633 Galileo is summoned to Rome to be tried by the Inquisition for criticizing the Ptolemaic cosmology upheld by Catholic dogma. Ordered to produce a recantation, he is sentenced to house arrest in Florence.

Monteverdi and Venetian opera

When the English diarist and traveller **John Evelyn** went to the opera in Venice in 1645, he was overwhelmed by his first encounter with the new form. 'Comedies and other plays,' he wrote, 'are represented in recitative musiq by the most excellent musicians vocall and instrumental, with variety of scaenes painted and contrived with no lesse art of perspective, and machines for flying in the aire, and other wonderfull motions; taken together it is one of the most magnificent and expansive diversions the wit of man can invent.'

Claudio Monteverdi, the first great composer in the history of **opera**, had died in Venice only two years earlier. His *Orfeo*, first performed in Mantua in 1607, had developed the music-drama form first produced in Florence in 1581 into a convincing theatrical narrative. Apart from a lost work, *Arianna*, known only from its libretto and a single surviving *lamento*, Monteverdi composed no more operas until the masterpieces of his very last years: *Il ritorno di Ulisse in patria* and *L'incoronazione di Poppea*. Together these works, written in short, intensely vivid scenes and featuring a wide variety of characters, set the path

1635 **France** declares war on **Spain**. Though the Spanish are reckoned to field the best armies in the world, France boasts more skilful commanders and will now challenge Spain's century-old dominance as the major European power. Italian states begin to reappraise their alliances in the light of the conflict.

1637 The **Teatro San Cassiano**, the world's first public opera house, opens in **Venice**.

1641 **Pope Urban VIII** annexes the town of **Castro** in Lazio, using the financial mismanagement of the **Farnese** family as his justification. Many feel his true motivation is exacting revenge for the insulting behaviour of the Farnese towards one of his nephews.

Venetian opera was to follow for the next fifty years. The basic musical form was **recitative**, free-flowing dialogue accompanied by a bass line provided by string and keyboard instruments. Out of this grew short songs known as **arias**, which gradually became more elaborate over succeeding decades. The recitative was interspersed with occasional **choruses** and **ballet** sequences.

Venetian audiences favoured complicated plots, with plenty of disguise, adventure and 'near-death experience', invariably culminating in a happy ending. The typical cast included comic figures such as nurses, gardeners and slaves, mingling with real-life historical personalities, romantic princesses and noble warriors. Scenery, in a city so full of exceptional artists, became ever more ornate (at least one famous painter, the 18th-century master **Canaletto**, started his career in a theatrical 'paint shop'). Monteverdi's operas owe their survival (unlike most other 17th-century Venetian music drama, which has proved more ephemeral) to his concentration on convincing plot lines and consistently believable characters, conveyed in the form of a richly expressive musical discourse.

1642 **Claudio Monteverdi** composes his opera *L'Incoron-azione di Poppea* (*The Coronation of Poppaea*) for performance in Venice.

1643 Claudio Monteverdi dies in Venice, aged 83, after many years as Maestro di Cappella at the basilica of **San Marco**.

The long and eventful papacy of **Urban VIII** comes to an end with his death in Rome. He is succeeded by Giovanni Battista Pamphilj, as **Innocent X.**

1644 The **Papal armies** are worsted in the continuing **war of Castro**. French mediation persuades Pope Innocent to yield the city and its territory to the **duke of Parma**, head of the **Farnese** clan.

1645 The **Ottoman Turks** prepare to invade the island of **Crete**, the last important Venetian colony in the Aegean. On 23 June, an army lands at Canea (Khania) and lays siege to the town, which yields after two months' resistance. The 'war of Crete' will continue for over twenty years, as the Turks step up military and naval operations and **Venice** desperately seeks help among European powers, including the papacy, France and England.

The sculptor, architect and painter **Gianlorenzo Bernini** (1598–1680) begins work on the **Cornaro Chapel** in Rome. The highlight of its sculptures is *The Ecstasy of St Teresa*, a virtuoso expression of Bernini's infallible dramatic instincts and his daring use of mixed media. It later comes to be viewed as a quintessential work of the **Italian Baroque**.

1646 After a disastrous harvest in **Sicily**, rioting breaks out across the island in protest against **Spanish mismanage-ment**. Local officials are murdered and their houses looted. The revolt is led by a goldbeater, **Giuseppe Alessio**, who calls for lower taxation, the restoration of ancient privileges and the removal of the Spanish viceroy.

© SCALA

The Ecstasy of Saint Teresa, part of the ornate altar of the Cornaro Chapel, Santa Maria della Vittoria, Rome

1647 Masaniello (Tommaso Aniello), a fishmonger and charismatic orator from Amalfi, leads a revolt in **Naples** against the heavy taxes imposed by the Spaniards. A vast crowd of his supporters marches on the palace of the viceroy, the **duke of Arcos**, forcing him to flee. Masaniello is soon assassinated on the orders of a group of nobles but the revolution makes a powerful impact, both in Italy and abroad, and the fishmonger is hailed as a proletarian hero and martyr. Four hundred priests and one hundred thousand lay people are said to have attended his funeral.

The **Sicilian revolution** fails, owing to irreconcilable differences between the supporters of Spain and those of France, which has been trying to foment anti-Spanish feeling for some time. **King Philip IV** sends a new **viceroy** to restore order.

© SCALA

The *Revolt of Masaniello* by Domenico Gargiulo

1648 The **Peace of Westphalia** ends the **Thirty Years' War**. Toleration of **Protestantism** is guaranteed within the Holy Roman Empire, implicitly defeating the Counter-Reformation initiatives begun with the **Council of Trent**.

1649 Pope Innocent X resumes the **war of Castro** against the duke of Parma, seizing the town for the papacy once more. In an extraordinary move, the pope's domineering sister-in-law, **Donna Olimpia Maidalchini**, orders its total destruction. Her agents remove everything lootable, including the church bells, while the fabric of the town is reduced to rubble. The ruins are never resettled.

1654 **Queen Christina of Sweden** abdicates her throne to her cousin Carl Gustaf and leaves for Rome, having converted to Catholicism. She will spend her last years as patroness of painters and musicians, living happily in a palace on the south bank of the Tiber.

1655 Cardinal Fabio Chigi becomes pope as **Alexander VII**. A brilliant theologian and diplomat, he renews the artistic impetus fostered in Rome by Urban VIII.

1656 **Gianlorenzo Bernini** starts work on a pair of magnificent curving colonnades designed to frame the basilica of **St Peter's** in Rome.

1662 In response to attempts by **Pope Alexander VII** to check his influence on ecclesiastical affairs within the kingdom (over which his effective rule started only the previous year), **King Louis XIV of France** sends the duc de Créqui to Rome with secret orders to make himself a nuisance to the papal court. On 20 August, a papal guardsman fires on the duke's coach, killing and wounding his servants. Louis uses this as a pretext for war and seizes the city of **Avignon**, in the possession of the papacy since the Middle Ages.

Roman Baroque art

Stimulated by the patronage of popes and cardinals, Roman Baroque art was a cultural offshoot of the Counter-Reformation, a deliberately orchestrated antithesis to the austerity and restraint of Protestantism. In the sculpture of **Gianlorenzo Bernini**, the architecture of **Francesco Borromini** and the work of painters such as **Carlo Saraceni**, **Orazio Gentileschi** and **Pietro da Cortona**, the emphasis lay on dramatic impact and a calculated appeal to the emotions. Acts of worship, prayer and even mourning were given a purposeful dramatic dimension and the creation of architectural features, such as Bernini's curving colonnades embracing St Peter's basilica, added theatricality to the urban environment of Rome itself.

Other art forms reflected this stress on the entertainment of the senses. Poets, led by the prolific and versatile **Giambattista Marino**, used rhetoric and bizarre conceits to play elaborate games with every kind of verse from epic to sonnet. In music, meanwhile, a new kind of religious drama developed from the re-enactment of biblical episodes with the help of voices and instruments. Its name, *oratorio*, derives from the oratory (prayer-hall) built in 1577 by the priest **Philip Neri** for his followers, next to the Roman church of Santa Maria in Vallicella. Early performances taking place here were soon imitated throughout Italy, and *oratorio* became an essential feature of Lent in churches and court chapels. Opera singers began appearing in these presentations, which grew more theatrical as a result. The narrative scope of the works themselves was extended to include personified abstracts such as **Time**, **Vanity** and **Repentance**, as well as allusions to current political events.

The new art of *oratorio* survived the age which created it. As the power and wealth of the Church declined during the late 17th century, so too did the flamboyance and imaginative excess of Baroque religious art. The presence of so much creative impetus in Rome, however, had a beneficial effect on the city's life as a cultural capital, confirming its international status as a mecca for artists for at least another two hundred years.

1664 Pope Alexander VII and Louis XIV conclude the **Treaty of Pisa**. Avignon is ceded to France and Louis demands that a column should be raised in Rome with an inscription detailing the outrage against the duc de Créqui. The pope's nephew is summoned to the French court at **Fontainebleau**, where he is made to read out a lengthy apology. This humiliation is an important indicator of the **decline of papal power** over the previous fifty years.

1669 With the fall of their last stronghold at Candia (Herak-leion), the **Venetians** are forced to surrender the island of **Crete** to the **Turks**. Of Venice's former Greek maritime empire, only the **Ionian islands** and a few mainland fortresses are now left.

1673 **Maria Beatrice, princess of Modena**, is married to **James, duke of York**, brother of King Charles II of England and heir to the English throne. The marriage has been arranged by her mother Laura Martinozzi, sister of the French politician **Cardinal Mazarin**, with the blessing of **King Louis XIV** of France, who sees it as an opportunity both to extend his influence over Italian sovereigns and to revive Catholicism in England.

1675 The citizens of **Messina** rise in revolt against their Spanish overlords, who have imposed crushing taxation on the island of **Sicily**.

1676 A French fleet, sent by **Louis XIV**, thwarts Spain's efforts to regain control of Messina. The French king promises to restore the ancient rights of the city's Senate, but once peace has been made with Spain by the Sicilian nobility, he ignores his pledge and abandons Sicily to **ruthless reprisals** by the Spanish. These include mass executions, abolition of local privileges, exaction of indemnity payments and the removal of priceless art treasures and manuscripts to Spain.

1683 On 13 July, a huge **Turkish army**, having swept through the Balkans and Hungary, lays siege to **Vienna**, which is eventually relieved by a combined Austrian and Polish force. The event inspires terror and apprehension throughout northern Italy, and especially in the **republic of Venice**.

Venice forms an alliance against the Turks with **Pope Alexander VII**, **Emperor Leopold I** of Austria and **King Jan Sobieski** of Poland. **Francesco Morosini**, captain general of the Venetian forces, begins a series of successful assaults on Turkish fortresses in the **Greek Peloponnese**, aimed at avenging the loss of Crete and recapturing Venice's former possessions in mainland Greece.

Francesco Morosini

In order to achieve its military successes, whether on the Italian mainland or in the Mediterranean, the Venetian republic had always relied on the help, or outright leadership of its forces, given by commanders from other states. Francesco Morosini (1618–94), who took control of military operations against the Turks in 1684, was in this and other respects an unlikely hero. Born into a Venetian noble family, he had begun his career as a naval officer and had been responsible for the surrender of the last fortress on Crete to hold out against the Ottoman attackers. The island's loss was traumatic for Venice, and though Morosini's capitulation was prudent and honourably negotiated, he was greeted with threats of imprisonment on his return home.

Tempers in the Venetian senate eventually cooled and his appointment as **commander-in-chief** in a new campaign was unanimously approved. As his army successfully besieged Turkish forts along Greece's **Adriatic coast**, imperial Venice seemed to have found her champion. Not since **Doge Francesco Foscari** in the 15th century had a native Venetian directed the republic's

Louis XIV prepares an expedition against **Genoa**, to punish the republic for its assistance to Spain during the recent rebellion in Sicily. A French fleet bombards the city, destroying or damaging nearly 3000 buildings, while an army ravages the suburbs. This show of strength serves to keep Genoa out of European wars for the next fifty years, while it maintains a benevolent neutrality towards France.

1687 After winning a decisive victory over the Turks at Argos, **Francesco Morosini** and his Swedish second-in-command Karl von Koenigsmark capture **Corinth** and **Patras** and lay siege to **Athens**. During the Venetian bombardment, one of Koenigsmark's gunners scores a direct hit on the Turkish powder magazine inside the **Parthenon**. The resulting explosion blows the roof off the building and

military enterprises so brilliantly. Hopes were high of recovering not just Crete, but also the islands of **Chios** and **Euboea**. Morosini, meanwhile, marched boldly into the Peloponnese, an area which had never been part of the empire, placing the whole of southern Greece under Venetian domination.

A stern disciplinarian, ruthless and arrogant, Morosini felt fully justified in accepting the honours conferred on him by the republic, including a bust, a medal and the title *Peloponnesiac*. In 1688 he was invested as **doge of Venice** but his health had begun to give way under the huge burden of rescuing the state's international reputation, at a time when Ottoman military might offered a genuine threat to Europe. When Morosini died Venice could find no adequate replacement for him among his lieutenants. The absorption of the conquered territories was bungled in such a way as to damage the local economy and antagonize their Greek populations. While the new empire was soon lost, memories of 'the *Peloponnesiac*' continued to inspire Venice with nostalgia for a glory it never afterwards managed to recover.

brings Phidias's superb 5th-century BC frieze crashing to the ground. Its marble fragments will later be seized by the British traveller **Lord Elgin**, who eventually sells them to the **British Museum** in London

1688 While at sea off the Greek coast, Francesco Morosini receives news that he has been elected **doge of Venice**. He is the first doge to be appointed *in absentia* and the first to receive his appointment while waging a military campaign. Two years later, he makes a **triumphal entry** into Venice and receives the title of *Il Peloponnesiaco* from a grateful senate.

1694 After prolonged deadlock in the Greek campaign, Morosini returns to the Peloponnese with a fresh strategy against the Turks, but dies before his plans can be put into practice. His place is taken by **Antonio Zeno**, who launches an attack on the island of **Chios**.

1698 Its forces weakened by the success of combined Venetian and Austrian operations against the Turks, the **Ottoman empire** begins peace negotiations.

1699 The **Treaty of Carlowitz** guarantees Venice's possession of most of its reconquered territories, including the **Peloponnese** and **Ionian islands**.

1700 **King Charles II of Spain** dies, leaving his throne to Louis XIV's grandson, **Philippe, duc d'Anjou**. Fearing a possible union of the French and Spanish crowns and supporting its own claimant, Archduke Charles, **Habsburg Austria** seeks an alliance with England and the Netherlands against **France**.

1702 The **War of the Spanish Succession** begins, ranging the powers of the **Grand Alliance** (Austria, England and the Netherlands), later joined by **Portugal**, against **France**, **Bavaria** and **Savoy**.

Austria's army in Italy is commanded by **Prince Eugene of Savoy**, a cousin of Duke Victor Amadeus. Snubbed by Louis XIV, to whom he had earlier offered his services, he now serves Austrian Emperor Joseph I. His brilliant swoop on the army of Marshal Villeroy at **Cremona** will be glorified in the military annals of the 18th century as the 'Surprise of Cremona'.

1703 **Victor Amadeus of Savoy** abandons the French in order to join **Austria** and her allies.

1704 Led by the **duc de Vendôme**, French troops invade **Savoy** and overrun the territories belonging to Victor Amadeus.

1706 Led by Prince Eugene and Victor Amadeus, Austrian and Savoyard forces rout a French army besieging **Turin**. **Austria** now seizes control in northern Italy, attacking **Mantua** and forcing Duke Francesco Carlo into exile. He never recovers his domains, which are formally annexed by Austria the following year.

Joseph I of Austria declares the cities of Parma, Ferrara and Comacchio imperial (rather than papal) fiefs. Pope Clement XI prepares his army for war.

1707 **Clement XI** excommunicates Prince Eugene for refusing to halt troop movements and recruitment around Ferrara.

1708 A British fleet captures **Sardinia** from the French.

Supported by Victor Amadeus and Duke Rinaldo of Modena, Prince Eugene occupies **Comacchio** and its surrounding district. Pope Clement sends troops to the region. **Imperial forces** under Marshal Daun now advance on **Rome**.

1709 Pope Clement is forced to make peace with Austria. Partly as a result of this humiliating submission to a secular power, relations between the **papacy** and the **Habsburgs** will remain embittered throughout the century.

1713 The **Treaty of Utrecht** brings an end to the **War of the Spanish Succession**. **Naples** and **Sardinia** pass to Austria, while **Sicily** is given to **Victor Amadeus** of Savoy, who is granted the title of king of Sicily.

7
Enlightenment and reform

1714–1814

The Italian 18th century is often considered to be a period of national decadence and chronic inactivity, to which **Napoléon's invasion** in 1796 and the earliest stirrings of the **Risorgimento** put a richly deserved end. This is a short-sighted and unjust perspective on an era when many important reforms occurred in the various sovereign states, and when Italians began to develop an awareness of the **shared culture** that bound them together as a nation. Most notably this included a common **literary heritage**, stretching from Dante, Petrarch and Boccaccio to writers of the time such as **Pietro Metastasio**, whose style as a dramatic poet set new standards of expressive clarity in the written language. Meanwhile, **historians** such as **Ludovico Muratori**, who worked tirelessly away in Modena on the recovery of medieval documents, made a valuable contribution to this sense of a shared national experience. At the same time, the new travel phenomenon of the **Grand Tour** – an extended journey through Italy taken by affluent foreign visitors in search of **objets d'art** and lessons in **aesthetic taste** – bolstered the pride of Italians in the unparalleled virtuosity of their various schools of painting and sculpture over the previous centuries.

The French-inspired but commonly held view of the **Enlightenment** as having begun and ended in Paris has proved remarkably tenacious, and has had the effect of marginalizing the original work of Italian **intellectuals** during this period, in fields ranging from **economic theory** and **education** to **prison reform**, **demography** and **musicology**. Even though Venice had lost most of its political influence and nearly all its imperial possessions, the city still had enough vitality to nurture artists such as **Vivaldi**, **Goldoni** and **Casanova**. **Milan** during the 1760s and 1770s became a significant forum of the Enlightenment, while its surrounding province of **Lombardy** was shaken up by reforms in **agriculture**, **education** and the **power of the Church** over secular society. At the same time Tuscany underwent a much more carefully calibrated programme of change at the hands of **Grand Duke Pietro Leopoldo**, an enlightened absolutist and perhaps Italy's most successful 18th-century ruler. The region continues to acknowledge a debt to his benign and considered approach to rule. Only in the kingdom of **Naples**, where the Enlightenment was heralded by the work of **Giambattista Vico** and **Pietro Giannone**, was there an obvious clash between the aspirations of reformers, the entrenched interests of the **feudal aristocracy** and – once King Ferdinand IV and Queen Maria Carolina had taken the reins of power in 1768 – the avowed conservatism of the **monarchy**. In 1799 the **Parthenopean Republic** was brutally suppressed, with assistance from British warships under the command of **Admiral Horatio Nelson**.

Widespread unrest across Europe, in the wake of the **French Revolution**, wholly unnerved the Italian sovereigns. It was a relatively easy matter for **Napoléon's armies** to execute his design of annexing the entire peninsula, which Napoléon eventually divided into a series of larger kingdoms under various members of his family. Austria's military opposition to the French invasion ultimately boded ill for Italy's future, as did Napoléon's compromise with Austrian Emperor Francis I at **Campoformio**. One of the chief effects of the French **centralization of government** was to create a **strong bureaucracy** based on merit, with clearly defined administrative cadres. A corresponding meritocracy operated within the ranks of the Napoléonic army, in which many Italians from relatively humble social origins served with distinction as officers. Although the imperial government was ruthless in suppressing any sort of dissent or opposition, this new efficiency and fostering of initiative paradoxically added impetus to the growth of a sense of **national identity**. This would clash violently with the notions of submissiveness and resignation to the sovereign will that were the founding principles of **Austrian rule** after 1814.

1714 After winning a war with Russia, Turkey prepares to recover the territories it lost to **Venice** during the 1690s. A series of attacks on Venetian shipping by a newly equipped **Ottoman navy** provokes the Senate to declare war.

1715 A **Turkish fleet** of some eighty ships, together with a land army, attacks Venetian forts in the **Peloponnese**, while a second fleet captures the islands of **Tinos** and **Aegina**.

1716 The Turks besiege **Corfu**, but are driven off after a heroic defence conducted by **Marshal Schulenburg**, a German officer in the Venetian service. On the initiative of Pope Clement XI, a '**Catholic Fleet**' is formed, including ships from Portugal, Tuscany and Malta.

1717 Francesco D'Aguirre, a Sicilian jurist working for King Victor Amadeus of Sardinia, publishes his *Della fondazione e ristabilimento degli studi*, ('Concerning the foundation and re-establishment of studies'), urging the need for sweeping reforms in **Italian universities**.

Ludovico Antonio Muratori, librarian to the Duke of Modena, begins work on his *Antiquities of the Este Family*, the first of a monumental sequence of scholarly historical works.

1718 With the aim of reforming **taxation**, the Austrian government in **Lombardy** begins work on a comprehensive registry of **land ownership** or *catasto*, the first of its kind in the region. Its exposures of fraud and malpractice antagonize the entrenched interests of the Lombard nobility and the Church, but the Austrian example will soon be copied elsewhere in Italy.

Spanish forces land at **Palermo** and seize Sicily from King Victor Amadeus's Savoyard garrisons, at the instigation of **Cardinal Alberoni**, chief minister of King Philip V of Spain. An Italian of humble origins, Alberoni has risen to power as a protégé of Philip's queen, **Elisabetta Farnese**, daughter and sole heir of the **duke of Parma**. A **British fleet** under Sir George Byng enters the **Straits of Messina** to prevent Spain from invading the mainland kingdom of **Naples**, now under Austrian rule. Byng outguns the Spaniards and takes their admiral prisoner. The fleet remains in Italian waters for the next six months.

By the **Treaty of Passarowitz**, forced on it by Austria which needs troops for the war with Spain, the republic of Venice makes peace with the Turks. All its recent conquests in Greece are ceded to the Ottoman empire.

1719 The Austrian general **Prince Elbeuf** makes the first excavation of the ancient Roman town of **Herculaneum**, destroyed by volcanic mud from Vesuvius in 79 AD.

1720 **Sicily** passes from the Spanish crown to the Austrian empire.

1723 **Pietro Giannone** publishes his *L'istoria civile del Regno di Napoli*. A history of the evolution of Naples from antiquity to the Habsburg takeover of 1707, the work analyses the continuing conflict between **civil government** and **papal authority**. Accused of seeking to discredit the Church, Giannone becomes the victim of a smear campaign orchestrated by the **Jesuits**. Forced to flee

Naples, he settles in **Vienna**, where he starts work on a still deeper examination of the Church's role in politics. This will become known as the *Triregno*, a reference to the triple tiara traditionally worn by the popes.

In **Naples**, **Giambattista Vico** begins work on his *Principi di una scienza nuova* (*Principles of a New Science*), a magisterial study of the making of nations and the evolution of natural law. Over the next two decades the book will go into several editions.

Ludovico Antonio Muratori publishes the first volume of his *Rerum italicarum scriptores* (*Writers on the History of Italy*), an exhaustive compendium of major Italian charters and chronicles from 500 to 1500 AD, on which he will continue to work for many years to come.

1724 **Grand Duke Cosimo III** dies in **Florence** after reigning more than fifty years, leaving as his heir his only surviving son, **Gian Gastone de' Medici**.

1725 **Antonio Vivaldi's** *Il cimento dell'armonia e dell'invenzione*, a set of twelve violin concertos featuring his *Four Seasons*, is published in Venice.

1729 Under a series of new decrees known as the 'Constitutions', **Victor Amadeus of Sardinia** sets up a new **education system** throughout his kingdom, freeing it from the Church's influence. The state, now comprising Savoy, Piedmont and the island of Sardinia, is the first in Europe to introduce secular schooling from primary level to university, offering scholarships to poor students of outstanding merit.

1730 King Victor Amadeus II abdicates in favour of his son, who becomes **Charles Emmanuel III**.

The Venetian painter **Canaletto** (Giovanni Antonio Canal, 1697–1768) completes *The Stonemason's Yard*, one of his most admired works both then and now. Trained as a

Antonio Vivaldi

On the strength of a single composition, the set of violin concertos known as the *Four Seasons*, Antonio Vivaldi (1674–1741) has become one of the most popular classical composers. This was not always the case: in the half-century after his death his reputation rapidly declined, and for almost 150 years his work was completely ignored. It was the rediscovery of Baroque music in the 20th century that revealed his prowess in both instrumental and vocal composition, which had made his music a major cultural attraction for early 18th-century travellers to Venice.

Though ordained (his hair colour earned him the epithet the 'Red Priest'), Vivaldi never actually followed a religious vocation, choosing instead to live openly with the singer **Anna Giro**, for whom he wrote several operatic roles. His main employment, from 1703 onwards, was as director of the orchestra at the girls' orphanage of **La Pietà** where – if the concertos he wrote for them are anything to go by – his pupils were astonishingly talented. His works for violin, bassoon, cello, flute and oboe gained him an international reputation and revolutionized both the **concerto** form and the role of the **soloist**. The disparaging assertion by Igor Stravinsky that Vivaldi wrote the same concerto five hundred times has been comprehensively disproved by modern performers on authentic instruments. These performances have revealed not only the originality of his sound world and his uncanny sensitivity to the individual 'voice' of a particular instrument, but also the passionate physicality and rhythmic drive that make his idiom so unmistakable. He was also a greatly admired composer of **operas**, **Church music** and **chamber sonatas**.

Nobody is quite sure why he suddenly left Venice for Vienna in 1741. He died there the same year, of an unspecified ailment, and was given a pauper's funeral at St Stephen's Cathedral, where one of the choirboys who sang at the service was **Joseph Haydn**. But by then Vivaldi's radical influence, not to mention his brio, panache and inventiveness, had made an indelible mark on music across the length and breadth of Europe.

Detail from an anonymous eighteenth century portrait of Antonio Vivaldi

scene-painter, he has turned his talents to creating a series of Venetian views, acclaimed for their handling of light and colour, and especially popular with English visitors.

1732 **Pope Clement XII** grants free-port status to **Ancona**, with the aim of improving the maritime trade of the **Papal States**.

1733 During the **War of the Polish Succession**, France and Sardinia, at war with Austria, invade **Lombardy**.

1734 Following the Spanish defeat of the Austrians at **Bitonto**, **Charles of Bourbon**, son of King Philip V of Spain by Elisabetta Farnese, becomes **king of Naples**. The Bourbon dynasty will reign over the kingdom (later known as the **Two Sicilies**) for the next 126 years.

1735 The historian and political theorist **Pietro Giannone** settles in **Geneva** in order to avoid persecution in Italy for his **radical ideas** on the liberty of the subject and the nature of ecclesiastical authority in the secular state. While visiting relatives in **Piedmont**, he is kidnapped on the orders of Charles Emmanuel III, and spends the rest of his life in prison.

1736 **Gian Gastone de' Medici**, the last of his family to be Grand Duke of Tuscany, dies, having spent much of his reign in bed. The Tuscan throne remains vacant for the next two years.

1737 **Francesco III** becomes **duke of Modena**. During his 43-year reign he carries out **far-reaching reforms**, expropriating Church lands to relieve poverty, appointing special magistrates to settle landlord-tenant disputes, revising the duchy's legal code and establishing an independent appeal court.

At the age of 93, **Antonio Stradivari** dies in **Cremona**, the city his violins have made famous. He is the last and greatest of the *liutai* (makers of stringed instruments) who have worked here since 1550, and who include the renowned families of **Amati** and **Guarneri**.

King Charles III of Naples relaunches the excavations at **Herculaneum**, begun eighteen years earlier by Marshal Elbeuf.

In **Modena**, **Ludovico Antonio Muratori** publishes his *Antiquitates italicae medii aevi* (*Antiquities of Medieval Italy*), a six-volume history of the Middle Ages.

1738 The **Treaty of Vienna** ends the War of the Polish Succession. By its terms, Stanislaus Lesczynski, dispossessed king of Poland, is awarded the duchy of **Lorraine** in compensation. Its Austrian duke, Francis Stephen, is given the vacant duchy of **Tuscany** as a reward for his generalship of the Habsburg army in Germany.

1740 Prospero Lambertini becomes pope as **Benedict XIV**. During his eighteen-year papacy the **administration** and **finances** of the Papal States are overhauled, concordats (agreements) favourable to **secular governments** are signed with Spain, Naples and Sardinia, discreet encouragement is given to the study of **'new science'** (such as the discoveries of **Sir Isaac Newton**, still officially condemned by the Church) and public-private finance initiatives are tested. Benedict is later commended as the century's most enlightened pontiff.

Francis of Tuscany marries his distant cousin **Maria Theresa, Empress of Austria**. Habsburg control over the duchy is now complete. **The War of the Austrian Succession** begins, in which France, Bavaria and Spain, supported by Prussia, challenge Maria's claim to inherit the imperial throne.

1742 French and Spanish armies invade Austrian territory in **Lombardy**. Francesco III, duke of Modena, declares his intention of joining them. A joint Austro-Sardinian force lays siege to **Modena**, capturing the city and forcing the duke to flee. He will not re-enter his duchy for another seven years.

A British fleet threatens to bombard **Naples** unless King Charles III withdraws his support for France and Spain. He accepts the ultimatum, but concentrates on training a new army to re-enter the conflict at an opportune moment.

1743 The last surviving member of the **Medici** family, Anna Maria Luisa, Electress Palatine, daughter of Grand Duke Cosimo III, dies in Florence. She bequeaths her immense wealth of **art treasures** collected by her ancestors to Tuscany's new ruler, **Francis of Lorraine**, on condition that it remains within the frontiers of the Grand Duchy 'for the ornament of the state, the benefit of the people, and as an inducement to the curiosity of foreigners'.

The dramatist **Carlo Goldoni** presents his comedy *La donna di garbo* (*The Woman of Style*) at Venice's **Teatro di San Samuele**. His earlier plays have been partly scripted, partly improvised by comedians of his theatrical company. This is his first fully scripted comedy.

1744 **Giambattista Vico** dies in **Naples**, where he has become an honoured historiographer royal to King Charles. He leaves a corrected version of the *Scienza nuova*, a work which gains in importance over the next fifty years but finds its most appreciative readership in the 20th century. Among its latterday admirers are the philosopher Benedetto Croce and the historian of ideas Isaiah Berlin.

Ludovico Antonio Muratori begins work on his 21-volume *Annali d'Italia* (*Annals of Italy*), a digest of his researches over previous decades, aimed at the general reader. The work represents a significant step towards raising consciousness of a shared **national heritage** among Italians.

An Austrian army threatens to invade the kingdom of Naples. **Charles III** deploys his new army to crush a pro-Austrian uprising in the province of **Abruzzi**. Later, supported by Spanish forces, he inflicts a major defeat on Austrian forces at **Velletri**.

1745 The painter **Giovanni Battista Tiepolo** embarks on a lavish series of frescoes commissioned by the *nouveau riche* owners of the **Palazzo Labia** on Venice's **Grand Canal**. Portraying scenes from Roman history, including the famous *Banquet of Cleopatra*, they represent the verve, fantasy and brilliant colouring of an artist who is seen as the natural heir to earlier Venetian painters such as Veronese, Tintoretto and Titian.

1746 During the **War of the Austrian Succession**, an Austrian army occupies **Genoa**. In December the people, resentful of the invaders and angry at the compromises made by Genoese patricians, rise in revolt. Ferocious street battles succeed in driving out the Austrians. This event is later seen as foreshadowing the Risorgimento of the next century, becoming part of the folk history of **Italian independence**.

1748 After peasants digging on the southern edge of Mount Vesuvius discover statues and bronze implements, King Charles III of Naples orders excavations to begin on the site, and the first traces of the city of **Pompeii**, devastated by volcanic eruption in AD 79, are uncovered. Excavations will continue until the present day.

The **Treaty of Aix-la-Chapelle** ends the War of the Austrian Succession. One of the treaty's clauses forbids Charles III from passing the crown of **Naples** to his descendants once he inherits the throne of Spain from his childless half-brother Ferdinand V. In a skilful diplomatic coup by Neapolitan envoys, the clause is swiftly annulled. Charles's younger brother Philip becomes **duke of Parma**. Though married to an Austrian archduchess, Philip aligns himself politically with his French Bourbon relatives, turning Parma into a miniature centre of Parisian culture in Italy.

Pietro Giannone dies in prison at Turin. His *Triregno*, a study of the Church's obsession with worldly power, remains suppressed throughout Italy but, circulated in manuscript form, it becomes widely influential throughout the rest of Europe.

1750 **Ludovico Antonio Muratori** dies, aged 78, in Modena. Though the Church has attempted to silence his questioning approach to its authority and moral integrity, he has earned admiration for his scholarship and balanced attitude towards his sources. His scrupulous methods have in many ways anticipated those of modern academics.

1751 The Neapolitan intellectual **Ferdinando Galiani** publishes *Della moneta* (*On Money*), a significant contribution to the debate in Enlightenment Europe on the role of economics in the survival of states.

1755 The **Accademia Ercolanese** is established in Naples by King Charles to undertake in-depth investigation of the antiquities of **Herculaneum**. Over the next forty years, its nine published volumes of research, picked up and circulated by travellers to Naples on the **Grand Tour**, will exert an important influence on European **decorative taste**, as well as on the evolving science of **archaeology**.

King Charles III leaves **Naples** to become **king of Spain**. A regency council, headed by **Bernardo Tannucci**, will govern for the next twelve years.

The Austrian government in **Milan** reforms municipal administration in **Lombardy**. Membership of local councils is now to be based on property qualifications rather than on titles of nobility, facilitating the political rise of a **bourgeoisie** based on wealth, landowner status and professional skills.

Parma's Enlightenment pleasure palaces

However small their territories, princes all over Europe during the 17th and 18th centuries aspired to the unparalleled grandeur of the court of **King Louis XIV** of France. An out-of-town palace after the fashion of **Versailles** was absolutely *de rigueur*. Italian rulers produced several splendid examples, beginning with **Sassuolo**, created for Duke Francesco II of Modena during the 1670s, and the spectacular royal hunting lodge at **Stupinigi** near Turin, designed by the Sicilian architect Filippo Juvarra in 1729 for Victor Amadeus of Sardinia. In 1752 at **Caserta**, outside Naples, Charles III ordered the building of an immense palace, rectangular in plan, set in splendid grounds featuring an 'English' park, with a lake, garden ornaments and a cascade. Perhaps the most truly French in spirit, however, was the palace at **Colorno** near **Parma**, begun for Philip of Bourbon in 1759 on the site of an earlier building, under his chief minister Guillaume du Tillot.

Du Tillot was a Frenchman, whose father had been a court functionary of Louis XIV. With Philip's encouragement, he initiated a far-reaching programme of **reforms** inspired by the ideas of the **Enlightenment**. The **Jesuits** were expelled from Parma and a new **state education system** introduced, with the university **law faculty** becoming Italy's finest. The **clergy's privileges** were curtailed and **mortmain** (the law preventing the sale of Church lands) abolished, along with the Inquisition forced on Parma by the popes, who believed that as its founders they had special claims on the duchy. The French philosopher **Etienne de Condillac** was invited to Parma as tutor to **Prince Fernando**, who nevertheless dismissed du Tillot as soon as he became duke in 1771.

Though Parma's age of reforms ended, many of the minister's wise edicts had by now taken beneficial effect. After the duchy became part of the kingdom of Italy in 1860, the palace at Colorno was turned over to military uses and then became a **mental hospital**. Almost nothing of its splendour survives, but the park, reflecting 18th-century **French garden design**, is a last remaining symbol of Duke Philip's attempt to bring Parma a little closer in spirit to Paris in the Age of Enlightenment.

1756 **Giacomo Casanova** flees from imprisonment in the **Piombi**, the prison next to the Palazzo Ducale in **Venice**. The escape, almost unprecedented in the annals of the republic, becomes a prominent episode in Casanova's memoirs, written some forty years later.

1759 **Count Karl von Firmian** arrives in Milan as Austrian governor of **Lombardy**. He embarks at once on a

The Grand Tour

The Grand Tour was the name given during the 18th century to the educational visits to Europe undertaken by young noblemen, accompanied by a tutor (known in England as a 'bear leader') and sometimes by friends. Although the journey might also take in trips to Germany, Holland and Switzerland, and nearly always started with an extended stay in **Paris**, its real object was Italy. Here the traveller would refine his artistic tastes by viewing **classical antiquities**, learning to distinguish between various styles of **painting**, and invariably building up a collection of statues, cameos, pictures and other *objets d'art* to display as evidence of his connoisseur status. Musically inclined tourists would also seek out the more important **operatic centres**, such as **Venice** and **Naples**, where they might even hire the services of Italian singers and composers.

By the mid-18th century, these rich foreign patrons had become such a conspicuous feature of Italian life that an entire economic subculture had come into existence to cater for them. New **inns** and **hotels** sprang up in larger cities; dozens of couriers and guides (known as *ciceroni*) offered their services; **dealers** sold a wide variety of antiques, genuine or fake; **ancient sites** were pillaged for their treasures; and a tribe of professional connoisseurs was ever eager to assist the traveller in forming his aesthetic sensibilities. Many of these experts were not Italian. Some were **Scottish Jacobites** (supporters of the exiled Stuart kings of Britain), others were artists of various nationalities attracted by the soft climate and visual charms of Naples and Rome, where living was cheap.

programme of important **fiscal and social reforms**.

1760 The Lombard *catasto* is finally completed, under supervision of the Florentine university professor **Pompeo Neri**. It provides the basis for an entirely new system of taxation, based on state assessment rather than voluntary personal declarations of income.

The Grand Tour phenomenon had a profound effect on affluent and cultivated lifestyles in Europe and America (the very name of Thomas Jefferson's estate in Virginia, Monticello, is a nod in its direction). Architecture, painting, sculpture, music and garden design all reflected influences absorbed in Italy. Travel was so seriously disrupted by the **Napoléonic War**, however, that the Grand Tour failed to recover its cultural significance after hostilities ended in 1815. Aristocrats continued to visit Italy, but more for pleasure than instruction and, although *ciceroni* still loitered around the principal monuments, the novelty of the Grand Tour of Italy had worn off and 'bear leaders' became a thing of the past.

❝ I have seen the ruins of Rome, the Vatican, St Peter's, and all the miracles of ancient and modern art contained in that majestic city. The impression of it exceeds anything I have ever experienced in my travels. ... We visited the Forum and the ruins of the Coliseum every day. The Coliseum is unlike any work of human hands I ever saw before ... The interior is all ruin. I can scarcely believe that when encrusted with Dorian marble and ornamented by columns of Egyptian granite, its effect could have been so sublime and so impressive as in its present state. **❞**

Percy Bysshe Shelley, letter to Thomas Love Peacock

View of the Colosseum (1761) by Piranesi, from his Le vedute di Roma engravings

1762 After more than twenty years as a successful playwright in Venice and other Italian cities, **Carlo Goldoni** accepts an invitation to become official dramatist of the troupe of Italian comedians based in **Paris**. He will never return to Italy.

Luigi Galvani becomes professor of anatomy at **Bologna**. His experiments will lead to the discovery of **electricity** in living creatures, while his name is remembered in the word 'galvanize'.

1763 **Pietro Verri** publishes his *Discorso sulla felicità* in Milan. This *Treatise on happiness* also embraces wider themes, such as the **social responsibility** of the privileged classes, the development of a **secular morality** and the idea of **progress** towards higher levels of civilization. In so doing, it offers a direct challenge to Jean-Jacques

Rousseau's proto-Romantic idealization of the savage and the primitive.

Carlo Goldoni

Although only half-Venetian by birth, his father having originally arrived in Venice from Modena, Carlo Goldoni (1707–93) enchanted the Venetians with his impressive ear for the rhythms of their **dialect**, and for the **realism** with which his comedies reflected their daily lives. *Il servitore di due padroni* (*The Servant of Two Masters*) is his best-known play today. Although it is not necessarily his finest or most characteristic, like many of his works it makes use of characters from the time-honoured Italian tradition of *commedia dell'arte*. Just as striking are his realistic portrayals of contemporary manners among the Venetian **bourgeoisie**, which depend for their success on his shrewd observation of **human foibles** such as social ambition, competitiveness, envy, greed and self-deception. Masterpieces such as *La locandiera* (*The Hostess*) and *Il ventaglio* (*The Fan*) mock their characters' pretentiousness and petty obsessions, while their dialogue is natural, fluid and spontaneous.

None of the characters inhabiting Goldoni's dramatic world is ever exaggerated or implausible, and he often brings them closer to us by spiking their comic experiences with a drop or two of bitterness and disappointment. In this respect, one of his greatest achievements is the *Villeggiatura* trilogy of 1761. All of its characters are flawed or unappealing in some way. Yet the heroine Giacinta, having foolishly refused the hand of the man she really loves, is able to move the audience by suddenly stepping out of the action to address us in the person of the actress playing the part: a persuasive advocate for a character we have been led to think of as wayward, selfish and materialistic. No other 18th-century European playwright displays Goldoni's power, range and originality – his British contemporaries Sheridan and Goldsmith, for example, appear old-fashioned and contrived beside him – and he is deservedly regarded not only as Venice's but also as Italy's greatest dramatist.

Pantalone, one of the stock comic characters of the *commedia dell'arte* put to use by Goldoni in plays such as *The Servant of Two Masters*

Edward Gibbon, an Englishman in Rome on the Grand Tour, conceives the idea of a *History of the Decline and Fall of the Roman Empire*, though he will not begin work on it for another eight years.

In Milan, **Giuseppe Parini** publishes *Il mattino* (*Morning*), the first instalment of a cycle of poems to be entitled *Il giorno* (*The Day*), a devastating **satire** on morals and manners among the **Milanese aristocracy**. One of their number ominously warns the poet, 'If you wish to live until evening, do not publish *Midday*', but Parini courageously goes on to produce most of the remaining sections, leaving only part of *Night* unfinished at his death.

Antonio Galli Bibiena's splendid **opera house** in **Bologna** opens with a performance of Christoph Willibald von Gluck's *Il Trionfo di Clelia*. Galli Bibiena, who has also designed the **Teatro Scientifico** in **Mantua**, belongs to a family which has dominated the world of Italian theatre architecture and scene-painting over four generations.

1764 **Pietro Verri**, together with his brother **Alessandro** and the Milanese aristocrat and writer **Cesare Beccaria**, starts a new magazine, *Il Caffè* (*The Café*). Lasting barely two years, it nevertheless becomes a valuable forum for **new ideas** in such areas as legal and economic reform, the changing state of the Italian language and the world of science and the arts.

The most serious **famine** for many years devastates the kingdom of **Naples**. Poor harvests are accompanied by outbreaks of **plague** in the major cities, especially Naples itself, where some 40,000 people die.

1765 Inspired by British economic theorists and the philosophical essays of **David Hume**, **Antonio Genovesi**, a Neapolitan university professor, publishes the first of his two volumes entitled *Delle lezioni del commercio* (*Lessons of Commerce*), a comprehensive analysis of the social impact of

Edward Gibbon

'It was at Rome, on the 15th of October 1754, as I sat musing amidst the ruins of the Capitol, while the barefoot friars were singing vespers in the Temple of Jupiter, that the idea of writing the decline and fall of the city first started to my mind.' This, as described by Edward Gibbon (1737–94) in his *Autobiography,* was the genesis of the most celebrated of all the literary works directly inspired by the experience of the **Grand Tour** and contact with the spectacular remains of ancient Rome: *The Decline and Fall of the Roman Empire*.

In his youth, Edward Gibbon had led a somewhat footloose and mercurial life, abandoning his studies as an undergraduate at Magdalen College, Oxford, and spending five years in Switzerland. There he made the acquaintance of **Voltaire** and became sufficiently fluent in **French** to write a book on literary appreciation in the language. After serving as a soldier in the Hampshire militia, he set off on a two-year Grand Tour, and in Rome conceived the idea for his great history. Back in London, he produced further volumes of **literary criticism**, in both English and French, and became a Member of Parliament. This, combined with a minor government appointment and a family inheritance, enabled him to live comfortably while working on the *Decline and Fall*, which he began in 1773 and completed in 1788.

wealth, luxury, trade and labour. The book has a powerful effect on those seeking to reform the ancient and complex structures of southern Italian society.

Pietro Leopoldo, younger son of Empress Maria Theresa of Austria and Francis, duke of Lorraine, becomes **Grand Duke of Tuscany** and embarks on an extensive programme of **reform** and improvement in various areas of state administration.

1766 Cesare Beccaria and Alessandro Verri leave for **Paris** to make closer contacts with French philosophers such as

This immense enterprise, encompassing a historical span stretching roughly from the 2nd century AD to the age of the Crusades, is still much admired for its literary qualities as well as for its spirited assault on the political role of the Church in both western Europe and the Byzantine empire. It is also an impressive feat of **historiography**, based on very wide reading and engagement with primary sources, while at the same time reflecting the scepticism and objectivity that were so characteristic of the 18th-century **Enlightenment**. Among **Gibbon**'s key influences were the Italian historians **Pietro Giannone**, whose *Civil History* he admired for its courageous anticlericalism, and **Ludovico Antonio Muratori**, whose broad range of scholarly enquiry provided the Englishman with much useful material. After publishing his final volume in 1788, Gibbon bade a fond farewell to his readers, and to his great project: 'I will not dissemble the first emotions of joy on the recovery of my freedom, and, perhaps, the establishment of my fame. But my pride was soon humbled, and a sober melancholy was spread over my mind, by the idea that I had taken an everlasting leave of an old and agreeable companion, and that whatsoever might be the future fate of my History, the life of the historian must be short and precarious.'

Diderot and **d'Holbach**. Beccaria begins a contentious correspondence with Pietro Verri, who resignedly decides to close down *Il Caffè*.

1767 **Ferdinand IV**, son of King Charles III, comes of age and assumes power as **king of Naples**. The following year he marries **Archduchess Maria Carolina of Austria**, daughter of Empress Maria Theresa and sister of the future queen of France, **Marie Antoinette**. The new queen of Naples becomes a dominant force, not always for good, in the affairs of the kingdom.

1769 In Paris, where he is directing concerts, the composer **Luigi Boccherini** of Lucca is invited by the Spanish ambassador to go to **Madrid**. He will spend the next thirty years in Spain, composing the chamber music which earns him international fame and the praises of Haydn and Mozart.

Cesare Beccaria

Stout and slothful, **Cesare Beccaria** (1738–94) was notorious among Milanese intellectuals for his indolence. It was only through the encouragement of his friends **Pietro** and **Alessandro Verri**, who had read an essay he had published on economic theory, that he was persuaded to begin work on *Dei delitti e delle pene (Of crimes and punishments)* in 1762. The work was to be the first major study of the relationship between crime and the penalties handed down for it, remaining of huge significance to the present day. Beccaria it was who coined the phrase 'the greatest happiness shared by the greatest number' as a civilized ideal, adopted by **social theorists** in France and Britain, such as **Jeremy Bentham**, **d'Holbach** and **Diderot**, who were admirers of his book. Examining the morality of punishment, he attacked the irrational nature of existing European legal systems and proposed revolutionary ideas concerning the **social rehabilitation** of criminals. He exposed the barbarous use of **torture** by various governments, questioned the efficacy of the **death penalty** and examined the moral basis of punishments as mere **revenge** for injury, theft or damage. His book attacked the social systems of the Ancien Régime, accusing them of contributing to a fundamental **inequality** in the administration of justice. **Poverty** and lack of **education** were also examined as major causes of criminal behaviour, and Beccaria was the first major writer to suggest that rulers who were tough on crime should also remedy the conditions which encouraged it.

First published in the Tuscan city of Livorno rather than Beccaria's native Milan, where somewhat stricter censorship

1773 In a bull entitled *Dominus ac Redemptor*, **Pope Clement XIV** responds to pressure from Austria, France and Portugal, and suppresses the **Society of Jesus** (the Jesuit order). The Jesuits have gained a reputation as the uncompromising intellectual shock-troops of **Catholic orthodoxy**, and Clement's gesture is later seen as the most significant of Church concessions to the **Enlightenment**.

operated, the book was immediately attacked by the clergy, one of whom notably condemned Beccaria's contention that all human beings are born **free and equal** as 'false and absurd'. Gaining instant popularity throughout Europe, his book was read (though not approved of) by **Frederick the Great** of Prussia, **Empress Maria Theresa** and **Tsarina Catherine the Great** of Russia. **Voltaire** wrote an admiring commentary on it, **Thomas Jefferson** copied whole sections into his notebooks, and the spirit of the work is clearly echoed in the constitution of the **United States** and the writings of several of the American **Founding Fathers**. The views proposed in Beccaria's momentous work have formed the basis of **penal reform** throughout the civilized world. It also gave the 19th-century Russian writer Fyodor Dostoevsky the title for his most famous novel.

       It is evident that the intent of punishments should not be to torment a sensible being, nor to undo a crime already committed. Is it possible that torments and useless cruelty, the instrument of furious fanaticism or the impotency of tyrants, can be authorized by a political body, which, so far from being influenced by passion, should be the cool moderator of the passions of individuals? Can the groans of a tortured wretch recall the time past, or reverse the crime he has committed?

Cesare Beccaria, *Dei delitti e delle pene*, trans. W. Gordon and W. Creech

Italian musical migrants

Luigi Boccherini was just one among hundreds of 18th-century Italian musicians who became what would nowadays be called '**economic migrants**' to other areas of Europe. Within Italy itself, against a background of widespread economic decline, the Church and the rulers of sovereign states could no longer afford to act as munificent patrons. Though **opera** flourished in many cities, singers could make better money at **foreign courts** and **theatres**. **Austria**, **England**, **Portugal** and the capitals of several **German princely states** all regularly presented lavish stage performances demanding the finest voices and players.

Italian composers, too, were tempted to seek their fortunes abroad. **Domenico Cimarosa** and **Giovanni Paisiello**, for example, worked for Catherine the Great of **Russia**; **Antonio Salieri** lived most of his later life in **Vienna** as a respected teacher of composition (to pupils who included **Beethoven** and **Schubert**); **Niccolò Jommelli** revolutionized opera during his stay at the court of **Saxe-Weimar**; and **Domenico Scarlatti** wrote most of his impressive range of keyboard sonatas while in **Spain**. Several ventured still further afield. Starting his career in Lucca, the violinist and composer **Francesco Geminiani** became director of concerts in **Dublin**, while his fellow townsman **Francesco Barsanti** lived in **Edinburgh**, where the Scots enjoyed his fusion of Italian styles with local folk music. Often, like Boccherini, the wanderer never came back to Italy. Those who did, such as the great castrato Carlo Broschi, known as **Farinelli**, returned as wealthy men.

The greatest singing star of the 1730s, Farinelli was invited to **Spain** by King Philip V's Italian queen Elisabetta. His brief was to cure the monarch's depression, which he did by singing the same four arias to the king nightly for nine years. Remaining in Madrid as a favourite of Philip's successor **Ferdinand**, he served as a benign influence on both sovereigns, interesting them in commercial and agricultural improvement schemes and impressing everyone with his intelligence and high-mindedness. Only when **Charles III**, who was not especially interested in music, came to the throne did Farinelli go home to Italy, living out a dignified retirement in a villa outside Bologna.

Interior of the Teatro alla Scala opera house, Milan, viewed from the stage

1775 Cardinal Giovanni Angelo Braschi is elected pope as **Pius VI**. He will soon be forced into a direct confrontation with **Emperor Joseph II of Austria** over the latter's sweeping attempts to limit the power of the Church in his dominions.

1776 Owing to the intrigues of his enemy **Queen Maria Carolina** of Naples, **Bernardo Tannucci**, appointed head of the regency council by Charles III 22 years earlier, resigns as King Ferdinand's chief minister. His attempts at reform have been hampered by a powerful **feudal aristocracy** and the obstructive tactics of the **Church**.

1778 The **Teatro alla Scala**, designed by the Umbrian architect **Giuseppe Piermarini**, is opened in Milan (the name is taken from the medieval church of Santa Maria della Scala, torn down to make room for the new opera house). The inaugural performance is *Europa Riconosciuta*, specially composed for the occasion by **Antonio Salieri**.

1779 **Alessandro Volta** is appointed professor of chemistry at the university of **Pavia**. He will go on to create the first electric **pile battery**, and to give his name to the 'volt' as a unit of **electricity**.

1781 **Emperor Joseph II** issues his **Edict of Toleration**, under which non–Catholics, including Jews, are allowed freedom of worship and the right to work and hold government appointments. Religious discrimination is outlawed in the Austrian empire.

1782 An anxious **Pope Pius VI** journeys to Vienna for talks with Emperor Joseph II regarding his proposed **ecclesiastical reforms**. It is the first time a pope has left Italy since the 14th century. The discussions are unproductive.

1785 At the **Synod of Pistoia**, the town's modernizing bishop, **Scipione de' Ricci**, tries to introduce new measures of **reform** within the Church, related to those of Emperor Joseph II of Austria. They are condemned at once by Pope Pius VI and Ricci's diocesan authority is soon removed from him.

1786 Continuing his programme of reforms, **Grand Duke Pietro Leopoldo** gives **Tuscany** a new **penal code**, recognizing the accused's right to defence, regulating the conduct of judges and trials and abolishing torture. By an article of the same code, Tuscany becomes the first state in the world to abolish the **death penalty**.

Johann Wolfgang von Goethe arrives in Italy on a Grand Tour which will last two years and have a crucial and lasting impact on his life. His memoir of the experience, the *Italenische Reise* ('Italian Journey') becomes a classic of European travel writing.

1789 King **Ferdinand of Naples** appoints the English admiral **Sir John Acton**, favourite of his wife Maria Carolina, as chief minister. Acton and the queen now press for

Pope Pius VI

By the time Pius VI (1775–99) became pope, the reputation of the papacy was at its lowest ebb for many years. The reforms instituted by **Benedict XIV** had been largely overshadowed by the stormy relationships between **Clement XIII** (1758–69) and **Clement XIV** (1769–74) and various European governments, and there was a sense that papal authority was seriously losing ground against the new secularist confidence generated by the **Enlightenment**. Pius himself had to contend immediately with **Febronianism**, a movement among influential Catholics in **Germany**, which challenged the authority of the pope on various matters and undermined the three archbishops who formed part of the princely electoral college that confirmed the appointment of successive **Holy Roman Emperors**. It was indeed an emperor, **Joseph II**, who presented Pius with his principal problem, by setting in train a series of **reforms** which included giving the sovereign the right to interfere in Church affairs, restricting papal authority to spiritual matters, and toleration of **Protestants** and **Jews**. Pius's journey to Vienna was symbolic both of his alarm on behalf of the Church and, ironically, of the papacy's weakness in the face of the ruthless determination of a typical late 18th-century enlightened despot.

The pope achieved nothing in this confrontation, and dug himself in yet further by condemning attempts within Italy to modernize various aspects of the liturgy and Church government. His condemnation of the **French revolutionaries**' drive, in 1794, to detach the clergy within France from Vatican authority was only to be expected, but it aligned him firmly him with the forces of **reaction** in Europe. Pius died a prisoner of the French at Valence, despondent at the prospects for the future of Catholicism, and saddened by the failure of his sincere initiatives on behalf of his papal office and of the Church in a fast-changing political landscape.

a firm line against liberal influences, freemasonry and revolutionary ideas.

The outbreak of the **French Revolution** is initially welcomed in Italy, but the Italian sovereigns soon become alarmed by developments and retreat towards increasingly reactionary political measures.

1790 The Austrian emperor Joseph II dies and is succeeded by his brother Pietro Leopoldo, Grand Duke of Tuscany, who becomes **Emperor Leopold II**. His son **Ferdinand** takes over as **Grand Duke of Tuscany**.

1792 Emperor Leopold II dies and is succeeded as ruler of the Austrian empire by his son **Francis II**. Unenlightened and undistinguished, Francis will soon become identified with the cause against the French Revolution, and later against **Napoléon**.

Venice's first theatre, the **Teatro La Fenice** designed by **Antonio Selva**, opens with a performance of Giovanni Paisiello's *I giuochi d'Agrigento* (*The Games of Agrigento*).

Without officially declaring war, the army of the **French revolutionary government** attacks the kingdom of **Sardinia**, occupying **Savoy** and **Nice**.

1793 Shocked by the execution of her sister Queen Marie Antoinette and her brother-in-law King Louis XVI of France, **Maria Carolina** of Naples encourages her husband King Ferdinand to sign an aggressive pact with **Britain**. Neapolitan land and sea forces now enter the ongoing European war with revolutionary France.

Carlo Goldoni dies in poverty in Paris, aged 88, after the revolutionary Legislative Assembly suspends the pension formerly allowed him by the French king.

1794 Alarmed by the spread of '**Jacobinism**' (the name loosely applied in Italy and elsewhere to any kind of sympathy with the French Revolution), the **Venetian repub-lic** makes multiple arrests, especially in the city of **Brescia**, where Jacobin sympathizers include members of the nobility and clergy.

1796 The 27-year-old general **Napoléon Bonaparte** is given command of the French '**Army of Italy**'. Forcing King Victor Amadeus III of Sardinia to allow French forces to occupy Piedmontese fortresses, Napoléon enters **Lombardy**. The **Austrians** send an army against him and are defeated at **Lodi**. The **French** occupy **Milan**, where they are welcomed by local Jacobins. In August, Napoléon forms the General Administration of Lombardy, which later becomes known officially – with **Modena**, **Mantua**, **Bologna** and **Ferrara** – as the **Cisalpine Republic**.

> ❝ Peoples of Italy, the French army comes to break your chains; the French people is the friend of all peoples; meet us with confidence. Your property, your religion, and your usages will be respected. We make war as generous enemies, and we have no quarrel save with the tyrants who enslave you. ❞
>
> Napoléon Bonaparte, proclamation, 1796

1797 Having occupied **Verona** and violated the declared neutrality of the Venetian republic, Napoléon threatens to destroy the city of **Venice** itself. An **Easter rising** in Verona is brutally suppressed by the French, and Napoléon declares war on Venice on 1 May. The ancient Republic hastily dissolves itself and Napoléon is welcomed by jubilant Venetians, who hail the dawn of liberty. Having arranged a separate peace with the Austrians, Bonaparte signs the **Treaty of Campoformio** on 17 October, under which he agrees to hand over Venice and her territories to **Emperor Francis II**.

1798 The French leave Venice on 18 January. **Austria** assumes control of the city and her territories on the same day.

A French army occupies **Rome**. **Pope Pius VI** is deposed and a **republic** is declared. Pius retreats to Siena, thence to the French town of **Valence**, where he dies in captivity the following year.

1799 **Naples** concludes an offensive alliance with **Austria**. The king and queen, with their friends Sir William and Lady Hamilton, the English ambassador and his wife, welcome **Admiral Horatio Nelson**, fresh from his victory over Napoléon at the battle of the Nile.

A combined **Austrian** and **Russian** force under **General Suvorov** invades **Lombardy**, driving out the French and remaining in control of the province for over a year. A **French** army invades **Tuscany**. **Grand Duke Ferdinand** and his family are given 24 hours to leave **Florence**, where French rule is unpopular. Reaction against French rule in southeast Tuscany results in the so-called **'Viva Maria' riots** in **Arezzo** and surrounding towns. Led by priests, monks and friars, the mob attacks **Jews** and suspected **Jacobins**, until finally dispersed by Austrian troops.

The French army enters the kingdom of **Naples**. Nelson hastily removes the king and queen to Palermo. Neapolitan liberals proclaim the **Parthenopean Republic** (Parthenope was an alternative name for the ancient Greek city of Neapolis). However, it fails to fulfil the hopes of the peasantry in the kingdom of Naples for an end to **feudalism**. Rural opposition to the new government is fostered by local clergy, led by **Cardinal Fabrizio Ruffo**. Forming a **monarchist army** he enters **Naples**, where his followers are allowed to murder, rape and pillage in the name of Christ and King Ferdinand. They are joined by the *lazzaroni*, the vast mob of unemployed with which the

Nelson and the Parthenopean Republic

The English admiral Horatio Nelson's intervention in the affairs of the kingdom of Naples forms the most inglorious chapter in his career, and might well never have taken place at all had it not been for his infatuation with **Emma, Lady Hamilton**. The second wife of **Sir William Hamilton**, British ambassador to Naples and a noted collector and amateur archaeologist, Emma was a London prostitute whom her husband had picked up in a fashionable brothel called the 'Temple of Health'. Once in Naples, she formed an unlikely but close friendship with **Queen Maria Carolina**. Nelson had already met the Hamiltons on his way to confront the French fleet in Egypt, and was instantly smitten with Emma.

Arriving back victorious after the **battle of the Nile**, he allowed Emma and the queen to influence his judgement, and helped to suppress brutally the **Parthenopean Republic**, satisfying the royal family's desire for **vengeance**. Admiral **Caracciolo**, the elderly and distinguished commander of the republic's navy, was carried on board Nelson's flagship, given a summary trial and sentenced to be hanged at the yardarm of one of King Ferdinand's frigates. When Caracciolo begged for shooting rather than hanging as the more honourable execution, Nelson refused. His second-in-command, Captain Troubridge, meanwhile battered the combined French and rebel forces into submission, while the king and queen inflicted **ferocious reprisals** against Neapolitan republicans.

For these services, Nelson was rewarded with the Sicilian duchy of **Bronte** and a large estate, as well as a diamond-hilted sword. Lady Hamilton also returned with him to London as his mistress (an arrangement to which Sir William was quite agreeable). Though he contemptuously dismissed Italy as 'a country of fiddlers and poets, whores and scoundrels', he had been the willing tool of Naples's most reactionary elements, and for Emma's sake had actually chosen to disobey British admiralty orders to leave Naples for Malta. His role in destroying the Parthenopean Republic and restoring the **Bourbons** was never forgotten or forgiven by Neapolitan liberals of the future **Risorgimento**.

city teems. Ruffo guarantees the republic's leaders their freedom in return for surrender. On the return of the king and queen, supported by Nelson's fleet, over one hundred republicans are executed.

At a conclave held in **Venice** by cardinals exiled from Rome, Gregorio Chiaramonti is declared pope as **Pius VII**.

1800 Having become sole ruler of France after the coup d'état of 18 Brumaire, **Napoléon** marches into **Lombardy** and decisively defeats the Austrians at the battle of **Marengo**.

Captured by the French, who establish a **Ligurian republic** in place of its former oligarchy, **Genoa** is besieged by an Austrian army and a British fleet. During the two-month siege, 30,000 citizens die from disease and starvation before the defending commanders, generals Soult and Massena, are forced to surrender.

1801 The **Treaty of Lunéville** ends the war between France and Austria. Under its terms, **Tuscany** becomes the kingdom of **Etruria**, to be ruled by **Lodovico di Bourbon**, duke of Parma. The treaty guarantees the existence of the Cisalpine and Ligurian republics.

1802 Having succeeded his father as king of **Sardinia**, Charles Emmanuel IV abdicates as legitimate sovereign, retiring to Rome and taking holy orders. He is succeeded by his brother, **Victor Emmanuel I**.

1804 Napoléon appoints himself **emperor of France**, summoning **Pope Pius VII** to crown him in the cathedral of Notre Dame in Paris. At the ceremony it is in fact the emperor who crowns himself, while Pius looks on.

1805 Napoléon assumes the title **king of Italy**, and is crowned in Milan Cathedral with the historic Iron Crown of Lombardy. As his viceroy in the new kingdom he appoints his stepson, 24-year-old **Eugène de Beauharnais**.

War is resumed between France and Austria. Defeated at **Austerlitz**, the Austrians surrender **Venice** and her former Adriatic territories to the French. **British** forces occupy

Italian towns in Napoléon's empire

Napoléon's absorption of Italy into his empire was to have major repercussions on the appearance of a number of the peninsula's larger towns and cities. Determined to make their mark on the built environment, the French administrators were especially concerned to improve the **street layout** and **public hygiene** of designated urban areas. Not surprisingly, many Italian communities tended to resent this heavy-handed attempt to impose typically Gallic notions of **order** and **rationalism** on their beautiful Renaissance and Baroque townscapes. In **Florence**, for example, the French were known pejoratively as *nuvoloni* ('big clouds'), a pun on the words *nous voulons* ('we desire') which heralded every proclamation announcing a fresh government scheme.

In **Venice**, **Milan** and **Rome**, by contrast, the French attempts at improvement were acknowledged as strikingly successful. While the Venetians may initially have regretted the disappearance of the church of **San Geminiano** from Piazza San Marco's western end, they eventually applauded the elegant neoclassical **Ala Napoléonica** which replaced it, designed by **Giuseppe Soli** and begun in 1810 as a suite of grand reception rooms for the viceroy **Eugène de Beauharnais**. In Milan, streets were widened and the spacious **Fuoro Buonaparte** laid out around the old citadel of **Castello Sforzesco**. The new initiatives of Napoléon's proconsuls endured in Rome even after French rule had ended, when in 1814, following the return to the city of Pope Pius VII, the architect **Giuseppe Valadier** laid out the splendid **Piazza del Popolo**. With its terraces, steps and radial streets converging on an impressive prospect of churches and sculpture, the square epitomizes a new taste for grandiose town planning, which, encouraged by French influences during the years of Bonaparte's regime, was to take root in 19th-century Italy.

Sicily. Under the new administration, the island's economy improves and relative peace and order prevail.

1806 Troops under **General Sir John Stuart** defeat a French force at **Maida** in southern **Calabria**, effectively ending French occupation of the region. The only action fought by British soldiers on Italian soil before World War I, it will later be commemorated in the name of Maida Vale, an area of northwest London. A French army occupies **Naples**. Ferdinand and Maria Carolina flee once more to **Sicily**, and Napoléon's brother **Joseph Bonaparte** is made king.

1808 Napoléon's troops occupy **Rome**, declaring it a free imperial city. Pope **Pius VII** is arrested and taken to **Savona**, where he remains a prisoner. Having striven to rule justly in Naples, abolishing **feudalism** and instituting a *catasto* (which remains unfinished when the Bourbons are restored in 1815), Joseph Bonaparte is sent by Napoléon to become king of Spain. **Marshal Joachim Murat**, husband of the emperor's sister Caroline, is made king of Naples. Napoléon annexes the kingdom of **Etruria** and awards it to his sister, **Elisa Baciocchi**.

1811 **Lord William Bentinck** arrives in **Palermo** as ambassador to the Bourbon court and commander-in-chief of British sea and land forces. A diplomat and military man of energy, intelligence and courage, he is determined to reform the politics and administration of Sicily, so clashing head-on with **Queen Maria Carolina**.

1812 Pope Pius VII is taken from Savona to the palace of **Fontainebleau** outside Paris, where he remains a prisoner until 1814.

William Bentinck discovers that Maria Carolina has been plotting against him in secret negotiations with **Joachim Murat**. He insists that she be exiled outside a 25-mile radius of Palermo. Meanwhile he introduces **constitutional**

bicameral government to Sicily, abolishing **feudalism**. Sicily is given **independence** from Naples.

Napoléon invades **Russia**. Many Italian soldiers, as subjects of the French empire, will take part in the campaign and the subsequent retreat from **Moscow**. Those who survive will play an important role in the wars and revolutions of the coming **Risorgimento**.

1813 Bentinck exiles **Maria Carolina** from Sicily. She is forced to return to Austria via Constantinople and Odessa, and dies in **Vienna** the following year.

The British Foreign Secretary **Lord Castlereagh** overrules William Bentinck's constitutional experiment in Sicily, and the island is reunited with the crown of Naples. Feudal privileges are restored. Bentinck is sent to **India**, where his reforming instincts are more effective during his years as governor of Calcutta, but his initiative is remembered in

> ❝ If the era of the French Revolution was the most brilliant and glorious period of modern history, as its admirers believe, Napoléon, who was able to reach and keep the highest rank for fifteen years, was assuredly one of the greatest men that has ever been seen. If, on the contrary, he had only to rise like a meteor above the fogs of general dissolution, ... if he had to combat nothing more than opponents already enfeebled by a universal weariness, nothing more than powerless rivals and ignoble passions, nothing more than adversaries paralysed by their disunity both within and without the country, then it is certain that the lustre of his success diminishes in proportion to the ease with which he achieved it. ❞
>
> Prince Clemens von Metternich, Austrian ambassador to France, trans. Herbert H. Rowen

Sicily as one of the few periods of good government in its history.

Austria declares war on Italy. An Austrian army invades **Venetia** (Friuli and the Veneto) and British warships blockade **Venice**.

1814 Napoléon is defeated at **Leipzig**. Forced to abdicate his throne, he is exiled to **Elba**. Eugène de Beauharnais concludes an armistice with **Austria**, whose armies then enter **Lombardy**. Their commander, Marshal Bellegarde, promises that Austria will respect the liberties and privileges of her Italian subjects. It rapidly becomes clear that the **Habsburg** government has no intention of doing so. Austria will now become the dominant power in Italian affairs.

8
The Risorgimento

1815–70

Risorgimento – Italian for 'resurgence' or 'rising again' – is the term applied to Italy's struggle for **unification** and **nationhood** during the 19th century. As they carved up Europe among them, the **great powers** at the **Congress of Vienna** in 1814–15 (Russia, Prussia, Austria and Great Britain) assumed that the majority of Italians would happily welcome the fall of Napoléon's empire and the reinstatement of their legitimate sovereigns. The chief architect of this policy of **restoration** was the Austrian chancellor **Clemens von Metternich**. What he had failed to grasp was that, for all their severity towards political dissent, the **Napoléonic kingdoms** in Italy had encouraged personal initiative, administrative efficiency and social mobility. The **centralization** imposed by the French government had moreover had the effect of binding the Italians closer together as a people. Thus Metternich was dangerously wide of the mark when, in 1847, he famously dismissed Italy as merely a 'geographical expression'.

Once restored to their former thrones, the Italian sovereigns proceeded largely to squander their initial 'honeymoon period' in power, when they might have secured the affection and loyalty of their subjects. In **Piedmont**, **Naples**, **Sicily** and the **Papal States** they set out instead to undo any progress made under the French, and to reimpose **despotic regimes** of the most reactionary and oppressive nature. The **Austrian empire**, now the direct overlord of **Lombardy** and **Venetia** and the dominant superpower throughout Italy, was ruthless in suppressing rebellion and even criticism. Constantly chivvying local rulers in **Parma**, **Modena** and **Tuscany** (all of whom had family ties with the **Habsburgs**) to be more vigilant in putting down secret societies and liberal manifestations of even the most harmless variety, the Austrians fostered a degrading **subculture** of police spies, informers, denunciations, press censorship and bureaucratic obfuscation. Not surprisingly, this implacable and sinister **obscurantism** was widely resented by a growing number of Italians aware of political freedom and **progress** enjoyed elsewhere in Europe.

The growth of **revolutionary** feeling during the 1820s and 1830s was not necessarily accompanied by any firm idea of what form a united and free Italy should take. **Giuseppe Mazzini**, the dominant ideologue of the age, offered moral inspiration but no practical foundations, and the early revolutions carried out by his followers were often hopelessly unsuccessful, and significantly failed to carry the people with them. Rising **political tension** throughout Italy during the 1840s, exacerbated by **economic hardship**, eventually persuaded several sovereigns to introduce programmes of reform within their states. By the momentous year of 1848, many Italians were pinning their hopes on **King Charles Albert of Piedmont** and **Pope Pius IX**: these were the leaders popularly perceived as the most likely to bring about the longed-for **liberal revolution** which would rid Italy of Austrian influence and forge a stronger sense of nationhood among the Italian people.

The failure of either Charles Albert or Pius to meet these expectations was only one of the causes of the wave of **disillusion** that swept the peninsula in the wake of the numerous revolts that erupted in 1848–49. Too often, opportunities for a consensus among the various shades of

Italian nationalism were wasted, and after an initial loss of nerve, Austria coolly exploited this lack of unity and resolve to restore the status quo. Revolutionary idealism and the confidence enshrined in Charles Albert's famous phrase 'L'Italia farà da sè' ('Italy will do it by herself') never properly recovered from the experiences of 1848, and it was the more hard-headed, pragmatic solutions of international diplomacy and the intervention of the great powers offered by Camillo Cavour, as prime minister ten years later, that were to prove more effective.

Even during the wars of 1859 and 1860, unity of purpose and aspiration among the Italians could in no sense be described as secure. That most repressive of Italian sovereigns, the duke of Modena, was followed into exile by his loyal army, and the king and queen of Naples found many unlikely admirers of their heroic last stand at Gaeta. Giuseppe Garibaldi's brilliantly successful Sicilian expedition had originally been sparked off by his anger at the cession of Nice to France, and his role as iconic liberator was to prove unwelcome to both King Victor Emmanuel and Cavour. The Italy that emerged from unification was none the less a dissatisfied one, unworthy in the view of many of the massive sacrifices made by the thousands directly involved in the Risorgimento.

> **"** Throughout Italy, one stroke of the pen has erased all our liberties, all our reform, all our hoped ... We Italians have neither parliament nor hustings, nor liberty of the press, nor liberty of speech, nor possibility of lawful public assemblage, nor a single means of expressing the opinions stirring within us. **"**
>
> Giuseppe Mazzini on the Congress of Vienna, trans. Bolton King

1815 Following the **Congress of Vienna**, the former **Italian sovereigns** ousted by Napoléon are **restored** to their thrones. To salvage some royal dignity, Bonaparte's ex-empress **Marie Louise** is awarded the duchy of **Parma**, whose ruling **Bourbon** family are compensated with a duchy created from the extinct republic of **Lucca**. **Lombardy** and **Venetia**, both economically important, become provinces of the Austrian empire. With the exception of Marie Louise and **Grand Duke Ferdinand of**

ITALY c.1815

SWITZERLAND
TYROL
KINGDOM OF HUNGARY
LOMBARDY VENETIA
KINGDOM OF SARDINIA
Pavia
Mantua
Padua
ISTRIA
PARMA
Cuneo
Genoa
MODENA
Ferrara
OTTOMAN EMPIRE
Pistoia
REPUBLIC OF SAN MARINO
Pisa
Florence
LIGURIAN SEA
Livorno
TUSCANY
PAPAL STATES
ADRIATIC SEA
ELBA
CORSICA
Rome
KINGDOM OF THE TWO SICILIES
Naples
Salerno
KINGDOM OF SARDINIA
Sapri
Cágliari
Cotrone
Duchy
Messina
0   100 kms
N
SICILY
Syracuse

Tuscany, all the restored rulers are dedicated **reactionaries**, firmly under the direction of Austria and her chancellor, **Prince Clemens von Metternich**.

Joachim Murat, king of Naples under his brother-in-law **Napoléon**, tries to negotiate with the Austrians to keep his throne. When Napoléon is defeated at **Waterloo**, Murat appeals for Italian nationalist support to help him remain in **Naples**. An Austrian army sent to restore the Bourbon king Ferdinand defeats Murat's forces at **Tolentino**. Fleeing to Corsica, he organizes an expedition to regain Naples, but is captured and shot.

1816 Bad harvests throughout Italy lead to widespread **famine**, particularly in **Lombardy** and **Venetia**. Austrian relief measures in these provinces are introduced too late, and **government incompetence** in the face of the catastrophe antagonizes all sectors of society.

The first performance of **Gioacchino Rossini's** *Il barbiere di Siviglia* (*The Barber of Seville*) is given in Rome.

1818 In **Milan**, **Luigi Lambertenghi** and **Federico Confalonieri** found *Il Conciliatore*, a literary and scientific review with strong liberal sympathies which attracts contributions from most of Milan's best writers. After only a year it is closed down on government orders, but it remains an important symbol of **free intellectual expression** among Italian patriots.

1820 **Duchess Marie Louise of Parma**, assisted by her lover (and later husband) Count Neipperg, introduces a new and skilfully framed **legal code** for her state, retaining many of the laws brought into force under the **Napoléonic regime**.

1821 A revolt led by **army officers** breaks out in the Piedmontese city of **Alessandria**. King **Victor Emmanuel I** resists demands for a constitution, but is forced to abdicate

Gioacchino Rossini

The Barber of Seville made Rossini's name as an inspired master of *opera buffa*, the comic opera form in vogue throughout Italy since the mid-18th century. Archetypally Italian in its tunefulness, elegance and sparkle, this opera has always been his most popular work. In his own time however, Rossini (1792–1868) was also admired for his **experimental** approach to serious opera, and when he settled in **Naples** after 1815 it was as a lofty lyric dramatist that he gained success. Operas such as *Mose in Egitto*, with its magnificent choral prayer and storm scene; *Maometto Secondo* and *Ermione*, striking in their original treatment of traditional aria and ensemble forms; and *La donna del lago*, combining a romantic theme from a Walter Scott poem with brilliant coloratura singing, were cutting-edge works which set new standards in music drama. By 1822, when *Semiramide* received its premiere in Venice, Rossini, aged only 30, was Europe's most popular composer.

After his death in 1868, these serious operas were quickly forgotten, partly because of changing fashions, and partly because singers had lost the vocal style needed to tackle them. Soon the composer was known only for *The Barber of Seville*, *La Cenerentola* and a handful of overtures. Late 20th-century revivals and recordings have since enabled us to reappraise this great Italian master, admired by composers as varied as Beethoven, Schubert and Wagner, and Rossini *serio* is nowadays as highly appreciated as Rossini *buffo*.

after a further mutiny breaks out in **Turin**. His official heir is his brother Charles Felix, but instead he names a young relative, **Prince Charles Albert** of Savoy Carignan, as regent. Both the ex-king and the heir leave the country, and Charles Albert comes to terms with the rebels. With military assistance from Austria, **Charles Felix** returns to crush the revolt. Charles Albert goes into a brief 'proba-tionary' exile in Spain, where he regains Austria's favour by fighting against the liberal constitutionalist government.

> **“** We halted in Terracina; and there ... we were invited to take supper with a party of travellers newly arrived out of Naples ... My eyes lighted upon a fair-haired young man, of some five or six-and-twenty years of age, astonishingly handsome in spite of a slight touch of baldness. I pressed him for news of Naples, and in particular, of music in that city: he answered my curiosity with answers that were clear-cut, brilliant and humorous. I enquired of him whether, when I reached Naples, I might still hope to see Rossini's *Otello*. I pursued the topic, asserting that, in my opinion, Rossini ... was the only living composer who had true genius as his birthright. At this my man seemed faintly embarrassed, while his companions were grinning openly. In short, this *was* Rossini. **”**
>
> Stendhal, *Rome, Naples and Florence in 1817*,
> quoted in *A Book of Travellers' Tales*, Eric Newby

1822 Austria removes the **customs barriers** which divide **Lombardy** from **Venetia** and separate both provinces from the rest of the empire, so facilitating a free market within Habsburg domains. Barriers with neighbouring states and markets in Germany, France and Britain continue to stifle commercial enterprise, however, creating further grounds for resentment of the Austrian government in northern Italy.

Antonio Canova dies in Rome. As Europe's finest Neo-classical sculptor working in stone he has produced many memorable images, including a massive statue of **Napoléon** as a classical hero, a recumbent nude figure of the emperor's sister **Pauline Borghese**, and the famous *Three Graces* group. He has also played an important part in recovering works of art **looted** from Italy by the French in the years 1796–1814.

The revolutions of 1821

The numerous discontents that simmered beneath the surface of many areas of Italian society in the years after the fall of Napoléon came to a head in the revolutions of 1821. The terrible and widespread **food shortages** of 1816–17 had created continuing economic hardship which governments had failed to tackle efficiently. The **Church** appeared to be exploiting the conservatism of the newly restored monarchies in order to claw back its lost **privileges**. The sovereigns themselves, meanwhile, found their armies were now under the command of a **disillusioned officer class**, all too easily inclined to remember the incentives to glory offered by their former master **Bonaparte**. **Secret societies** mushroomed in **Piedmont**, **Lombardy** and **Naples**, including most notably the **Carbonari** ('charcoal burners' or 'charcoal makers'). Led by army officers, it was these who spearheaded **revolutions** in both Piedmont and the Two Sicilies.

The uprising in the **Two Sicilies**, which began at **Nola** on 1 July, succeeded in forcing King Ferdinand to accept a **constitution**, but was ultimately brought down by a lack of unity between its various elements (military, bourgeoisie and peasantry), coupled with a mutual **distrust** between Sicilians and mainlanders. The revolutionaries in **Piedmont** – mostly **aristocrats** and professional **soldiers** – counted too heavily on the support of **Charles Albert**, the youthful heir to the Sardinian throne. But after a brief reign following the abdication of King Victor Emmanuel I, Charles Albert was forced to hand over power to his uncle **Charles Felix**, who was wholly unsympathetic to the rebel demands and backed by an Austrian army. The revolutionaries were seized, tried and condemned, as the Austrian government in Milan displayed a remorseless efficiency and ruthlessness in trawling in political suspects. In Naples, thirty of the condemned were executed; Austria and Piedmont, meanwhile, were content to award harsh prison sentences or terms of banishment. These political **exiles** carried their **Risorgimento** ideals abroad with them, and became influential throughout Europe in promoting the image of Italy as a country ground down by **alien oppressors**.

Charles Albert abdicates, following the Battle of Novara

1824 **Ferdinand III of Tuscany** dies and is succeeded as Grand Duke by his son **Leopold II**, who continues his father's policy of prudent and **mild government**, combined with **agricultural reforms** and the promotion of **industrial initiatives**.

1827 **Alessandro Manzoni** publishes the first version of his novel *I promessi sposi* (*The Betrothed*).

1830 **Ciro Menotti**, a Neapolitan businessman based in **Modena**, plans a **nationalist uprising** with the ultimate aim of creating a unified **Italian state**. Other revolutions are planned in **Bologna** and **Romagna**. Modena's **Duke Francesco IV**, who has pretended to encourage the conspirators, retreats temporarily to the safety of the Austrian fortress at **Mantua**, though not before arresting Menotti, whom he takes with him. A **provisional government** assumes power in Modena. In **Parma**, rioting crowds force

Alessandro Manzoni

Although it was not the first Italian novel, *I promessi sposi* is significant as the earliest attempt to raise the **novel form** in Italian to the levels of seriousness and substance that characterized the best fiction published in **Britain** and **France** at this period. Alessandro Manzoni (1785–1873) was already well known as a **poet** and **dramatist**, and had gained a reputation in his native **Milan** as a writer on important questions such as the links between literature and history, and the role of Christian teaching in secular life.

A love story set in 17th-century Lombardy, *I promessi sposi* lays great emphasis on the importance of **faith** and the sage acceptance of **reality**, as well as on the individual's power of **moral choice**. Also significant is the book's **political subtext**. Although Manzoni was himself a conservative Catholic aristocrat, much of his earlier writing had reflected **anti-Austrian** views but also a sense of **resignation** with regard to the political destiny of Italy. In his portrayal of Milan's Spanish rulers during the 1630s, many readers therefore detected a correspondence to their 19th-century counterparts, as embodied in the **Habsburg** administration. After a pivotal visit to Florence, which he described as 'dipping my rags in the Arno', Manzoni revised *I promessi sposi*, using the **Tuscan** dialect rather than his native Milanese as his literary idiom. This change was to have lasting consequences for the standardization of language in Italian literature.

The novel became a national classic, representing both a belated coming-of-age of the novel form in Italian and more importantly a source of pride among Italians in the vitality of their native talent, at a time when many people in Europe viewed them as merely a **slave race** crushed under the heel of the Austrian empire.

the unpopular chief minister **Baron Werklein** to flee the duchy. **Duchess Marie Louise** retreats to **Piacenza**, protected by its Austrian garrison, before returning to Parma with a firm pledge never to reinstate Werklein.

On 9 March, **Francesco IV** returns to **Modena** with Austrian military backing. **Ciro Menotti**, who has escaped the duke's clutches, is rounded up during a dramatic street battle, tried and executed. He becomes a **Risorgimento martyr**, after whom **Giuseppe Garibaldi** will name one of his sons.

Sporadic uprisings break out in the cities of the **Papal States**. **Bologna** establishes a provisional government and **Ancona** is seized by a revolutionary force under **Giuseppe Sercognani**. An Austrian force now enters papal territory, ocupying **Ferrara** and driving the rebels from Bologna.

Giuseppe Mazzini, a member of the **Carbonari**, is arrested in his native city of **Genoa**. While in prison at **Savona** awaiting trial for involvement in the activities of a secret society, he evolves his vision of Italy as a republic born from a **democratic nationalist revolution**.

Gaetano Donizetti's *Anna Bolena* is produced at Milan's **Teatro Carcano**. Starring the legendary prima donna **Giuditta Pasta**, the opera is an instant success and marks the emergence of this highly influential composer's mature style.

1831 Charles Albert becomes **king of Piedmont**. Noted for his piety, he has pledged to the Austrians that he will

> **❝** The people must be the basis of nationality; its logically derived and vigorously applied principles its means; the strength of all its strength; the improvement of the life of all and the happiness of the greatest possible number its results; and the accomplishment of the task assigned to it by God its goal. This is what we mean by nationality. **❞**
>
> Giuseppe Mazzini, *Nationalité. Quelques Idées sur une Constitution Nationale*, trans. Donald Weinstein and Herbert H. Rowen

maintain the conservative stance of his predecessors. His attitude to Italian affairs will undergo a notable shift during the next decade. His unpredictability and his refusal to make up his mind earn him the nickname *il re tentenna* ('the wobbly king').

Acquitted for lack of evidence, **Mazzini** goes into exile in **France**, where he founds the revolutionary cell *La Giovine Italia* ('**Young Italy**').

Mauro Capellari, a Camaldolite monk, is elected pope as **Gregory XVI**. During his reign, government in the Papal States reaches a nadir of **oppression**.

At Milan's Teatro alla Scala **Vincenzo Bellini's** *Norma* is given its premiere. Built around the talents of prima donna **Giuditta Pasta**, the opera is a classic example of the bel canto style, in which a romantic plot is brought to life through virtuoso singing.

1832 **Ancona** is attacked and seized by a French expeditionary force despatched by **King Louis Philippe**, with the aim of preventing Austria from becoming a dominant military presence in the **Papal States**.

1833 *Giovine Italia* members, encouraged by **Mazzini**, plan an insurrection in **Piedmont**. This is brutally repressed and its leader, **Jacopo Ruffini**, commits suicide. Dissidents throughout Italy are subject to mass arrests and imprisonment over the next two years.

1834 After taking part in the failed Mazzinian uprising, the sailor **Giuseppe Garibaldi** of Nice (then part of **Piedmont**) escapes to South America, where he becomes a successful general in campaigns in **Argentina** and **Uruguay**.

1835 Donizetti's *Lucia di Lammermoor* receives its première at the Teatro San Carlo, **Naples**. The archetypal romantic bel canto opera, based on a novel by Sir Walter Scott, this will be the only one of the composer's serious stage works to survive the decline of his reputation during the second half of the 19th century.

1837 After spending three years in Switzerland, **Mazzini** seeks refuge in **London**, which will become his permanent base for the next ten years. Admired by the British intelligentsia, including **Charles Dickens**, **Robert Browning** and **Thomas Carlyle**, he continues to plan revolutions and maintain contacts with Italian dissidents.

The poet **Giacomo Leopardi** dies in **Naples**, aged 39. Born to a noble family in the **Marche**, he has led a wandering life among various Italian cities, writing a series of lyric poems combining a deep Romantic gloom with a love of nature and a sense of the vastness of the universe. His work – like Manzoni's – will contribute to the growing sense of unity among the Italian people.

1838 An Austrian **amnesty** in **Lombardy** and **Venetia** allows political exiles to return to both provinces.

1839 The Milanese teacher and intellectual **Carlo Cattaneo** founds *Il Politecnico*, a journal of contemporary ideas on socio-economic subjects. Though it carefully avoids political topics, during its five years of publication *Il Politecnico* becomes required reading for Italian liberals.

1842 **Giuseppe Verdi's** *Nabucco* is produced at Teatro alla Scala, Milan. Written while the composer is in the depths of a depression following the deaths, within two years, of his wife and children, the work is a runaway success, bringing him important new commissions. Its chorus, *Va pensiero sulla ali dorat'* (***The Chorus of the Hebrew Slaves***) will become an unofficial national anthem of united Italy.

1843 **Vincenzo Gioberti,** an exiled Piedmontese priest, publishes *Del primato morale e civile degli italiani* (*The Moral and Civil Primacy of the Italians*) in Brussels. Proposing a federation of free Italian states under papal leadership, it has an overwhelming impact in Italy.

Giuseppe Verdi and the Risorgimento

During the Risorgimento, Italian **opera houses** became the unlikely venues for subversive expressions of **patriotic zeal**, with patriots showering the stage with bouquets in the colours of the Italian flag. The enthusiastic cries of '*Viva Verdi!*' that punctuated performances of Verdi's (1813–1901) operas, meanwhile, were testimony not only to the composer's popularity but also to the nationalistic fervour of the audience: 'Verdi' being an acronym for *Vittorio Emmanuele, Re D'Italia*.

In fact Verdi's music was linked with the Risorgimento cause well before Victor Emmanuel became king in 1849. Although his famous *Chorus of the Hebrew Slaves* did not gain its anthemic status until long after unification, the opera's story of a people held in brutal captivity was clearly resonant with parallels to life in **Austrian-occupied Italy**. *Attila*, another early work full of patriotic references to **Italian independence**, was premiered in Venice in 1846 and thereafter frequently revived there. Choruses in both *I Lombardi* and *Ernani* both roused **patriotic passions**, fomenting unrest that the authorities put down with a heavy hand.

While all Italian theatres remained closed in the aftermath of the **risings of 1848**, Verdi composed *La battaglia di Legnano* expressly for performance in Rome under **Mazzini's triumvirate republic**. After 1849, the restored regimes continued to favour Verdi's music, and his name was not on any list of political dissidents. Nevertheless, the composer persisted in sporting a Mazzini-style beard and associating freely with Milanese patriots such as **Giovanni Visconti Venosta** and the critic **Carlo Tenca**, both of whom had taken part in the *Cinque Giornate*, Milan's revolutionary uprising of 1848. In 1861, following **unification**, Verdi was briefly elected a member of the **Italian parliament** in Turin.

1844 The **Bandiera brothers**, Attilio and Emilio, both former officers in the Austrian navy, lead an abortive **revolutionary expedition** to **Calabria**, which ends in their execution by a Bourbon firing squad.

In *Delle speranze degli italiani* (*The Hopes of the Italians*) **Cesare Balbo** proposes an international diplomatic solution to the Italian question, with Austria being offered part of the **Balkans** in compensation for losing **Lombardy** and **Venetia**.

1845 Massimo d'Azeglio, a Piedmontese artist and writer from an aristocratic military family, makes contact with revolutionaries in **Romagna**. Their attempt to stage an **uprising** in **Rimini** (in which d'Azeglio plays no direct part) is savagely suppressed by papal forces of law and order, including the thuggish gangs known as *centurioni*.

1846 D'Azeglio publishes a study of the Romagna revolt, entitled *Degli ultimi casi di Romagna* (*On the recent events in Romagna*). Though espousing moderate nationalism rather than violent revolution, he nevertheless condemns the papal government and urges **major reforms**.

Pope Gregory XVI dies and is succeeded by Giovanni Maria Mastai Ferretti, bishop of Imola, who takes the name **Pius IX**. Greeted with excitement by Italian liberals, the election is initially welcomed by Austria, which had begun to be concerned about the long-term effects of Gregory's conservative regime. The new pope grants an **amnesty** to all political exiles and prisoners.

> **❝** We were prepared for everything, except a liberal pope. Now we have got one, there is no accounting for anything. **❞**
>
> Clemens von Metternich

1847 Pius IX permits relaxation of the laws on **press censorship** in the Papal States.

Austrian troops, garrisoned in the fortress of **Ferrara**, violate an earlier treaty with the papacy by occupying the entire city. The pope issues a formal protest to the imperial chancellor, **Prince Metternich**, becoming a hero of Italian liberals.

The Bandiera brothers, patriot martyrs

The fatal expedition of Attilio and Emilio Bandiera to **Calabria** in the summer of 1844 was to become one of the most celebrated and inspirational episodes in the martyrology of the Risorgimento. Like their friend **Domenico Moro**, who died beside them, these young Venetians had been officers in the **Austrian fleet** (their father, Baron Bandiera, was a rear-admiral). Fingered as members of a secret society named '*Esperia*', in contact with the exiled **Mazzini**, they fled to **Corfu** (then a British colony). There they gathered together twenty other patriots with the aim of mounting a raid on Calabria in the kingdom of Naples, the scene of recent political unrest.

Landing near the town of **Cotrone**, they marched through the local villages in a fruitless attempt to muster support among the local peasants. Members of a government militia eventually surprised the rebel band as they rested wearily by the roadside, killing several of them in a desperate fight before taking the remainder to **Cosenza**, where they were put on trial. There the townsfolk proved so sympathetic towards the rebels that the court commuted many of the death sentences originally handed out. The ten who were finally condemned, including the two Bandieras and Domenico Moro, went gallantly to their deaths before a **firing squad**, singing an operatic chorus and crying '*Viva l'Italia!*' as the soldiers took aim.

Though ostensibly a spectacular failure, the whole episode handed the Italian cause a huge **propaganda victory**, as news of the rebels' heroic end spread throughout Europe. Over the next few years their example was to spur countless young men to join the revolutionary movement, and to prompt Massimo D'Azeglio's shrewd reflection: 'To an unjust government a martyr does greater harm than a rebel.' After Italy's unification, the bodies of the Bandieras and Moro were given **state funerals** in Venice, and streets and squares throughout Italy were named after them.

Richard Cobden, radical British member of parliament and apostle of free trade, visits Italy and is welcomed by liberals in various cities. The political character of the banquets given in his honour is noted by the police, wary of the opportunities they create for voicing dissident opinions. The British diplomat **Lord Minto** also arrives, on a **fact-finding mission** for the British government. Following meetings with Italian heads of state, he spends nearly a year in Italy, witnessing the outbreak of **revolution** and acting as intermediary in the affairs of the **Two Sicilies**.

Following King Charles Albert's concession of **press freedom** in **Piedmont**, the politician **Camillo Cavour**, in collaboration with **Cesare Balbo**, founds the progressive journal *Il Risorgimento*.

> " The term 'Italy' is a geographical expression, a linguistic qualification, without any of the value set upon it by the efforts of revolutionary ideologues. "
>
> Clemens von Metternich

1848 In January, a revolt against the Bourbon government of King Ferdinand II in the Sicilian capital **Palermo** marks the beginning of Europe's momentous '**Year of Revolutions**'. Sicily breaks away from the mainland kingdom, but its new administration becomes locked in fruitless negotiations with Naples, using **Lord Minto** as a mediator. Demonstrations in the streets of **Naples** force King Ferdinand to proclaim a **constitution**, a **free press** and a **civil guard**. The conservative nature of the constitution will prove a useful tool for Ferdinand as he gradually claws back his authority during the coming months. A public campaign to boycott smoking, designed to cripple the Austrian state monopoly on **tobacco**, begins in **Milan**. Noisy protests at army officers smoking in the streets erupt into

rioting, with a number of civilian casualties. In **Venice**, a tribunal considers the case of **Daniele Manin** and **Niccolò Tommaseo**, imprisoned for having submitted a petition to the Austrian government demanding changes in the administrative process.

In March five days of rioting in **Milan** – the famous '*Cinque Giornate*' – force **Marshal Radetzky**, commander of Austria's army, to withdraw his Austrian garrison. He retreats with his troops to the safety of **Verona**. In **Venice**, **Daniele Manin** and **Niccolò Tommaseo** are released from prison. Following a confrontation between Austrian soldiers and angry citizens in Piazza San Marco, Manin successfully forces the Austrians to withdraw from the city altogether, and becomes leader of a **provisional government**. Apart from a brief interval in July, when it becomes part of the kingdom of Piedmont, Venice will remain independent for the next eighteen months.

Charles Albert of Piedmont declares war on **Austria**, rejecting proffered diplomatic assistance from **Britain** and military help from republican **France** with the words, '*L'Italia fara da se*' ('Italy will go it alone'). Many suspect his real motives are territorial expansion and a desire to crush republicanism in the newly liberated Austrian provinces.

In April **Pope Pius IX** reluctantly allows an army of combined professional and volunteer brigades, under **General Giovanni Durando**, to march north in order to join the war against Austria. The **Piedmontese** win battles at **Goito** and **Pastrengo**. Charles Albert now concentrates his army's efforts on besieging the key fortress of **Peschiera**.

Nervous of losing support among **German Catholics** critical of his apparently anti-Austrian stance, Pope Pius IX issues a document known as the **Allocution**, condemning the current war and effectively forbidding his soldiers to fight. Papal troops in the **Veneto**, however, continue to oppose Austria's southward advance.

In May **Neapolitan troops** under General Pepe enter the **Veneto** to aid the Italian war effort. The **Lombard** provisional government in **Milan**, controlled by anti-republican nobles, votes for fusion with **Piedmont**. An Austrian force defeats Papal troops under General Ferrari at Cornuda, near **Treviso**. Having routed the Austrians at Goito for the second time, Charles Albert captures **Peschiera**, but fails to follow up either success with further attacks on the main body of Radetzky's army.

In **Naples**, King Ferdinand and his conservative supporters exploit the muddle and failures of the new constitutional government, provoking fear among the bourgeoisie of **working-class unrest**. A royalist **coup d'état** on 15 May effectively ends revolution in the mainland kingdom, though **Sicily** is still ruled by its provisional government. **Parma** and **Modena** vote to become part of an expanded kingdom of **Piedmont**.

The towns of the **Veneto**, including **Treviso** and **Padua**, fall to Austrian forces in June. Only **Venice** and the Friulan fortress of **Osoppo** remain to challenge Austria's push to recover the entire province for the empire. **Venice** votes for integration with **Piedmont** in July. **Daniele Manin** stands down as president, a new provisional government is formed, and Charles Albert's royal commissioners arrive to superintend the transfer of power.

Radetzky and **Prince Felix Schwarzenberg** persuade the Austrian government to reject a planned armistice with **Piedmont**. Continuing the war, Radetzky inflicts a crushing defeat on Charles Albert at **Custoza**. A treaty restores **Lombardy** to the Austrians and Charles Albert withdraws his army. Following the Piedmontese defeat, the royal government in **Venice** is overturned and **Daniele Manin** returns, to popular acclaim, to head a new administration.

Pius IX appoints **Count Pellegrino Rossi** as his chief minister. Unpopular for his known opposition to **Mazzini** and his ideas, Rossi becomes a target for conspirators, and on 15 November he is murdered. Following **anti-papal demonstrations** in Rome, Pius flees the city to seek refuge in the Neapolitan fortress of **Gaeta**, where he remains for the next six months.

The triumph of Mazzini

The Victorian sage **Thomas Carlyle**, sceptical and conservative as he was, observed of Giuseppe Mazzini, 'He, if ever I have seen one such, is a man of genius and virtue, a man of sterling veracity, humanity and nobleness of mind, one of those rare men who are worthy to be called martyr souls.' It was this supreme **integrity** which led many Italians to admire Mazzini even if they questioned his political ideas, or indeed his practical grasp of what was required to make a revolution work.

Carlyle's judgement was triumphantly vindicated by the **Roman Republic** established by Mazzini in 1849, when he ruled as a member of the **triumvirate**, with a programme proclaiming: 'No class war, no hostility to existing wealth, no violation of property rights, but a constant readiness to improve the condition of those least favoured by fortune.' Combining tolerance with efficiency, Mazzini demonstrated how enlightened government could work for the good of all sectors of society. The **death penalty** was repealed, **banditry** and **terrorism** were sternly dealt with, the **Church** was protected and the **spiritual authority** of the fugitive Pope Pius IX guaranteed. Some attempt was even made at overhauling the **economy**, a noble but hopeless endeavour in a city that was perpetually under siege from French and Neapolitan armies.

Short-lived though the Roman Republic proved to be, Mazzini's principles of **humanity** and social inclusiveness won him lasting and widespread admiration, while at the same time making France's treacherous intervention in the name of conservative Catholicism appear all the more sordid and ignoble.

1849 **Emperor Ferdinand of Austria** abdicates. He is succeeded by his young cousin **Franz Josef**, who will reign over the Habsburg empire for 67 years, until his death during the Great War. On 15 February the **Costituente**, an assembly including representatives of governments from all over Italy, holds its first meeting, organized by republicans in Rome. **Giuseppe Mazzini** arrives in Rome and

Portrait of Mazzini by an anonymous painter, Museo del Risorgimento, Milan

© SCALA

assumes leadership of the **Roman Republic**, assisted by Carlo Armellini and Aurelio Saffi. His rule is admired for its combination of enlightened tolerance and prudent efficiency.

In exile at Gaeta, **Pius IX** calls for assistance from other European powers against 'the enemies of religion and society'. **France** despatches an **expeditionary force** under General Oudinot to destroy the Roman Republic.

Charles Albert resumes Piedmont's war against **Austria**, having failed to achieve a satisfactory negotiated peace. Defeated once again by Radetzky at **Novara**, he abdicates and leaves Italy for the Portuguese city of **Oporto**, where he dies later in the year. An **anti-Austrian uprising** at **Brescia** is suppressed with appalling savagery. **General Haynau**, the garrison commander responsible, achieves international notoriety, proving himself, in the words of a contemporary, to be 'an atrocious tyrant to his prostrate foe'. On a visit to London later that year he is attacked, while inspecting a Southwark brewery, by a mob of workmen chanting 'General Hyena!'

King Ferdinand of Naples bombards the **Sicilian revolutionaries** into submission, and the island is re-incorporated into the kingdom of the **Two Sicilies**. Ferdinand becomes known to Italian liberals as '**King Bomba**'. **Grand Duke Leopold** flees **Florence** to seek refuge at **Gaeta**. Tuscany is now controlled by **radical democrats**, but loyalist revolts among the peasantry encourage moderates to challenge the authority of the new republican government. **Domenico Guerrazzi**, popular champion of liberty, is made dictator, but antagonizes radicals and moderates alike. The latter form a new **provisional government** and recall the Grand Duke.

Rome is threatened by a large **Neapolitan** army marching in support of Oudinot's **French** force. **Giuseppe**

Garibaldi, summoned to Rome, defeats the Neapolitans at **Velletri**. **Ancona** falls to the **Austrians** after a month-long siege.

On 3 July, **Rome** falls to the French, following a heroic defence of the city by **Mazzini** and **Garibaldi**. Mazzini goes into exile in **London**, while Garibaldi, accompanied by his followers, makes a dramatic escape through the **Apennines** to the mouth of the River Po. His wife and inseparable companion Anita dies on the journey, and he himself narrowly escapes capture.

Following a heroic defence of **Venice** against prolonged Austrian bombardment, **Daniele Manin** and his government finally surrender on 24 August. Though their city is devastated by **famine** and **cholera**, the Venetians have gallantly and steadfastly supported Manin in his avowed determination to resist at all costs.

1850 **Pope Pius IX** returns to **Rome** amid cheering crowds. Having formerly governed from the Quirinal Palace, he now removes his official residence to the **Vatican**. Henceforth his chief minister is the corrupt and ultra-conservative **Cardinal Giacomo Antonelli**.

1852 **Camillo Cavour** becomes prime minister of **Piedmont**.

Following the death of his chief minister Felix Schwarzenberg, **Franz Josef** assumes autocratic control of the Austrian empire, putting the final touches to a restoration of the pre-1848 **police state** in the two Italian provinces, **Lombardy** and **Venetia**.

1853 Moving to Switzerland, **Mazzini** tries to organize an uprising in **Lombardy**. Many of those involved are arrested and executed by the Austrians. An imperial decree announces the **sequestration** of all property belonging to **political exiles** and fugitives.

Camillo Cavour

Born into Piedmont's military aristocracy, Count Camillo Benso di Cavour (1811–61) studied at the **Royal Military Academy**, but soon found himself at odds with his commanding officers for asking too many questions. Sent to cool his heels at a frontier fortress, he began a course of serious reading, mainly in **politics** and **economics**, which encouraged him to leave the army and go on a fact-finding tour of **France** and **Britain**. In London and Manchester he met leading industrialists and economic theorists and studied banking and new methods of agriculture, as well as developing a lifelong enthusiasm for railways. Returning to Piedmont in 1835, he settled down to manage his family's estates, while beginning a part-time career as a journalist. In 1848 he won a seat in the recently opened **Piedmontese parliament**, and two years later he became minister of agriculture.

When the government fell in 1852, **King Victor Emmanuel** asked Cavour to lead a **new administration**, and he remained in office until his death nine years later. His gifts as an **orator** were complemented by his self-confidence, iron determination and subtle talent for the kind of **compromise** which concealed ruthless manipulation in order to achieve results. **Unscrupulous** in rigging elections, bribing journalists and muzzling extremist elements, he was no more in tune than Victor Emmanuel with the loftier ideals of Risorgimento visionaries, yet he remained devoted to freeing Italy from Austrian domination and expanding the Piedmontese realm.

Traditionally Cavour has been seen as the architect of the new kingdom emerging from the war of 1859, but this earliest form of a joined-up Italian state was based on his ambitions for **Piedmont** rather than a belief in an Italy unified from north to south. After his death (probably from malaria) in 1861, streets and squares were nevertheless named after him as one of the nation's founding fathers, and his papers were carefully edited in order to present him in the guise of a true Italian patriot. Viewed from a dispassionate modern historical perspective, however, a less

idealized figure emerges, whose skilful parliamentary and
diplomatic manoeuvres for the sake of achieving realistic goals
anticipate in striking fashion those of Italian politicians of our own
day.

Portrait of Cavour by Francesco Hayez, Pinacoteca di Brera, Milan

1854 At the outbreak of the **Crimean War**, **Cavour** commits **Piedmont** to fighting alongside Britain and France against Russia.

1855 Fighting the Russians in the Crimea, the 15,000-strong Piedmontese army, under the command of **General Alfonso Lamarmora**, wins the battle of **Chernaya**.

1856 **Cavour** attends the **Paris peace conference** concluding the Crimean War; here he is able to canvass British and French opinion as to the likelihood of establishing a **united Italy**.

1857 The Neapolitan socialist and political commentator **Carlo Pisacane** plots a Mazzinian uprising in **Calabria**. Landing at Sapri, the rebels are attacked and overcome by local peasants and gendarmes. In the débâcle, Pisacane commits suicide. Thanks in part to a much-admired poem written soon afterwards by **Luigi Mercantini**, *La Spigolatrice di Sapri* ('The Gleaner of Sapri'), this ill-fated venture, with its curious echoes of the **Bandiera** expedition of 1844, becomes part of Risorgimento martyrology.

1858 **Luigi Orsini**, an Italian exile living in England, crosses to Paris, where he attempts to assassinate **Emperor Napoléon III** and **Empress Eugénie** by throwing bombs into their carriage. Orsini believes that if the emperor is killed France will become a republic, which will then offer armed support to Italian revolutions. He is executed, but not before urging Napoléon to go to Italy's aid. At the French spa town of **Plombières**, a crucial meeting takes place between **Napoléon III** and **Cavour**. Cavour proposes that, in return for being allowed to annex **Savoy** and the town of **Nice,** France should drive the Austrians out of Italy. The compact is sealed by the betrothal of the emperor's nephew **Jerome Bonaparte** and **Princess Clothilde**, daughter of **King Victor Emmanuel**.

1859 Leaked news of the Plombières agreement prompts **Austria** to **mobilize** its troops. **Piedmont** follows suit, and on 19 April Austria delivers an **ultimatum** to Cavour, demanding immediate demobilization. Cavour rejects the ultimatum, and Napoléon III declares war. At the inconclusive battle of **Magenta**, the Austrians are forced to retire in disarray. Fierce fighting at **Solferino** forces the Austrians to retreat from Lombardy into the Quadrilateral. The horrifying carnage at this battle inspires the Swiss businessman **Henri Dunant** to found the international **Red Cross** organization for the relief of suffering in wartime.

Revolts break out in the duchies of **Tuscany**, **Parma** and **Modena**, partly inspired by the success of the Franco-Piedmontese army, and partly orchestrated by Piedmontese agents. The dukes flee, abandoning their states to provisional governments overseen by **Piedmontese commissioners**. A further revolt takes place in **Romagna**, the northeastern territory of the Papal States. In July **Napoléon III**, fearing that **Prussia** will come to Austria's aid and alarmed by the speed of unification, makes peace with **Emperor Franz Josef** at **Villafranca**. Austria cedes **Lombardy** to France, which then confers it on **Piedmont**. **Venetia** remains part of the Austrian empire. The uneasy peace that follows depends on Napoléon's willingness to allow Piedmont to annex the duchies, Romagna and the Legations (**Bologna** and **Ferrara**). **British** diplomatic pressure encourages him to accept the creation of an **Italian kingdom**.

> ❝ You shall pay me the cost of the war, and we will talk no more of Nice and Savoy. ❞
>
> Napoléon III to Victor Emmanuel, 1859

1860 **Plebiscites** held in the **duchies** and the disputed areas of the **Papal States** are all favourable to annexation. **Nice** and **Savoy** are ceded to France. **Garibaldi**, furious at the annexation of Nice (his home town), organizes an expedition to prevent it.

Revolts against the Bourbon government break out in various parts of **Sicily**. Garibaldi hastily abandons his unrealistic scheme for defending Nice against the French and reroutes his '**Thousand**' to Sicily. Most of this company of '**Redshirts**' are from Lombard cities, but the expedition also includes foreign volunteers, one woman and an 11-year-old boy. On 11 May, Garibaldi and the Thousand land at **Marsala**. Five days later, they defeat the Bourbon army at **Calatafimi** and advance to **Palermo**, where they establish a provisional government. A second battle at **Milazzo** proves a tougher struggle, but enables Garibaldi to capture **Messina**. Crossing the straits, the augmented liberation force sweeps through the mainland kingdom. On 7 September, Garibaldi enters **Naples** in triumph, while King **Francis II** and his queen retreat to the fortress of **Gaeta**.

A **Piedmontese** army invades the **Papal States**. The pope's army is defeated at **Castelfidardo**, and the Piedmontese advance into the former kingdom of **Naples**. At the head of a large army, **Francis II** moves to recapture Naples. **Garibaldi** halts his advance at the **River Volturno**. Francis retreats to Gaeta, where he and the queen will earn praise for their heroism in sustaining a four-month siege.

Plebiscites in **Naples** and **Sicily**, heavily influenced by the local **Camorra** and **Mafia** organizations, favour **annexation** to the new Italian kingdom.

Victor Emmanuel meets **Garibaldi** at **Teano**. Immortalized in numerous paintings and engravings, the encounter is not only symbolic but also friendly. The king refuses to allow Garibaldi to act as temporary dictator in the newly acquired southern realms, however. After driving in triumph into **Naples** at the king's side, the hero retires to farm on the little island of **Caprera**.

> " Garibaldi is one of the few whom Nature created to have great influence over the masses ... His thorough self-devotion to the noblest interests of mankind, his lion-like power in battle, and his almost feminine gentleness in private life, his single-mindedness, and his thoroughly democratic habits, the very weaknesses of his impressionable nature, make him the thorough man of the people, the poetic hero of a nation. "
>
> Anonymous British tribute, written during Garibaldi's lifetime

1861 On 13 February the siege of **Gaeta** is brought to an end as the Bourbon defenders run out of food and ammunition, and **King Francis of Naples** and his wife go into exile in **Rome**. On 17 March the **kingdom of Italy** is proclaimed. **Rome** is still in the hands of the **pope**, backed by troops provided by **Napoléon III**, who is anxious to appease French Catholic opinion. **Venetia** remains part of the **Austrian empire**. The first **Italian parliament**, meeting in **Turin**, confirms Victor Emmanuel as king. He styles himself **Victor Emmanuel II**, implying that the realm has always been the fiefdom of the House of Savoy. The choice provokes disapproval and suspicion among various patriotic factions.

Camillo Cavour dies at the early age of 51, probably of malaria. With **Garibaldi** and **Mazzini**, he will be regarded as one of the three main architects of unified Italy, and streets and squares in towns all over Italy will bear his name.

1862 **Garibaldi** raises a volunteer army in **Sicily** for the attempted capture of **Rome**. When the army reaches the mainland the **Italian government** intervenes and, during

Giuseppe Garibaldi

Most of Garibaldi's life (1807–82) was spent as a subversive figure, admired by those with ideals and imagination, mistrusted by kings, ministers and bureaucrats who feared the power of his appeal to ordinary people, including thousands all over the world who never met or even saw him but were fascinated by his image and achievements. Born in Nice (then a Piedmontese port) in 1807, he was a sailor until 1834, when his involvement in a naval mutiny drove him into exile in South America. There he met Anita Ribeiro da Silva, who became the mother of his three children and, in 1842, his wife. In Uruguay he gained international fame as a leader of revolutionary armies, commanding a legion of fellow Italian exiles, all wearing the red shirts that were to become the 'garibaldino' uniform.

Returning to Italy in 1848, Garibaldi initially offered his services to King Charles Albert of Piedmont, who rejected him as a potential troublemaker. In 1849, he joined Giuseppe Mazzini in the heroic defence of Rome against the French. When the city fell, he made a daring escape with his followers to the Adriatic coast, where Anita died in his arms as Austrian troops scoured the area in search of him. Managing to flee westwards, he spent some further years in exile before settling as a farmer on a small property on the Sardinian island of Caprera.

In 1858, Camillo Cavour, who appreciated his effectiveness as a guerrilla leader, asked for his help in the war against Austria. Two years later and without Cavour's blessing, Garibaldi masterminded a dramatic expedition to Sicily, to capture the island from the Bourbon monarchy. After a victorious campaign on the island, Garibaldi pushed on to Naples, finally defeating King Francis II's army on the River Volturno and organizing the plebiscites which presented the whole of southern Italy to King Victor Emmanuel II. The latter nevertheless deeply mistrusted

a brief skirmish on the slopes of Aspromonte in Calabria, Garibaldi is wounded in the leg. Kept prisoner for five weeks, he becomes the focus of sympathetic international

the hero's power and charisma, and the new Italian kingdom's political and military establishment found his presence a continuing embarrassment.

When Garibaldi tried to invade the **Papal States** in 1862 and 1867 he was arrested, but eventually allowed to retire to Caprera, where he spent his last years. His brilliance as a **military commander** and his **personal integrity** and **idealism** made him one of the most widely revered revolutionary figures of 19th-century Europe.

Garibaldi's armies at the battle of Volturno

> **❝** The Risorgimento was the spirit of sacrifice, it was suffering through exile or imprisonment, it was the blood of Italian youth spilt on the battlefields, it was the passion of a people for its Italian identity. **❞**
>
> Niccolò Rodolico, historian, 1960

attention. The continuing hero-worship is a serious embarrassment to **King Victor Emmanuel** and his ministers: Garibaldi is released and **prime minister Ratazzi** resigns.

1864 Under an agreement known as the **September Convention**, **Napoléon III** agrees to evacuate French troops from **Rome** within two years. The **Italian capital** is removed from Turin to **Florence**.

Pope Pius IX issues the *Syllabus Errorum*, in which most of the ideas of the Enlightenment and recent scientific theory are condemned as **heretical**. This is a cause of deep distress to liberal Catholics.

1866 The Italian prime minister **Alfonso Lamarmora** signs a treaty with the Prussian chancellor **Otto von Bismarck**, preparing for war with **Austria**. In return for opening a second front, Italy is promised possession of **Venetia**. **Napoléon III** signs a secret treaty with Prussia, pledging neutrality in return for the cession of Venice to France, which will then give it to Italy.

War with Austria begins on 14 June. The Italians are defeated (for the second time within 25 years) at **Custoza** and at the naval battle of **Lissa**, off the Dalmatian coast. A Prussian victory over the Austrians at **Sadowa** secures peace. The war has lasted just six weeks. **Venice** at last joins a **united Italy**.

1867 After **French troops** leave **Rome** according to the September Convention, **Garibaldi** seizes his chance to

Florence, capital of Italy

No Italian city reflects the impact of **unification** on its appearance and layout more clearly than Florence. Chosen in 1864 as capital of the new kingdom (in place of **Rome**, still occupied by the pope as an independent sovereign), the former seat of the **Medici** and **Habsburg-Lorraine** Grand Dukes was given a drastic makeover. Its walls were replaced by **tree-shaded boulevards** and part of its historic centre, the **Mercato Vecchio**, was ripped out, to be replaced by a piazza (the fittingly titled **Piazza della Republica**) dominated by a **triumphal arch** in honour of King Victor Emmanuel II, topped by group of sculptures entitled '*Italy Enthroned*'. The unfinished façades of both the **Duomo** and the church of **Santa Croce** were completed with the advice of expert art historians, the stately **riverside frontages** on either bank of the Arno were further embellished and extended, and the area of the city on the south side of the river was radically altered by the architect **Giuseppe Poggi**, who laid out **Piazzale Michelangelo** and the winding road leading up to it.

Poggi's Florentine master plan was thwarted by the removal of the capital to Rome in 1870, but he made his mark elsewhere in the townscape with his imposing oval **Piazza Beccaria,** and by isolating the monumental **Protestant cemetery** from its surrounding thoroughfares so as to make it a dignified and intriguing feature of the city's rich architectural ensemble.

Florence had of course been a metropolis since the Middle Ages, first as an independent state and then as a Medici city. It was Poggi's inspiration, however, in the form of grand buildings and harmonious vistas which, after the city had lost its role as capital, renewed and enhanced its enduring cultural stature, both within Italy and throughout the world.

enter the **Papal States** at the head of his volunteers. The French return and, with the aid of their new **breech-loading rifles**, defeat Garibaldi at **Mentana**. Garibaldi retires once more to **Caprera**, and the French resume their defensive role in Rome.

Pius IX and the doctrine of papal infallibility

Greeted with excitement by Italian liberals on his election in 1846, Pius IX sealed his popular reputation as a **political reformer** and potential deliverer of the nation by granting an amnesty to political prisoners and lifting press censorship. But within two years he had refused to join the war for independence, and when Mazzini's **Roman Republic** was declared in 1849 his response was **excommunication** of his subjects. Restored as **absolute ruler** by France and Austria, he resorted to increasingly autocratic methods of imposing his power, and after the creation of the **kingdom of Italy** in 1860 he became more rather than less determined to hang on to whatever authority he could. Rejecting proposals for the separation of ecclesiastical and secular powers, encapsulated in Cavour's famous phrase 'A free Church in a free state', he aligned himself firmly with the forces of **political reaction**, secure in the protection offered by the French troops stationed permanently in Rome by **Napoléon III**. His *Syllabus Errorum* of 1864 confirmed this **ultra-conservative** shift, offering a sweeping condemnation of contemporary ideas on progress, tolerance, pluralism and individual liberty.

The following year, after the model of the Council of Trent, Pius IX began preparations for a **Vatican Council**, to which he invited Greek Orthodox and Protestant bishops as well as Catholic prelates. But by the time the Council met in 1869, many

1869 At the Vatican Council convened by Pius IX, he secures confirmation of his absolute authority over the Catholic Church and proclaims the doctrine of **papal infallibility**.

1870 The **Franco-Prussian War** begins. French troops are withdrawn from **Rome**, and after a brief bombardment the Italians enter the city through a breach in the walls at **Porta Pia**. **Pius IX** confines himself within the **Vatican**, while **King Victor Emmanuel** takes up residence in the

suspected its true purpose was to shore up Pius's authority not only as leader of the Roman Catholic Church but also of other communions, and only Catholic clergy attended the sessions, which were held in St Peter's Basilica. What ultimately emerged was the dogma of **papal infallibility** as expressed in the document *Pastor aeternus*. Although there was significant opposition to this doctrine among those present (indeed an influential minority believed that the power of the papacy within the Church should be curbed rather than increased), since few dared to vote against the pope's express wishes it was approved by a vote of 451 to 88. As the British diplomat Odo Russell wryly observed, Pius had 'safely reckoned on the unabating ignorance and superstition of mankind'.

Ironically – in view of the fact that this bid for personal power was motivated by Pius's own vanity, stubbornness and fear of contradiction – some theologians defended this absolutist dogma, on the grounds that it offered a steady and dependable spiritual authority amid the intellectual ferment and rapidly changing morals of the mid-19th century. Most Catholic intellectuals remained unconvinced, however, viewing the dogma as a contravention of the spirit of the Church and, in the words of the Catholic historian Lord Acton, a 'conspiracy against divine truth and law'.

Quirinal Palace. Italy is now wholly united, and the **Risorgimento** is officially at an end.

9
The kingdom of Italy

1871–1921

The new kingdom of Italy faced its first decade in a mood of **optimism**, tempered by a sense, among many Italians, of its **social backwardness** and the lack of a centralized administrative infrastructure to underpin a spirit of **national unity**. The need to get an independent state up and running was paramount, in order to fulfil expectations generated by the events of 1859–60, and politicians felt compelled to make use of institutions and administrative models already in existence before unification. For example, the statute issued by Charles Albert for the governance of Piedmont in 1847 formed the basis of the new **constitutional monarchy**, while the **public education system** was broadly based on that introduced by the Austrians in their provinces of Lombardy-Venetia after 1815. Governments of the 1870s and 1880s, dominated by the powerful presences of **Agostino Depretis** (a highly pragmatic follower of Mazzini) and his rival, the former revolutionary **Francesco Crispi**, relied for their survival on the doctrine of *trasformismo*. Striking inter-party deals and compromises, this successfully cut across political affiliations and broke down party loyalties, so rallying politicians of all persuasions behind the power of central government and a broad parliamentary base. Shrewd conciliation of vested interests and determined resistance to opposition from influential sectors of Italian society, in both north and south, further strengthened the newly unified kingdom. Predictably enough, the immemorial **socio-economic inequalities** between north and south grew more emphatic as the 19th century reached its end, with the famine-stricken and impoverished south lagging far behind the levels of development and prosperity attained by northern regions such as **Lombardy** and **Piedmont**.

There was a price to be paid for this comparative wealth, however, as accelerating **industrial growth** gave rise to bitter **social divisions** and an atmosphere of smouldering unrest in the **northern cities**, which during the closing years of the old century and the first decade of the new often erupted into **strikes** and **riots**. With its protectionism, its exploitation of the work force through wretchedly low pay and long hours, and its oppressive response to any kind of protest, the industrial boom alienated influential sectors of the Italian **liberal bourgeoisie**. **Giovanni Giolitti**, the dominant politician of the years 1900–15, saw it as his task to reduce tensions through consensus politics based on social reforms, while appeasing right-wingers with **nationalistic gestures**. His controversial and disastrous invasion of **Libya** in 1911 proved a step too far, however.

The inadequacy of Italy's preparations for a prolonged military operation became even more starkly apparent with her entry into **World War I** in 1915. Although the Italian troops fought bravely (despite the stereotypical images of military cowardice propagated later in the 20th century), they were poorly led and, despite a frantic drive towards increasing industrial output, often inadequately equipped with munitions and supplies. By the end of the war, the country's growing sense of the fruitless expenditure of human life and endeavour only aggravated the already volatile political situation that hung over Italy. The role of **parliamentary democracy** had been weakened by the necessity for the state to assume **emergency powers** during this national crisis, and the apathy and alienation of many

Italian voters played into the hands of right-wing interests, determined to exploit fears of Russian-style Communism. The stage was set for opportunism and demagoguery in the shape of the ex-socialist **Benito Mussolini**. His **Fascist** movement quickly contrived to ingratiate itself with the **bourgeoisie** and **industrial barons**, while gaining the approval of the **army** and encouragement from the hands-off attitude of **senior politicians** from the prewar liberal state. The so-called **March on Rome** in 1922 (which Mussolini actually undertook in a railway sleeping car from Milan) marked the end of united Italy's first experiment with **constitutional democracy**.

1869 The Chamber of Deputies passes the **Law of Guarantees**, defining the secular state's relationship with the **papacy**. The pope is acknowledged as a sovereign within the **Vatican**, with appropriate honours, prerogatives and the right to receive independent diplomatic representatives, as well as an annual income from the Italian treasury. **Pius IX** rejects this settlement, becoming metaphorically 'the prisoner of the Vatican'. Another 58 years will pass before his successors accept a political settlement with the kingdom of Italy.

1876 **Agostino Depretis**, a former adherent of **Mazzini**, becomes prime minister, leading a left-wing government. Depretis is the first statesman in the newly unified Italy to make use of the deals, alliances and bribes which will become typical of the nation's political culture during its periods of constitutional democracy. Known as *trasformismo*, this strategy aims at breaking down party alignments and transforming opponents into supporters. During the following decade, Depretis becomes one of the hardiest survivors on the Italian political scene.

1877 **Matteo Imbriani** founds *L'Italia Irredenta* ('unredeemed Italy'), a society dedicated to the recovery of territories inhabited by Italians but currently ruled by other European powers, such as Austria and France. **Irredentism**, active principally in **Trieste**, the **Trentino** area, and cities along the **Dalmatian coast** such as Zara (Zadar) and Sebenico (Sibenik), will become an important political force in the years leading to the Great War.

A new act of parliament makes **primary education** compulsory throughout Italy, though only for two years of schooling. In rural areas, especially in the south, the act is largely ignored by parents and local authorities, while it meets opposition from local clergy who are suspicious of secular encroachments on their authority.

1878 **King Victor Emmanuel II** dies and is succeeded by his son **Umberto I**. A less able monarch than his father, he

Church and state in the new Italy

From the outset, relations between Church and state in the new kingdom of Italy were complicated by the refusal of **Pope Pius IX** to renounce his **territorial sovereignty**, and by his ruling that Catholics (representing the vast majority of the electorate) should not vote in **parliamentary elections**. Despite the significance accorded to papal authority, the ban was widely ignored by those eager to exercise their **constitutional right** as voters. It nevertheless served to prevent the formation of any political party officially representing Catholic interests. The Church, whose immense social influence had survived the dismantling of the pope's temporal authority, sought instead to mobilize the faithful as a kind of **unofficial opposition** to the liberal state. In many areas, **village clergy** fulfilled an undeniably important role as teachers and intermediaries between peasants, landlords and state officials and, as the liberal politician **Sidney Sonnino** pointed out, Christian religious ideals often provided the only palliative to the daily grind of a harsh rural existence.

In his 1891 encyclical *Rerum Novarum*, **Leo XIII** made a serious

fails to give Italy the secure constitutional government it badly needs.

Pope Pius IX dies after a reign lasting 32 years, one of the longest, most eventful (and ultimately, in view of its early promise, most disappointing) in the history of the papacy. He is succeeded by Gioacchino Pecci as **Leo XIII**. The new pope encourages Catholics to embrace **liberal-democratic** politics and allows them to support **republican regimes**.

1881 The qualifying age for the electoral **franchise** is lowered from 25 to 21, and the tax qualification is also reduced. This increases the electorate from 600,000 to two million.

Italy fails to gain control of **Tunisia**, despite the presence there of a large Italian community, and a period of tension

effort to focus Catholic action on the growing problems of an **industrialized society**. While discouraging strikes, the encyclical permitted the formation of **trade unions** and urged better relations between workers and employers, based on moral responsibility. The Catholic movement meanwhile helped to establish **rural banks**, through which peasants could secure easy credit terms, while local priests were able to offer bank managers practical advice on the likely financial risks among their parishioners. Measures such as these did little, however, to stem the rising tide of **anticlericalism**. This was especially true of northern Italy, where the Church was often identified with conservative interests in politics and social issues.

As part of a gradual **rapprochement** over the years 1900–14, Leo XIII's successor Pius X relaxed the ban on voting, and Catholics began to take a fuller part in the political life of the nation. Another two decades would elapse before full accord was reached between Church and state in the 1929 **Concordat**, the political settlement established by the Fascist government and Pope Pius XI.

between Italy and **France** ensues. Having encouraged border raids by Algerian tribes, France eventually attacks **Tunis**, whose ruler capitulates without serious resistance. The Treaty of Bardo guarantees a **French protectorate**.

1882 Italy, Austria and Germany conclude an alliance guaranteeing mutual assistance in time of war. Renewed every five years, the **Triple Alliance** will last until 1915.

Guglielmo Oberdank, an Italian–speaking student from Trieste, is hanged by the Austrians for plotting to assassinate **Emperor Franz Josef**. The **Irredentists** quickly adopt Oberdank as a martyr for their cause. Removing the final 'k' (to make it less German-sounding), his name is given to streets and squares in towns all over Italy.

1885 Looking further afield for an **African empire**, Italy occupies the Sudanese port of **Massowa** on the Red Sea.

1887 Agostino Depretis dies while still in office as prime minister and is succeeded by his interior minister **Francesco Crispi**. A former member of Garibaldi's Thousand, Crispi is noted for his **anticlericalism**, his strongly **anti-French** foreign policy and his support for the **Triple Alliance**. He will gradually abandon his liberal attitudes in favour of a more authoritarian approach, on a number of occasions even encouraging the king to bypass or override parliament.

Italian troops leave for **Ethiopia**, to aid attempts to extend the colonial powerbase inland from Massowa. War breaks out between Italy and **Emperor John** of Ethiopia. At the battle of **Dogali** an Italian army suffers a humiliating defeat. Italy now turns to **dynastic intrigue** to secure its position, favouring **King Menelek of Shoah** in his bid to usurp the imperial throne.

1889 Menelek becomes emperor of Ethiopia on John's death. Under the terms of the Treaty of Ucciali, he accepts

Abyssinian painting championing the resistance to the Italian invasion, by an anonymous Abyssinian artist

an **Italian protectorate** and the establishment of the colony of **Eritrea** (later known as Italian Somaliland). The document is written in two languages, Italian and **Amharic** (the Ethiopian language), but the latter does not make the details of the protectorate clear.

1891 The Crispi government falls, to be succeeded by a moderate right-wing administration headed by **Antonio di Rudini**. An economic **anti-imperialist**, he seeks to balance the budget by reducing military expenditure, and announces his intention of withdrawing Italy from its costly colonial venture altogether.

Pope Leo XIII publishes the encyclical *Rerum novarum*, addressing the problems of **labour relations** in the newly industrialized societies and emphasizing the moral duties of employers to their workers.

1892 Giovanni Giolitti becomes prime minister. A mounting **financial crisis** hits Italy, the result of protectionist tariffs introduced by Crispi's government, which deter foreign investment, and the lira comes under serious pressure on foreign exchanges.

At a congress in **Genoa,** the Lombard lawyer **Filippo Turati** is instrumental in founding the **Italian Workers' Party**. This will eventually change its name to the **Italian Socialist Party**, the first such left-wing grouping in Italy.

1893 A spectacular series of **bank failures** destroys Italy's two largest credit institutions, the **Banca Generale** and the **Società Generale di Credito Mobiliare**. The **Banca Romana** has meanwhile been under surveillance for illegally printing money and advancing loans to politicians to cover election expenses. A treasury report reveals that several important political figures, including **Giolitti** himself, have benefited from the scam, and that the dirty money may even have passed to the royal family. The Banca Romana collapses and its chairman, **Bernardo**

Tanlongo, a Giolitti protégé recently nominated to the Senate, is arrested. Italy's first major **financial scandal** since unification forces the government to resign.

Rioting breaks out in rural areas of **Sicily**, which has been badly hit by a slump in grain prices, a phylloxera epidemic in the wine-producing regions and a falling market for sulphur, one of the island's main exports. Social alliances, or *Fasci*, are founded at various levels among the rural community, their name deriving from the ancient Roman symbol of unity: a bundle of sticks around an axe. Their leaders are **socialist intellectuals**, who become the mouthpiece of peasant demands for fairer wages and reduced rents. Following Giolitti's fall, **Francesco Crispi** enters on a second term of office. The Sicilian **peasant revolt** is ruthlessly suppressed with the help of 40,000 troops, but Crispi also tries to introduce **land reform** on the island's larger estates.

1894 Crispi dissolves the **Socialist Party** and arrests its deputies; **anarchists** are also legally proscribed at the same time. He also contrives to reduce the electorate by disenfranchising 800,000 voters, and closes the **Chamber of Deputies** for five months in response to the disclosure of his involvement in the **Banca Romana** scandal.

1895 Infuriated by the deliberate mistranslations in the Amharic text of the **Treaty of Ucciali**, which has obscured the introduction of the Italian protectorate in **Ethiopia**, **Menelek** repudiates the agreement and declares war.

Crispi sends troops to Ethiopia. Owing to economy measures undertaken by the finance minister **Sidney Sonnino**, the army is critically under-equipped and over-confident. Its advance is dogged by disaster. Serious setbacks at **Amba Alagi** and **Makalle** make Crispi determined to avenge the dishonour of **Dogali** with a major victory.

© MEPL

Contemporary poster advertising Puccini's *Tosca*

1896 At the battle of **Adua,** a force of 25,000 Italians is massacred or taken prisoner by a huge Ethiopian army. Italy is compelled to sue for peace. The **Treaty of Addis Ababa** confirms Ethiopia's independence and restricts Italian colonial authority to **Eritrea**. Widespread demonstrations in Italy lead to **Crispi's** downfall. **King Umberto's** support for him and for the African venture has also weakened the prestige of the monarchy. In the wake of the Ethiopian débâcle, the new ministry, under **di Rudini**, embarks on a diplomatic rapprochement with **France**. Italy agrees to renounce its claims to **Tunisia**.

Giacomo Puccini's opera *La Bohème* receives its first performance at the Teatro Regio in **Turin**.

1898 Bad harvests and food shortages lead to a rise in the price of **bread**. This touches off a series of **riots** in both urban and rural areas throughout Italy. Demonstrators on the streets of **Milan** find themselves confronted by troops under government orders, led by **General Fiorenzo Bava Beccaris**. Believing that a Capuchin monastery, where the friars are busy feeding a queue of beggars, is a revolutionary headquarters, he brings up artillery to storm the building. The episode ends with 100 killed and 450 wounded. Bava is awarded with a decoration by King Umberto and the government introduces emergency measures, suppressing **trade unions** and **radical newspapers** and arresting **Socialist leaders**.

In the wake of the **national emergency**, **Antonio di Rudini** resigns as prime minister. The king chooses **General Luigi Pelloux** to lead a new government. Pelloux becomes Umberto's mouthpiece for the introduction of harsher measures against **industrial action** and **press freedom**.

1899 Pelloux is authorized to proceed with his repressive legislation by means of a *decretone* (major decree) from the king, which allows him to bypass parliament. This outrages liberal members of the chamber, led by **Giolitti**. On 30

Giacomo Puccini and *verismo*

Verismo was the name given to a kind of naturalistic opera which developed in Italy during the 1890s, following the runaway success of **Enrico Mascagni's** *Cavalleria Rusticana*. Based on a tale of Sicilian peasant life by **Giovanni Verga**, this opera spawned many imitations, reflecting the contemporary European taste for strongly realistic narrative material drawn from **working-class life**. In Italy this produced powerful artistic statements such as Medardo Rosso's portrait sculptures, the painter Pelizza da Volpedo's famous image of a resurgent proletariat *Il Quarto Stato* (*The Fourth Estate*) and the novels and short stories of writers linked to the Milanese **'Scapigliatura'** (literally 'tousle-haired') movement, whose object was to connect more closely with the French realist manner of Emile Zola and Alphonse Daudet.

In the world of opera the true master of *verismo* was Giacomo Puccini (1828–1924). *La Bohème*, *Tosca* and *Madama Butterfly* made imaginative use of local colour, offstage sound effects and convincingly paced dramatic dialogue to intensify their focus on raw, naked emotional confrontations, often between characters drawn from less than 'respectable' social backgrounds. The first two of these works achieved **classic status** almost instantly after their first performances (*Madama Butterfly*, meanwhile, was a fiasco at its La Scala premiere, only triumphing after a radical revision). While remaining faithful to the lyric qualities of Italian music theatre, which was essentially 'singers' opera', Puccini was also an innovator. In his later works, such as *La fanciulla del West*, set in the Californian Gold Rush, and *Turandot*, left unfinished at his death in 1926, he sought new dramatic styles and a more imaginative use of the orchestra. Italy has never subsequently produced an opera composer to rival him. During his last years, opera was rapidly losing ground to **cinema** among Italian audiences; many former opera theatres in small towns were adapted to present this new and irresistibly popular form of entertainment.

June, fighting breaks out during a debate and the army is summoned to restore order, while Socialist members remove two of the **urns** in which votes are cast. **Parliament** is closed for five months.

Following the example of other European powers, Italy seeks to establish an imperial foothold in **China**. Its demand to open a naval base at **San Mun** is rejected by the Chinese government. Italy sends an **ultimatum**. Four hours later it is withdrawn. Published throughout the world news media, this forces the resignation of Pelloux's foreign minister **Admiral Canevaro**.

Il Quarto Stato ('The Fourth Estate', 1901) by Giuseppe Pelizza da Volpedo

A group of ex-cavalry officers, led by **Giovanni Agnelli**, founds the Fabbrica Italiana Automobili Torino, soon known by its acronym '**FIAT**', in **Turin**. Over the next ten years the city becomes one of the world's major centres of automobile production.

1900 **King Umberto I** is assassinated by the anarchist **Gaetano Bresci** while visiting the town of Monza. He is succeeded by his son **Victor Emmanuel III**.

An agreement with **France** secures Italy's right to invade the North African region of Tripolitania (present-day **Libya**), hitherto under the control of **Turkey**. In return, France will be allowed a free hand to pursue its imperial interests in **Morocco**.

1901 A period of **industrial unrest** begins throughout Italy, exacerbated by earlier government attempts to suppress left-wing political activity and labour organizations.

The composer **Giuseppe Verdi** dies in **Milan**, aged 88. A huge crowd attends his funeral, and the nation mourns the passing of a cultural figure whom popular imagination has identified closely with the movement for unification in the previous century.

1902 Following industrial action by railway and gas employees seeking union recognition, a **general strike** is threatened.

1903 Pope Leo XIII dies, to be succeeded by Giuseppe Sarto as **Pius X**. During his eleven-year papacy relations between Church and state in Italy gradually improve, and the papal ban on voting in **parliamentary elections** is relaxed.

Giovanni Giolitti becomes prime minister once more. He will dominate the political scene for the next ten years, a period of unrestricted **capitalist enterprise**, **industrial unrest** and flamboyant **consumerism**. Practical and

Portrait of Verdi (1886) by the Ferrarese painter Giovanni Boldini

cynical as a political operator, he is nevertheless guided by a genuine desire to reconcile the nation and its government, a concern for the public good, and loyalty to the Italian monarchy.

'Italietta'

'Italietta', or 'little Italy', was a term of contempt applied to the seemingly easy-going, self-confident world of the Italian **bourgeoisie** in the years leading up to World War I. **Social unrest** in the form of strikes and riots was more or less continuous during this period, and political life see-sawed between Giovanni Giolitti's attempts at **liberal compromise** with the socialists, led by Filippo Turati, and the rise of **right-wing nationalism** and **irredentism**. By 1910, however, Italy was a prosperous nation, eager for international prestige and the chance to range itself alongside the great powers of Europe. **Consumerism** in Italian cities during this period was dominated by a love of **display** and a passion for **novelty**, which were to become the twin hallmarks of the lifestyle of the Italian middle classes throughout the 20th century.

   This ardent embrace of whatever was new and fashionable included the newly developed phenomenon of the **motor car**. In only a few years, Italy became one of the world's leading automobile producers, with Giovanni Agnelli's **Fiat** firm leading the way. Another contemporary invention, the **cinema**, now assumed an important cultural role in bourgeois society. 'Sword-and-sandal'

1904 Mounting tension between government and the workforce leads to widespread **strikes**, accompanied by violent clashes in **Milan** and other northern cities. **Socialist deputies** recently elected to parliament fail to provide real leadership for the workers, and Giolitti correctly anticipates the failure of the strikes. The Socialists are divided between **'reformists'**, keen to use the machinery of government to overhaul the state, and the more extreme **'intransigents'**, themselves split by a syndicalist movement among trade unionists.

1906 A new government, led by **Giolitti,** embarks on a major programme of **social reform** aimed at improving conditions in the workplace. A policy of low-level inter-

epics such as Giovanni Pastrone's *Cabiria* and *The Last Days of Pompeii* were produced on an opulent scale in film studios whose technicians later found work in Hollywood. Fashionable **resorts** along the Ligurian Riviera and the Adriatic developed handsome new boulevards lined with smartly appointed hotels, and the period was a golden age for **spas** such as Montecatini, Salsomaggiore and San Pellegrino.

The new atmosphere of brashness and ostentation was also reflected in **newspapers** and **magazines**, with their growing focus on high-life scandals and the latest **fashion statements**. Also attracting breathless coverage was the craze for **aviation** espoused by the **Futurists**, a group of iconoclastic young artists whose attack on the old, unmodernized Italy was launched through a series of headline-grabbing performances and manifestos. The biggest self-publicist of all was the poet and dramatist **Gabriele D'Annunzio**. Snobbish, dandified and a notorious sexual athlete, his meretricious flirtation with new media and new literary styles seems to sum up the freewheeling, superficial spirit in which Italy confronted the dawning 20th century.

vention in industrial disputes is designed to reconcile socialists and trade union leaders.

> **❝** Giolitti understood what Italy wanted, like the father who sees that his daughter is in love and therefore takes steps to secure for her the husband of her choice. **❞**
>
> Benedetto Croce

1908 A massive **earthquake** devastates **Calabria** and **Sicily**, destroying large areas of Reggio Calabria and completely flattening Messina. 150,000 people are believed to have died.

In the Piedmontese town of Ivrea, **Camillo Olivetti**

opens his first factory for the mass production of **type-writers**. The Olivetti brand name will soon become one of Italy's most famous market leaders.

1909 **Filippo Marinetti** publishes the first '**Futurist Manifesto**' on the front page of the French newspaper *Le Figaro*.

1911 Spurred on by France's pursuit of 'special political interests' in **Morocco** and her manoeuvres to deter German colonialism in the region, Italy declares war on **Turkey** over **Tripolitania**. Italian troops land in **Tripoli**, and despite the Turks' successful resistance inland, **annexation** is formally declared.

Futurism

In terms of its impact on popular consciousness, Futurism was the most successful of all modernist movements in 20th-century art. The present-day stereotype of artists as louche people behaving badly, while making noisy public statements about their work, ideas and intentions, owes much to the founder Futurist, **Filippo Tommaso Marinetti** (1876-1944). His 1910 manifesto, signed by the painters **Carlo Carra**, **Umberto Boccioni** and **Luigi Russolo**, proclaimed the overthrow of traditional notions of culture and reverence for the great achievements of Italy's artistic past. To replace them, Marinetti conjured up an art form which celebrated the hectic speed of technological change, manifested by the motorcar, the cinema, aeroplanes, telephones, phonographs, **saturation advertising** and mass-circulation newspapers. Futurist sculpture and painting hailed the arrival of a mechanized urban world, capturing its dynamism and headlong energy in works with titles such as '*The City Rises*', '*The Street Enters The House*' or '*What The Tramcar Said To Me*'. Long before high-rise residential units became a feature of modern cities, Futurist architects planned vast blocks in steel, glass and concrete. Russolo devised a new form of music based on specially created **noise machines**, their sounds inspired by factory sirens,

1912 Italian warships bombard **Turkish ports** and vessels in the **Red Sea** and along the **Syrian coast**. Turkey refuses to abandon Tripoli.

Italian forces occupy the **Dodecanese** (Rhodes and its surrounding islands). Peace talks begin but break down almost at once. Only war in the **Balkans**, which breaks out during the summer and puts pressure on Turkish military resources, forces a successful outcome. The Italians agree to evacuate the Dodecanese once the Turks have surrendered Tripoli and its surrounding territory, now called **Libya**.

foghorns, tramwhistles or even automobile accidents. Marinetti himself issued a Futurist cookery book, damning pasta in favour of bizarre marriages between unlikely flavours and foodstuffs.

The Futurists depended for their success on the use of shock tactics and mass audiences. Marinetti and his fellow artists toured Europe, giving 'Futurist Evenings' as elaborately publicized spectacles in Paris, Berlin and Moscow, and appearing on the bills at London's smartest music-hall, the Coliseum. Their advent on the international art scene in the years before World War I thrilled a generation which included Picasso, Stravinsky, Diaghilev and **Kandinsky**, but the war itself put an end to this cultural circus troupe. It was not the cleansing conflict, the moment of 'mathematical and **aesthetic intoxication**', which Futurism had so eagerly anticipated. Several of the movement's founders, including Boccioni, its most gifted painter, were killed in action, and Futurism's motor swiftly broke down. After 1918 surviving Futurists such as Marinetti and Carra shifted towards compromise with Fascism. Carra altered his style and joined Italy's artistic establishment, while Marinetti, romanticizing Mussolini (who had for a time been his ideological pupil) realized too late that *Il Duce* had no time for anarchic revolutionary individualism.

The **Fiat** car factory in Turin, which has now extended its product range to lorries and buses, begins mass production of cheaper **automobiles**.

1913 In a general election, the **Socialists** increase their representation in parliament from 41 seats to 78.

1914 Following industrial unrest caused by new taxes to fund the war with Turkey, a **general strike** is proclaimed.

Cardinal Giacomo della Chiesa succeeds Pius X as **Benedict XV**, and almost immediately becomes involved in **peace initiatives** in the events leading up to the outbreak of **world war**.

Giolitti resigns as prime minister, prompted partly by industrial issues, and partly by his failure to pacify anticlerical radicals and Socialists with regard to **Catholic influence** on the government. **Antonio Salandra**, his more conservative political rival, takes over. After **rioting** in **Ancona**, **strikes** break out in surrounding areas of eastern Italy. During '**Red Week**', public buildings and railway stations are attacked, tax offices are ransacked and telephone wires cut. Several thousand troops are called out to suppress the rioters, who include **Benito Mussolini,** then editor of the Socialist newspaper *Avanti!*.

Following declarations of war by **Germany** and **Austria** on **France** and **Russia** between 31 July and 3 August, Italy announces its **neutrality** in the developing conflict. **Mussolini** advocates Italian intervention on the side of the **Allied powers** (Great Britain, France and Russia). Expelled from the PSI, he founds a new paper, *Popolo d'Italia*, which aggressively presses the **interventionist** case.

1915 The Italian foreign minister, **Sidney Sonnino**, demands Austrian cession of **south Tyrol**, northern **Istria** and various **Dalmatian** islands, as well as the establishment of an international zone around **Trieste**.

Italy concludes the secret **Treaty of London** with the Allied powers (Great Britain, France and Russia), under which it is conceded all disputed territory, as well as the **Dodecanese** islands and additional territory in **Eritrea** and **Libya**. In return, Italy repudiates the **Triple Alliance** with Austria and Germany. Italy mobilizes its troops, declaring **war on Austria–Hungary** on 23 May. During the autumn, tension develops between Italy and **Serbia** (one of its new allies) over claims to ports in **Albania**. By 20 December, Italian forces are installed in the towns of Valona and Durazzo (Durres).

Commanded by **General Luigi Cadorna**, Italian troops try to break through the Austrian front line along the **River Isonzo** in northern Friuli. The next two years will see no fewer than eleven similar attempts.

> **❝** I am more than ever convinced of the complete worthlessness of treaties or agreements on paper – and paper is indeed all they are worth. The only real strength lies in bayonets and guns. **❞**
>
> King Victor Emmanuel III

1916 The Austrian high command, under **General Conrad**, urges **Germany** to support a **rearguard attack** on Italy along the valleys of the **Trentino**. German troops are too heavily committed to the Western Front, however, so Austria embarks on an independent offensive, eventually to be beaten back by Italian reserve forces.

1917 **Prince Sixtus of Bourbon-Parma**, member of one of the princely families driven into exile by the events of the Risorgimento, tries to negotiate a **peace agreement** between **Austria–Hungary** and the **Allies**. The sticking point is Austrian reluctance to make full concession to Italy of the territory demanded by the terms of the **Treaty**

of London. Though France and Britain are willing to accept Austria's offer, **Italian intransigence** forces them to reject it.

The eleventh battle of the **Isonzo** produces few more encouraging results for Italy than its forerunners and the strategy of pressure on the Austrian front line is temporarily abandoned.

On 24 October, combined **Austrian** and **German forces** (the latter recently sent to Italy by **Field Marshal Erich Ludendorff**) begin a sustained attack on Italian troops at **Caporetto** in the upper Isonzo valley. The battle, which drives the Italians back behind the River Piave, is a spectacular success for the **Central Powers**, though the Austrians are unable to maintain their pursuit for lack of sufficient mechanized transport.

> **"** In his rare intervals of leave the Italian soldier would return from the scorching limestone plateau of the Carso to find his family starving on a maintenance allowance from the state which was wholly insufficient for its needs. In such circumstances it is not surprising that his will to victory faltered, that he listened to the priests if he were a Catholic or to the Soviets if he were a socialist, and from each of these very different sources learned that the war should be promptly stopped. **"**
>
> H.A.L. Fisher, *A History of Europe* (1936)

General Cadorna, held responsible for the defeat at Caporetto, is forced to resign his command and is replaced by **General Armando Diaz**.

Pope Benedict XV puts forward new **peace proposals**, the most drastic so far, including the evacuation of occupied territory and renunciation of threatened indemnities

Caporetto

The battle of Caporetto was one of the most devastating defeats suffered by the Allied armies during the Great War. Originally the assault on Italian positions had been designed to relieve pressure on Austrian troops battered by earlier action on the **River Isonzo**. The carefully planned advance, on a foggy October morning, overwhelmed the Italian front line, which held most of General Cadorna's artillery. German regiments, one of them led by **Erwin Rommel**, future commander of Hitler's armies in North Africa, easily stormed the surrounding heights, taking many prisoners. After several days of heavy fighting and huge Italian losses, over 100,000 Italian troops had fled in confusion from their Alpine positions, leaving Cadorna's defensive strategy in ruins.

In a desperate attempt to stem the panic, Italian military police were ordered to shoot every tenth man among the stampeding troops. Following in their wake, **Austrian** and **German** battalions (as far as their lack of motorized transport would allow) swept forward on to the **Veneto plain** (Venice itself still bears the scars of wartime bombardment), and only prompt action by **French** and **British** regiments holding the line along the **River Piave** prevented Austria from recovering what it still regarded, after fifty years, as its rightful domains in northern Italy.

The **psychological impact** of Caporetto on ordinary Italians was immense. The disaster contributed to a vengeful, bellicose mood that paved the way for the rise of **Fascism**, not the least of whose implicit pledges was to restore the nation's lost honour and validate its claim to be taken seriously as a military power.

by the **combatant powers**, as well as independent examination of conflicting claims to the **Trentino**. These are rejected by **Britain** and **France** on the basis of Germany's reluctance to give ground on the question of **Belgium**, currently occupied by German troops, and **Alsace-Lorraine**, seized from France in 1870.

1918 The **Austrians** cross the **River Piave**, but are driven back, with heavy losses, by Italian forces. **General Diaz**, under pressure from the Allies, launches a assault on the entire Austrian front. Italian forces break through at **Vittorio Veneto**, scattering demoralized Austrian troops and taking over 100,000 prisoners. On 29 October, Austria offers **unconditional surrender** to Italy. The Italian war effort has achieved comparatively little in terms of increased international prestige or territorial gains, and although Italy is represented at the Paris Peace Conference, the terms of the **Treaty of London** are not guaranteed by the **Treaty of Versailles**. The nation emerges from the conflict heavily in **debt** and politically **unstable**, its society **disillusioned** and **directionless**.

> **"** Their incapacity and vanity are extraordinary. They are in my opinion the most odious colleagues and allies to have at a conference, the beggars of Europe, well known for their whining alternated by truculence. **"**
>
> British diplomat Sir Charles Hardinge, on the Italian delegates at the Versailles Peace Conference

1919 **Benito Mussolini** forms the first *Fascio di Combattimento*, the basis of a right-wing political movement which gains rapid support among all classes.

President Woodrow Wilson of the USA blocks Italian claims to former Austrian territory on the **Adriatic**. The Italian delegates, prime minister **Vittorio Emmanuele Orlando** and foreign minister **Sidney Sonnino,** quit the **Paris Peace Conference** in protest and are welcomed home as heroes.

Universal suffrage and **proportional representation** are introduced under a new electoral law.

The poet, aviator and nationalist **Gabriele d'Annunzio** leads an expedition to seize the port of **Fiume**, then assigned to the new state of **Yugoslavia**.

The Socialist writer **Antonio Gramsci** founds *L'Ordine nuovo* (*The New Order*) a newspaper reflecting the ideals of his left-wing group within the party.

> **❝** Fiume today represents Italy herself. She is the point of honour for our conscience, that great Latin conscience which alone formed the truly free men of past centuries and forms them today. **❞**
>
> Gabriele D'Annunzio, *Italy or Death*

1920 A treaty with **Greece** confirms Italy's claim to the **Dodecanese** islands, including **Rhodes**.

Giovanni Giolitti becomes prime minister for the last time. **D'Annuzio**, still occupying **Fiume** with his expeditionary force, declares war on the Italian government, and troops are sent to bombard him into submission.

1921 **Rioting** between **Fascists** and **Communists** breaks out in **Florence**. **Liberals** and **Democrats** win the first election held under the new universal suffrage law. Giolitti's government falls and he is succeeded as prime minister by **Ivanoe Bonomi**.

Bonomi resigns as prime minister and **Luigi Facta** leads a **Liberal-Democrat coalition**. **Fascists** gain control of key local governments in Italy, including **Milan** and **Bologna**. Fearing the rise of **communism** and the power of the **trade unions**, **business** and **industrial employers** are lending increased support to the Fascists. Though offered a ministry in the Facta cabinet, at the Fascist party congress in Naples **Mussolini** rejects all cooperation, calling on the prime minister to resign.

In the midst of a worsening political and economic crisis, Facta advises **King Victor Emmanuel** to impose **martial law**, but he refuses to do so. In the **March on Rome**, Mussolini and his Fascist cohorts converge on the capital to exploit the prevailing atmosphere of **tension** and **panic**. This proves to be a brilliantly successful manoeuvre for the Fascists. The king summons **Mussolini** to form a government. He is granted **dictatorial powers** for a year and the triumph of **Fascism** is assured.

After quitting the Socialists, Antonio Gramsci joins the **Italian Communist Party**.

10
Fascist Italy and World War II

1923–45

D uring the period immediately following **World War I**, Fascism had gathered support in Italy among widely differing sections of society. All of these groups shared a sense of **disillusion** with peacetime politics and **impatience** with attempts by the parliamentary old guard, represented by figures such as **Giovanni Giolitti**, **Vittorio Emmanuele Orlando** and **Antonio Salandra**, to maintain the democratic consensus of the post-unification era. **Mussolini** gathered support not just among the lower middle class and the business community, but also from conservative aristocrats, army officers and many of the conscripts who had fought under such gruelling conditions on the **Isonzo** and at **Caporetto**. His triumph after 1922 was ensured only as long as he kept up the sense of victory and excitement generated by Italy's involvement in the war. The renewed impetus he gave to **colonialism**, leading to the annexation of **Ethiopia**, provided the most obvious example of the *Duce's* need to keep Italians focused, active and on the move. But this restlessness, coupled with a craving for sensationalism, characterized every aspect of Fascism. **Rhetoric**, **spectacle** and a sense of **occasion**, all perennial features of Italian life, were as essential to the regime's survival as its **militaristic** approach to social and economic problems. The sense of well-being, harmony and order it was intended to generate, however, were an illusion that became ever harder to sustain in the 1930s, as Mussolini's colonial ventures and foreign policy generally drove him into ever closer alliance with **Nazi Germany**.

Adolf Hitler had himself been inspired by the example of Fascist Italy, but by 1938 it was Mussolini who was aping his German counterpart in increasingly extreme measures and gestures, culminating in the infamous **racial laws** removing civil rights from the Italian **Jewish community**. Many Italians who had earlier viewed Fascism as an effective response to Italy's postwar problems and territorial disappointments now became alienated from it. The **anti-Fascist initiatives** that resulted from this disenchantment nevertheless lacked organization, and never posed any real threat to the regime. Distinguished intellectuals such as **Benedetto Croce** kept their distance from the movement, its ideology and its political solutions, but any attempts at **direct resistance**, whether open or clandestine, were ineffectual in the face of police informers and media censorship. Although the population at large was indifferent to the more posturing and histrionic aspects of Fascism, Mussolini was increasingly determined to follow in the footsteps of Nazi Germany, casting Italy in the role of a saviour of western Europe from the sloth, indecisiveness and cowardice of its politicians. Thus it was that, as Germany's chief ally, the country found itself propelled into war in 1940 on a tide of expectant triumph, ill-prepared though the Italian armed forces were for global conflict.

With the **Allied victory** in **North Africa** and conquest of **Sicily** in 1943, Mussolini was finally ousted by the efforts of senior members of his own government, the military high command and anti-Fascist leaders. As an **armistice** was concluded between Italy and the Allies, **Hitler** responded by turning the country into a battleground, as the German forces who held the north of the country sought to block a full-scale British and American invasion from the south. While Mussolini, at Hitler's behest, established an even more brutal

Fascist republic in northern Italy, thousands of Italians joined or gave assistance to the **partisans**. Fearful that it would develop links with Soviet communism – or indeed that it might already have done so – Allied generals from the outset gave inadequate support to this heroic and often remarkably successful resistance movement, and later actively obstructed it.

It was almost another two years before German forces in Italy surrendered, and Mussolini was captured by partisans and shot. The Fascist era died with him. What remained, however, was the fundamental yearning among conservative Italians for **political stability** at any price, a yearning which had brought the *Duce* to power in 1922. The same desire had helped to defeat the patriot revolutions of 1848 and would provide a basis for the political consensus which ensured the survival of successive Christian Democrat governments during the Cold War era. That this spirit is by no means dead has been proved in recent years by the success of the right-wing coalition under Silvio Berlusconi's leadership. Within this group is the **Alleanza Nazionale** party, whose leaders openly acknowledge a debt to Fascism and advocate a revisionist approach to Mussolini and his achievements.

> ❝ I organized a 'column of fire' to extend our reprisals throughout the province ... We went through Rimini, Sant' Arcangelo, Savignano, Cesena, Bertinoro, all the towns and centres in the provinces of Forli and Ravenna, and destroyed and burned all the red buildings, the seats of the Socialist and Communist organizations. It was a terrible night. Our passage was marked by huge columns of fire and smoke. The whole plain of the Romagna was given up for the reprisals of the outraged Fascists determined to break for ever the red terror ... ❞
>
> Italo Balbo, diary entry for 1 January, 1922 (*Diario 1922*)

1923 Mussolini is prime minister, foreign minister and interior minister. To his party members he is *Il Duce* ('the leader', from the Latin *dux*), a title by which he is soon hailed throughout Italy. In order to reward his supporters, Mussolini prevails on **King Victor Emmanuel III** to sanction the creation of a **militia** designed to become the *Duce*'s private army and to 'defend the values of the Fascist revolution'.

The **Popular Party**, representing Catholic interests, agrees to support the Fascist regime. Its leader, the Sicilian priest **Don Luigi Sturzo**, announces his resignation.

After Italian members of a commission determining the Graeco-Albanian frontier are assassinated, Italy blames **Greece** for the murder and sends warships to bombard **Corfu**. Greece appeals to the **League of Nations**, and under international pressure Italian forces are withdrawn.

Mussolini introduces a new **electoral law**, decreeing that the party that gains the largest number of votes in a general

> Mussolini is the biggest bluff in Europe ... Get hold of a good photo of Signor Mussolini some time and study it. You will see the weakness in his mouth which forces him to scowl the famous Mussolini scowl that is imitated by every 19-year-old Fascisto in Italy. Study his past record. Study the coalition that Fascismo is between capital and labour and consider the history of past coalitions. Study his genius for clothing small ideas in big words. Study his propensity for duelling. Really brave men do not have to fight duels, and many cowards duel constantly to make themselves believe they are brave. And then look at his black shirt and white spats. There is something wrong, even histrionically, with a man who wears white spats with a black shirt.

Ernest Hemingway in the *Toronto Star*, 27 January, 1923

election shall be allotted two-thirds of all parliamentary seats.

1924 A treaty with **Yugoslavia** recognizes **Fiume** as an Italian city.

In a **general election** on 6 April, the Fascists gain 65 percent of the votes, so increasing their seats in parliament from 35 to a spectacular 356 (out of a total of 535). This follows a campaign marked by the brutal intimidation of voters by **Fascist militia squads**.

On 30 May, the Socialist deputy (member of parliament) **Giacomo Matteotti** denounces the corruption and illegality surrounding the recent elections. Ten days later he is kidnapped and subsequently murdered, his body afterwards found dumped on scrubland in the countryside near Rome. The episode alienates political moderates from Mussolini, who initially seeks to distance himself from the assassination. Led by the Socialist **Giovanni Amendola**, outraged opposition deputies leave parliament in protest, a gesture known as the '**Aventine secession**' (after the Aventine hill, where they set up an alternative assembly). Mussolini seizes the opportunity to suppress the opposition and introduce **emergency legislation** controlling national newspapers (which have been highly critical of him).

1925 In a speech to parliament on 3 January Mussolini confronts his critics, taking responsibility for the consequences of **Fascist violence**, and announcing that he will move swiftly to crush all opposition to Fascism. The chamber makes no move to impeach him. The Fascists at once toughen **press censorship laws** (newspapers and journalists are made subservient to government-appointed directors), expel the **Aventine secessionists** from parliament, institute a nationwide purge of **anti-Fascist elements,** and embark on the reform of **local authorities** with a system of nominated mayors. **Trade union**

> **"** If two irreconcilable elements are struggling with each other, the solution lies in force. There has never been any other solution in history, and there never will be ... I declare that I and I alone assume the political, moral and historical responsibility for all that has happened ... If Fascism has been a criminal association, if all the acts of violence have been the result of a certain historical, political and moral climate, the responsibility for this is mine. **"**
>
> Benito Mussolini, *Discorsi del 1925*

organization is now strictly controlled by government, and **strikes** are declared illegal.

Italy acts as guarantor ensuring the fulfilment of the terms of the **Locarno Pact**, a treaty between Britain, France, Germany and Belgium guaranteeing the security of European frontiers.

1926 Mussolini is authorized, as prime minister, to govern by decree in the event of a **national emergency**.

A **Fascist youth movement** is founded and named after **Balilla**, boy hero of the Genoese revolt against the Austrians in 1746. The name will also be applied to a popular make of cheap automobile produced during this period by Fiat.

Antonio Gramsci is imprisoned for political subversion. While in jail he begins the work later known as the '*Prison letters*', developing his political philosophy.

Inflation forces a revaluation of the lira, a process known as **Quota 90**, which after prolonged negotiations with the Bank of England finally fixes the exchange rate at 90 lire to the British pound sterling, Although this attracts **foreign investment** in Italy, its knock-on effect on **wages** and

working conditions will ultimately endanger the stability of the regime.

With Mussolini's encouragement, **Cesare Mori**, prefect of Palermo, begins a successful campaign against the operations of the **Sicilian Mafia**. The island's murder rate declines dramatically, and landowning interests bolster Mori's drive to arrest and imprison most of the organization's bosses, or to at least force them abroad.

> " I believe in the genius of Mussolini, in our Holy Father Fascism, in the communion of the martyrs, in the conversion of the Italians and in the resurrection of the Empire. "
>
> From the creed recited by the 'Balilla' Fascist youth movement

1928 The **Fascist militias** are incorporated within Italy's regular army. **Universal suffrage** is abolished: the franchise is restricted to males over 21 who pay tax at a rate above 100 lire. **Electoral candidates** are to be scrutinized by the Fascist Party's grand council.

Italy concludes a treaty of friendship with **Ethiopia** and supports her admission to the League of Nations. Italy, with Germany and Japan, sign the **Kellogg-Briand Pact** devised by America and France, under which the international powers renounce the pursuit of aggressive war.

1929 The government concludes the **Lateran Treaty** with **Pope Pius XI**, recognizing the pope as an independent sovereign within the Vatican City. A concordat (agreement) guarantees the Catholic Church privileged status within Italy.

In a rigged **general election** the Fascists score an easy victory, with eight million votes against just 135,000.

The Fascist aesthetic

Mussolini saw Italy in terms of what he considered its rightful place as a great nation on the world stage, but always doubted the Italians' capacity to fulfil the true expectations of Fascism in achieving this. His own obsession with public image and photo opportunity, a posturing famously satirized by foreign cartoonists, could be seen as an exaggerated form of a typically Italian preoccupation with style and '*bella figura*'. Amid all the vainglorious trappings adopted by the burgeoning Fascist movement in the years leading up to 1922, the iconography of **imperial Rome** played a central part. The term 'Fascist' itself derived from the **fasces**, a bundle of rods around an axe, which had been the Roman symbol of **strength in unity**. As *Il Duce*, Mussolini encouraged a spirit of 'romanita' ('Romanness'), referring to his followers as 'legions' and 'centurions' and exhorting his architects to destroy much of the Italian capital's medieval and Renaissance centre in order to transform it into a city worthy of a new Roman empire. Fascist architecture, as exemplified in works such as **Milan railway station**, the model town of **Sabaudia**, the Rome **Olympic stadium** and the city's **EUR suburb** (originally designed to showcase an international exhibition) dwelt on the massive, monumental and muscular. The cult of sport and fitness promoted in Nazi Germany influenced the Italian regime in other respects, notably its various youth movements, and the *passo romano*, the Fascist version of the Prussian goose-step. New rules were laid down for everyday social customs, such as forms of address and the traditional handshake, which most party members replaced with the **Fascist salute**. With such gestures went other paraphernalia intended to distinguish the regime, including the uniform of **black shirt**, black tasselled cap and riding breeches. Public buildings displayed the *Duce*'s slogans and sayings, and books and newspapers were forced to include a Roman-numbered '**year of the Fascist epoch**', dated from 1922, beside its conventional calendar equivalent. By gestures like these, Mussolini considered, he could begin to persuade a people he privately scorned as 'sheep' and 'slaves' that theirs was a nation in the vanguard of progress and social change, under the guidance of a wise and dynamic leader.

The Palazzo della Civiltà Italiana, designed by Bruno La Padula for Mussolini's *Esposizione Universale Roma*

1930 In an effort to stem the tide of **rural unemployment** and migration to the cities, the regime embarks on a major land reclamation programme in the swampy area southwest of Rome known as the **Pontine Marshes**.

1932 King Zog of Albania rejects Italy's proposal of a customs union, one of several attempts by Mussolini to influence the affairs of Albania, which is already heavily dependent on Italian loans and investments.

1933 The **National Socialists** (Nazis), led by **Adolf Hitler**, gain control of the government in Germany. Anxious to create European power blocs with Italy as a major player, Mussolini signs a **Four-Power Pact** with the new German regime, Britain and France.

Pope Pius XI concludes a concordat with the **Nazi government** in Germany. Catholics are guaranteed the right to practise their religion, and Church property and the independence of Catholic schools are protected. In return for these concessions, Germany demands that **priests** be forbidden to take part in political activities of any kind.

Fascist agricultural policies

Rural Italy – or at any rate the idea of rural Italy – was immensely important to the Fascist regime. In common with many right-wing ideologies, Fascism was suspicious of urban elites and the educated bourgeoisie, seeking support instead among landowners, farmers and peasants. Mussolini presented his government's goals and programmes to these sections of society in the form of symbolic battles which had to be won if Italy was to survive. Thus self-sufficiency in grain supplies during the late 1920s, for instance, was to be achieved through the so-called '**Battle for Grain**'. In a radical transformation of the landscape, parts of Italy such as Lazio and Sicily, which had traditionally supported pastureland and orchards, now came under the plough – an initiative which was to have the unfortunate effect of undermining traditional **export markets** in fruit and olive oil on which these areas depended.

More positive in terms of immediate results was the **reclamation of marshland** for farming in the Tuscan Maremma and the Pontine Marshes around Rome (a scheme in which the government consolidated work started by earlier Italian rulers). By the mid-1930s such projects had dramatically reduced the incidence of **malaria**, scourge of peasant communities, and had proved useful in stemming rural unemployment. But broader economic factors, such as the major postwar slump in world markets of the 1920s, meant that Fascism was never to achieve its self-proclaimed goal of returning more small farmers to the land. The pattern of **rural exodus**, drift to the cities and emigration which had marked Italian life so strongly during the 1870s continued, even if the pace of rural change was now somewhat slower, and it was to remain constant throughout the period 1922–40. Always dreaming of grand transformations in Italian society, Mussolini ultimately failed to make a real impact on age-old lifestyles and work habits in the countryside, and he never managed to establish a genuine core of support for Fascism among Italy's agricultural working class.

1934 Hitler visits Mussolini in Venice, a first meeting which leaves the two dictators mutually unimpressed. The main bone of contention is **Austria**, where the Nazis are planning a **coup d'état**. Mussolini opposes this, suspicious that Germany is trying to extend its sphere of influence towards the Mediterranean.

By concentrating troops around the **Brenner Pass**, on Italy's northern frontier, Mussolini thwarts Nazi activists in **Austria,** who in an abortive coup on 25 July assassinated the country's chancellor, **Engelbert Dollfuss**, and seized the Vienna radio station.

Determined to safeguard Italian control over **Albania**, Mussolini sends a fleet to the port of Durres (**Durazzo**). King Zog and his government accept what is essentially a protectorate status under the Italian government.

1935 At the **Stresa Conference**, Italy joins **France** in protests against **German rearmament** and the recent attempted coup in Austria.

Using the pretext of a dispute with **Ethiopia** over her frontier with **Italian Somaliland**, Mussolini threatens military action in the area. Ethiopia appeals to the **League of Nations** as arbitrator. In an attempt to stave off outright war between Italy and Ethiopia, Britain sends **Anthony Eden**, minister with special responsibility for the **League of Nations**, to Rome to offer a number of concessions to Mussolini. When the League's attempts at arbitration break down, Mussolini authorizes an Italian **invasion of Ethiopia**. The League reacts by voting to apply **economic sanctions** against Italy.

1936 Under **Field Marshal Pietro Badoglio**, Italian troops seize the Ethiopian capital, **Addis Ababa. Emperor Haile Selassie** seeks asylum in Britain. On 9 May, Italy formally announces its **annexation of Ethiopia**, of which **King Victor Emmanuel** is now declared emperor. The failure of the League of Nations to prevent the invasion, the inadequacy of its sanctions policy and its willingness to sacrifice Haile Selassie to **realpolitik**, reveal its fundamental weakness as an international peacekeeper.

Civil war breaks out in **Spain** between the Republican government and Nationalist forces led by **General Francisco Franco**. Mussolini supports Franco by sending some 70,000 troops to Spain.

In October, a secret pact between Italy and Germany is signed in Rome. Dubbed the **Rome-Berlin Axis**, it pledges mutual cooperation in international affairs.

The Austrian chancellor **Kurt Schuschnigg** visits Mussolini in Venice to ask for continued Italian support against Germany. Mussolini, now in need of German backing for Italian aggression in Ethiopia and Spain, offers no further guarantees. Germany acknowledges Italy's annexation of Ethiopia.

Released from prison on grounds of declining health, Antonio Gramsci dies in hospital in Rome.

1937 Italy joins Germany and Japan in the **Anti-Comintern Pact** against communism. Italy formally withdraws from the **League of Nations**.

1938 Mussolini offers no protests when German troops enter **Austria** (the *Anschluss*, or 'union') and the country is absorbed into the **Third Reich**. Influenced by **Hitler**, Mussolini introduces the first of a series of **racial laws** restricting the civil rights of Italy's Jewish population. Jews are forbidden to teach in schools and universities and are prohibited from marrying non-Jews.

Italy secures **British recognition** of the annexation of **Ethiopia**, in exchange for a promise to withdraw Italian forces from Spain once the civil war has ended. Tension develops between Italy and **France** when hard-line Fascist

Antonio Gramsci

Antonio Gramsci (1891–1937) is an interesting example of a writer and thinker whose influence was far greater after his death than during his life. Born in **Sardinia**, the son of a lowly official, Gramsci suffered from curvature of the spine and a series of lingering illnesses which plagued him throughout his life. In 1911 he gained a scholarship to Turin University, where he studied political science, became absorbed in **Marxist theory** and at length joined the Socialist party. Besides writing theatre reviews for the party's paper *Avanti!*, Gramsci founded his own journal *L'Ordine Nuovo* in 1919. Around this time he began moving further to the left, finally joining the newly formed Communist Party, whose secretary he later became. After spending two years in post-revolutionary Russia as a member of the Comintern's executive committee, he returned to Italy to fight Fascism as an elected **member of parliament**. The Fascists, determined to crush political opposition, introduced tough new security measures, under which, in 1926, Gramsci was arrested, accused of subversion and imprisoned in a bleak fortress near Bari. Here he spent most of the remaining eleven years of his life.

While in prison he was allowed to write, and in his *Quaderni del carcere* (*Prison Notebooks*) he developed his own political philosophy, rejecting the determinist view of history espoused by earlier Marxist theoreticians, proposing instead that the individual

elements revive 'historic' Italian claims to **Tunisia** and **Corsica**.

At the **Munich Conference**, Italy is represented by Mussolini's foreign minister and son-in-law **Galeazzo Ciano**, who purports to act as **peacemaker** in the dispute among Germany, Britain and France over the fate of **Czechoslovakia**, where Hitler has threatened to annex the German-speaking **Sudetenland** area. The failure of the British and French to resist Hitler's demands confirms Mussolini in his determination to forge closer links with

and the intellectual had a freer, more creative role to play in the historical process. Central to his concept of class struggle was the notion of **hegemony**, the rise to power of a single elite or social grouping. The working class, he argued, could establish its own counter-hegemony through the moral influence of its intellectuals in the civil society of political parties, academia and the Church. This would enable the proletariat to dominate public institutions, such as the civil service, the judiciary and the armed forces.

Gramsci died of a **brain haemorrhage** a week after his release from prison in 1937. The *Prison Notebooks* were finally published ten years later, and their ideas had a lasting influence on Italian intellectual debate, not just in the field of political theory but in literature and art criticism. In the 1970s his work achieved a positively totemic significance among left-wingers at a time when the Italian Communist Party was scoring its greatest electoral triumphs, and cultural life in Italy became heavily politicized. Gramsci's name was invoked, during this period, like that of a patron saint, and countless books and articles were devoted to his writings. One of the more notable ironies of modern Italian history was that a man whose influence on events had been so disastrously thwarted during his lifetime should now become a figure of central importance in the evolution of a political consciousness among Italy's postwar generations.

Nazi Germany and reject any further alliance with the western democracies.

1939 Pope Pius XI dies and is succeeded by Cardinal Eugenio Pacelli as **Pius XII**. A former papal secretary of state, the new pope is known for his **pro-German** sympathies and is less inclined than his predecessor to criticize the regime.

Emboldened by the outcome at Munich, Mussolini now orders an invasion and occupation of **Albania**. King Zog flees to Greece, and the Albanian constituent assembly votes for full union with Italy. Mussolini concludes the **Pact of Steel** with Hitler, a political and military alliance based on the *Duce*'s assumption, shared by Ciano, that Germany is unlikely to engage in full-scale war for another five years. The pact obliges either side to lend support to the other in the event of both defensive and offensive campaigns.

Visiting Berlin in August, **Ciano** is alarmed by German

The racial laws

> **The population of Italy is of Aryan origins and its civilization is Aryan. There now exists a pure Italian race, and the Jews do not belong to that Italian race.**

From the text of the Fascist Racial Laws

In 1938, the Jewish population of Italy stood at not much more than 45,000. Italian Jews had nevertheless played a significant role in the life of the nation since their emancipation by **Napoléon** at the beginning of the 19th century, taking a major part in the **Risorgimento** and **post-unification** politics: prominent Jews included prime minister **Sidney Sonnino**. The Jewish community even broadly supported Fascism, and Mussolini's secretary, his dentist and at least one of his finance ministers were all Jews. Unlike France and Germany, Italy had no tradition of **anti-Semitism**, and although Catholic dogma, which proclaimed Jews to be Christ's murderers, had ensured their confinement to **ghettos** in the medieval and Renaissance periods, **pogroms** were much rarer here than in other parts of Europe.

When Mussolini introduced his racial legislation programme, he intended its effects to be far-reaching. In addition to the restrictions on **marriage** and **education**, Jews were barred from professions such as the **law**, **banking** and **journalism**, in which they were traditionally well represented, and they were made to renounce their membership of the **Fascist Party**.

preparations for the invasion of **Poland**. The Italian ambassador to Berlin, **Bernardo Attolico**, reveals the scale of Italy's lack of military preparation to Hitler, who resigns himself to releasing Mussolini from the Pact of Steel. The *Duce* apologizes to the **Führer** for being 'compelled by forces beyond my control not to afford you real solidarity at the moment of action'.

Whatever their loyalty to the regime, many Italians viewed the new decrees as inherently vulgar and discreditable to Italy. **King Victor Emmanuel**, who loathed Germany and feared its influence, infuriated Mussolini with his expressions of 'infinite sorrow for the poor Jews'. Dr Salim Diamand, a Polish-born Jew interned in Italy (quoted by Martin Gilbert in *The Righteous: The Unsung Heroes of the Holocaust*), observed that 'throughout my years of confinement in various camps during the war years in Italy I never found racism in the Italians. Of course there was militarism; but throughout the war years, I never found any Italians who approached me, as a Jew, with the idea of exterminating my race'. And **Pope Pius XII,** in the Christmas message in 1942, provoked a furiously indignant response from the Reich Security Main Office: 'In a manner never known before, the pope has repudiated the National Socialist New European Order … Here he is virtually accusing the German people of injustice towards the Jews and making himself the mouthpiece of the Jewish war criminals.'

Until the *Duce*'s fall and Italy's surrender in 1943, no attempt was made to follow Germany's example in pursuing a **'final solution'**. Although deprived of their civil rights Jews remained largely unmolested. However, under the Nazi occupation, **concentration camps** were set up in northern Italy (at Fossoli near Modena and at Risiera di San Saba near Trieste). Many hundreds of Jewish Italians were rounded up and deported to slavery in German **labour camps** or execution in the gas chambers of **Auschwitz**.

On 3 September, **Great Britain** and **France** declare **war** on Germany following its invasion of Poland. Italy remains **neutral**, although Mussolini increasingly regards this position as a disgrace to the nation.

1940 Fearing that Germany will seize **France**, which he has long seen as his enemy and ultimate prey, Mussolini declares **war** against the **Allied powers** on 10 June.

In Berlin, **Germany** and **Japan** conclude a military pact with Italy, guaranteeing each other support in all operations over a period of ten years.

In October, Mussolini prepares for an invasion of **Greece**, announcing this to Hitler as a *fait accompli* when the Führer arrives in Florence for talks. Hitler has already advised against the plan, partly because he fears **Russian intervention**, but mostly because the campaign may require support from German forces already committed to the war in **North Africa**. The Italian invasion of Greece is a spectacular **fiasco**. Fighting furiously, Greek forces drive the Italians back across the Albanian border. Weather conditions during these winter months are severe, and Mussolini's army is badly equipped: many of the soldiers are issued with cardboard-soled boots, which disintegrate in the snow. **Germany** is compelled to offer support and renews the attack, subsequently occupying **Greece** and **Yugoslavia**. Hitler later claims that of all the events during the early phases of World War II, Mussolini's **Greek campaign** did the most serious harm to Germany's long-term military objectives.

In North Africa, a **strategic British retreat** in the Western Desert lures Italian troops to within 100 kilometres of the **Suez Canal**. The British turn and fight, rapidly driving the Italians back and capturing **Libya**, where they take more than 25,000 prisoners. British forces invade **Ethiopia** and **Italian Somaliland**, seizing **Addis Ababa** on 6 April. The **duke of Aosta**, Italian commander in the region and a son of King Victor Emmanuel, surrenders.

Hitler accepts Mussolini's offer of an **Italian expeditionary force** to fight alongside German troops in their attack on **Russia**. Some 200,000 men are despatched on what proves to be a disastrous mission for the Axis powers, culminating in their momentous defeat at **Stalingrad** in January in 1943.

On 11 December, following the Japanese attack on **Pearl Harbor** four days earlier, Italy declares war on the **United States of America**.

> This whipped jackal [Mussolini], who, to save his own skin, has made Italy a vassal state of Hitler's empire, is frisking up by the side of the German tiger with yelps not only of appetite – that could be understood – but even of triumph.
>
> Winston Churchill, House of Commons, April 1941

1942 At the head of specially trained German divisions, **General Erwin Rommel** assumes supreme command of Axis troops in **North Africa**. Capturing the British-held port of **Tobruk**, he sweeps on towards Alexandria, but is defeated on 23 October by the Eighth Army under **General Bernard Montgomery** at **El Alamein**. The victory spells an end to any effective Italian military presence in Africa. The Fascist government's relationship with Germany begins seriously to deteriorate.

Living conditions in Italy are seriously affected by **austerity measures**. Food rationing is introduced; all available metal, including kitchenware, is requisitioned; silk and cotton clothing are withdrawn from sale; electricity

Mussolini's image

Mussolini came from a **rural working-class** background and always prided himself on having risen to power entirely through his own strength of will and iron determination. An expert communicator and **gifted propagandist**, he made a virtue of adaptability, never tying Fascism too closely to an inflexible programme and ideology. He too, after all, had famously shifted political positions, early in his career, from left to right. Much of his success, whether with fellow Italians or with impressionable and credulous foreign politicians, diplomats and journalists, depended on the skill with which he projected his image as a simple, inherently modest **man of destiny**. The homage of adoring crowds, ready to hail him as Italy's saviour and greatest son, was adulation he took for granted. His strutting gait, puffed-out chest and protruding jaw may have been a gift to Charlie Chaplin in his film *The Great Dictator*, but to Mussolini's many admirers they embodied his passionate, restless nature: keen for action, change, answers and results.

In conversation he was lively, engaging and seldom at a loss for ideas, but never particularly embarrassed at changing his mind on a subject about which he might have offered categorical views only a short time earlier. He enjoyed posing as inscrutable and unfathomable, and many of his vaunted virtues, such as an appetite for hard work and an **encyclopedic memory**, were little more than clever bluffing. His reputation as a **womanizer** certainly did him no harm in Italy, although – as leader of a regime which gave prizes to proud mothers – he was also keen to cultivate his image as a devoted family man. His wife, the shrewd but humourless **Rachele Guidi**, was, bizarrely, the daughter of his first mistress, between whom and her best-known, ill-fated successor **Claretta Petacci**, there stretched a long line of conquests.

Mussolini never succeeded in his ultimate goal of transforming the Italians into the kind of dogged radical modernists he believed himself to represent, and he was exasperated by what he considered the national vices of disobedience, irresponsibility and political cynicism. Yet he continued to believe that Italians would

Benito Mussolini

fully accept Fascism once they learned to respond to it
emotionally and ceased making intellectual demands of a regime
which had no real philosophy at its heart. His seemingly infallible
abilities as a **public orator** were devoted to wooing audiences
with his rhetoric so as to convince them that their collective
destiny was safe in the hands of a wise and provident leader. It
was the failure of this superficially benevolent **authoritarianism**,
as much as the simple fact that the *Duce* had deluded them both
in image and substance, that the Italians found hard to forgive.

supplies are reduced; and travel on public transport is limited to essential journeys.

1943 A series of **strikes** in **Turin** and **Milan**, the first such working-class protest in Italy for over twenty years, reveals the growing unpopularity of the war and its effect on ordinary Italians. In response, the government promises wage increases. In February, Mussolini reshuffles the Fascist government. **Dino Grandi**, minister of justice, and **Giuseppe Bottai**, education minister, are both ousted, and the *Duce* himself replaces **Galeazzo Ciano** as **foreign minister**. The changes are designed to persuade Hitler that Italy is still committed to the war effort, but all three sacked ministers will now begin plotting the *Duce's* downfall.

The **British Eighth Army** occupies **Tripoli** and the **Axis** forces retreat into **Tunisia**. Axis forces attempting to stem the **American advance** into Tunisia are defeated at the **Kasserine Pass**.

On 9 May, after returning from a visit to Hitler, Mussolini addresses the Roman crowd from the balcony of the **Palazzo Venezia**, declaring that their sacrifices will be rewarded by final victory. Such speeches, accompanied by the *Duce's* characteristic gesticulations and facial contortions, have been a significant feature of his public style as dictator. This will be the last of them.

With the Allied capture of **Tunis** and **Bizerta**, the combined German and Italian armies are conclusively defeated in **North Africa**, with 200,000 men killed, wounded or captured. British and American generals now plan an invasion of **Sicily**.

On 9 July, Allied troops under the command of **General Dwight D. Eisenhower** land in Sicily. **Allied bombing raids** on Italian mainland targets begin, focusing on **Naples** and **Rome**.

Hitler flies to Italy to meet **Mussolini** at **Feltre**, where he lectures him on the need for further commitment to the Axis war effort and demands that Italian troops be put under German command.

> **❝** The Italians are extremely lax in their treatment of Jews. They protect the Italian Jews both in Tunis and in occupied France and will not permit their being drafted for work or compelled to wear the Star of David. This shows once again that Fascism does not really dare to get down to fundamentals, but is very superficial regarding problems of vital importance. **❞**
>
> Josef Goebbels, quoted in *The Righteous: Unsung Heroes of the Holocaust*, Martin Gilbert

At a meeting of the **Fascist Grand Council** on 24 July, the *Duce* shocks his audience with a rambling and inept address, full of self-pity, lies and accusations, delivered in an uncharacteristic monotone. Dino Grandi, supported by Ciano, demands **Mussolini's resignation** and the return of power to constitutional authority, headed by King Victor Emmanuel.

> **❝** You believe you possess the devotion of the people. You lost it the day you tied Italy to Germany. **❞**
>
> Dino Grandi to Mussolini at the last meeting of the Fascist Grand Council

On 25 July, Mussolini has an audience with **Victor Emmanuel**, who urges him to confront the reality of Italy's predicament. Mussolini resigns, and **Marshal Pietro Badoglio** takes over as leader of the government. Now placed under arrest, the *Duce* is taken first of all to the **prison islands** of Ponza and Maddalena, and then to a hotel on the mountain of Gran Sasso d'Italia, in the **Abruzzi** region.

On 2 September, **British** and **American** forces land in **Calabria**. The next day an **armistice** between the new Italian government and the Allies is signed at Algiers, ending the state of war between them with an unconditional **Italian surrender**. Following news of the surrender, German troops seize control of all the principal Italian cities. Their commander-in-chief, **Field-Marshal Kesselring**, proclaims all Italian territory behind the German front line to be a **war zone**, subject to **martial law**. Any act interpreted as potential sabotage is considered a capital offence.

On 12 September, **Mussolini** is rescued from Gran Sasso by an Austrian Wehrmacht officer, Otto Skorzeny, using gliders, and is flown to **Vienna**. After meetings with **Hitler** and German propaganda minister **Goebbels**, Mussolini agrees to form a new Fascist administration operating within the northern part of the country controlled by German forces. On 17 September, the **Italian Social Republic** is proclaimed, with its headquarters at **Salò** on Lake Garda.

American troops enter **Naples** on 1 October. Any further advance is halted by strong German positions around the great Benedictine monastery of **Monte Cassino**, on the route north towards Rome.

During the autumn and winter months, clandestine **Committees of National Liberation** are formed and **partisan units** begin to organize throughout northern and central Italy. Their main aim, in which they are largely successful, is to destabilize both the German war effort and Mussolini's 'Salò Republic' by means of acts of **sabotage** and **assassinations** calculated to provoke savage reprisals. By this means they will be able to divert valuable military resources and increase the hatred of ordinary Italians for the Nazis and their Fascist puppets.

In December, Italian forces occupying the Ionian Islands make a nominal surrender to the Allies, but this is thwarted by German troops, who embark on a massacre of Italian service personnel.

1944 **Galeazzo Ciano** is captured by the Germans, tried in Verona and sentenced to death. He is executed on 14 January. Despite frantic appeals from his daughter Edda, Ciano's wife, **Mussolini** refuses to intervene.

On 22 January, **Allied forces** land at **Anzio**, south of Rome. Defence of the beachhead involves heavy Allied losses, and the operation fails in its attempt to outflank the Germans.

On 23 March, a dustcart filled with explosives kills a wagonload of German soldiers in Via Rasella in **Rome**. As a reprisal, **335 civilians** are arrested at random and taken to the **Fosse Ardeatine** caves outside the city, where they are shot and buried. The barbarity of the outrage hardens **popular resistance** to the Nazi occupation.

Monte Cassino falls to the Allies on 18 May, after a prolonged bombardment during which most of the ancient monastery and its priceless collections of manuscripts and art treasures are destroyed. Allied troops under **US General Mark Clark** enter **Rome** on 4 June.

> **❝** A generation of men has destroyed your youth and your nation, hurling you into a heap of ruins. Amid these ruins you must carry the torch of faith and the impetus to action, rebuilding both youth and nationhood. Betrayed by fraud, violence, cowardice and criminal servility, you must fight alongside the workers in town and country to create for Italy a new history and a new people. **❞**
>
> Message left for his students by Concetto Marchesi, Rector of Padua University, before himself joining the resistance in Milan on 9 November, 1944, quoted in *Storia dell'Italia Partigiana*, Giorgio Bocca

Partisans and other war heroes

The heroism of thousands of ordinary Italians in the period 1943–45 provides ample evidence to refute – if any such rebuttal were needed – the glib popular joke according to which the 'Book of Italian War Heroes' would be the shortest in the world. The **partisan movement** in northern Italy mobilized many more fighters than the French Resistance and it proved itself more than capable, in a short space of time, in its operations against the Germans. 'Most partisan bands developed along political lines. One group in the Piedmontese district of Cuneo, for example, divided into republicans and monarchists, another in the same region was composed of ex-soldiers, while in the Veneto many were Communists. Other groups spread their net wider, even relying on the support of local industrialists who, aware of the drift of events in the Allies' favour during 1944, were reluctant to cooperate with the German war effort.

The partisans' success in pinning down German divisions, liberating major cities and asserting the triumph of anti-Fascism was assisted by innumerable acts of personal bravery in **civilian communities. Catholic clergy** aided, joined and in certain cases led partisan units, while **farmers** and their families hid and protected **Allied prisoners** on the run. As M.R.D. Foot observes in *Resistance*, 'None of these [Allied] escapes in Italy would have been conceivable without the self-sacrifice and cooperation of hundreds of thousands of the Italian rural poor: small peasants,

Following the Allies' capture of **Florence** in August, they make little progress in their advance. While partisans harass the occupation forces and those of the Salò government in towns and cities, the Germans hold the '**Gothic Line**' of defence, remaining in control of the Po valley, Lombardy, Piedmont and the Veneto over the next six months. In anti-partisan **reprisals** on 28–30 September, German troops murder nearly seven hundred people in the village of **Marzabotto**, near Bologna.

charcoal-burners, shepherds, old women tough as the soil they tilled. Even the names of most of them are lost to history. Their achievement is the more memorable as a tribute to the impact of popular feeling of twenty years of Fascism.'

It is to Italy's credit, moreover, that a larger proportion of its **Jewish community** survived the war unharmed than was the case among similar populations elsewhere in Europe. Jews were sheltered in cupboards, attics, cellars and wells, passed off as servants, nuns or priests, given false identities and smuggled along contact networks across Italy. With the knowledge of the Catholic hierarchy led by Pope Pius XII, they were hidden, along with escaped prisoners, in the neutral territory of the **Vatican** itself. Though Pius remained strongly pro-German, he made no effort to interfere with attempts by priests and bishops to save the lives of those in danger in occupied areas.

Very little of this widespread **civilian contribution** to the eventual defeat of Nazism and Fascism has ever been properly acknowledged, and Italians, for whatever reason, have never been tempted to romanticize it. In nearly every case it was offered at the greatest possible personal risk, without complaint and with no expectation of reward, in a spirit recalling the **humanity** and **solidarity** shown by Italians during the Risorgimento a century earlier.

Mussolini orders the formation of the *Brigate Nere* ('Black Brigades'), civilian **vigilante forces** intended, supposedly, to guarantee public order and the peaceful life of ordinary citizens under the Salò Republic. Their violence and brutality will become notorious during Italian Fascism's final months.

1945 In January, **Allied armies**, including **Soviet Russian** forces, break German resistance on the **Rhine** and in **Poland**, and begin to menace **Berlin**. Using the Cardinal

Archbishop of Milan, **Ildefonso Schuster**, as go-between, German SS officers now begin negotiations for the surrender of German forces in Italy. In April, Allied armies begin a major advance northwards, seizing **Bologna**, **Modena**, **Cremona** and **Mantua**. **Mussolini**, now in Mantua, evacuates his wife **Rachele** and their children to Monza, from where they will be flown to **Spain**. Remaining with him is his mistress, **Claretta Petacci**. His attempt to bargain with Cardinal Schuster and the Liberation Committees over his surrender ends in failure. On 25 April he and Claretta leave for Como with an SS escort.

On 27 April, disguised as a German soldier, Mussolini attempts to escape into **Switzerland**. Near Dongo on Lake Como he is captured by partisans and taken, with Claretta Petacci, to a farm at Azzano. On 28 April, the pair are driven to the nearby Villa Bellini, where they are shot dead by the partisan colonel **Walter Audisio**. Their bodies are taken to **Milan**, where they are hanged upside down from the girders of a half-built garage in **Piazzale Loreto** while a jeering crowd looks on. Among those forced to watch is the former secretary of the Fascist Party, **Achille Starace**, who is condemned to a similar fate. On the same day, German forces in Italy offer their **unconditional surrender**. The war in Italy is over.

> ❝ The contribution of the partisans to the Allied victory in Italy was a very considerable one, and far surpassed the most optimistic forecasts. By armed force, they helped to break the strength and morale of an enemy well superior to them in numbers. Without the partisans' victories there could not have been an Allied victory in Italy so fast, so complete, and with such light casualties. ❞

Secret report to Allied HQ by Colonel Hewitt, commander British Special Force No. 1, April 1945, quoted in *Resistance*, M.R.D. Foot

11
Modern Italy

1945–2003

taly's political reconstruction after the end of World War
II took place with startling speed. Having rejected a
return to constitutional monarchy in 1946, the nation
became a **democratic republic**, with an elected president as head of state. The Catholic Church, which remained
a powerful force in national life both socially and politically,
gave its unreserved support to the right-wing **Christian
Democrat** party. Effectively, with its numerous governments
being made up largely of the same reshuffled politicians, this
became the party of government for the next thirty years.
During this period its grip on power was reinforced by the
influence of the **USA**, which during the **Cold War** viewed
Italy as a soft target, and early on grew alarmed at the success
of the **Communist Party** in gathering popular support at
all social levels. The full extent of American intervention in
Italian affairs is still a matter of conjecture, and is unlikely –
given the culture of secrecy and suppression endemic to
Italian political life – ever to be fully disclosed. All that can
be said with certainty is that, of all Europe's postwar democracies, Italy was most obviously overshadowed by a succession of vigilant US administrations.

The **economy** of Italy during the late 1950s and 1960s
was a major success story, owing to the mobility of its population, the expansion of the public sector and a degree of
autonomy in regional and municipal government (although
both these spheres remained, broadly, under party political

control). What had endured unchanged since 19th-century unification, however, was the tangible **economic** and **social** divide between north and south. **Industry** remained concentrated largely in northern regions such as **Piedmont**, **Lombardy** and **Emilia–Romagna**, so that the **Po valley** eventually became one of the most affluent areas in Europe. But **Calabria**, **Puglia** and **Sicily** still lagged far behind, dogged by poverty, illiteracy and high unemployment. Ancient systems of **social bonding**, involving family and patron–client relationships, together with the deliberate suppression, by employers and vested interests, of independent initiative in local government were bound up in many areas with powerful criminal organizations: the Sicilian **Mafia**, the Calabrese **N'drangheta** (from the Greek *andragathos*, meaning 'wise' or 'powerful' man) and the Neapolitan **Camorra**. The links between these organizations and Christian Democrat politicians were an open secret. Requiring this support as part of its power base, the party could never in any case govern with an outright majority, owing to the inherent weakness of a system of government designed originally to prevent a concentration of power in any single area of the executive. Italian postwar politics thus became a series of **deals** and **compromises** involving all parties, including, during the early 1970s, the Communists under Enrico Berlinguer. The electorate grew increasingly cynical and disillusioned in the face of a political subculture in which the same names (**Giulio Andreotti**, with his fifty years in parliament, being the most suspiciously resilient) jockeyed for personal advantage while remaining apparently indifferent to the nation's problems. The formation of the extremist **Red Brigades** in 1970 was an inevitable by-product of this alienation.

Since the fall of the **Berlin Wall** in 1989 and the ending of the Cold War, there have been clear opportunities for change. Parties have regrouped and renamed themselves, the electoral system has been adjusted and some notable efforts have been made to improve standards in public life, chiefly by making Italy's rulers more accountable. Curiously, the most significant resistance to this process has come not so much from the politicians themselves as from Italian voters. Busy rejoicing in Italy's international leadership in such areas as fashion, football or industrial design, all too often it can seem as if the modern heirs of Dante, Verdi, Galileo, Machiavelli and Michelangelo are in general strikingly uninterested in their own history (much of which is documented and analyzed by foreigners). Paradoxically, it is precisely because of Italy's historic legacy of bad government by selfish and despotic rulers, followed by the failure of the liberal monarchy and the fraudulent triumph of Fascism, that Italy now feels reluctant to face the challenging task of reorganizing her executive structures. A strong feeling of 'better the devil you know' has made Italians reluctant either to strengthen the still frail democratic system or to introduce adequate levels of accountability into public life. The collapse of the '**Clean Hands**' judicial investigations in 1996 and the re-election of **Silvio Berlusconi's Forza Italia** in 2001 suggest that modern Italy (still a deeply conservative society, its passion for consumer novelties aside) is happier with the traditions of its past than with the responsibility of shaping a political future.

1945 Following the end of hostilities in Italy, the form of the country's future government becomes a pressing issue. On 9 May, King Victor Emmanuel III abdicates in favour of his son Umberto. Though never crowned, the new king is known as **Umberto II**.

A caretaker government under Ivanoe Bonomi resigns, and **Ferruccio Parri**, leader of the powerful partisan grouping known as the **Action Party**, becomes prime minister. The new government is faced with a massive task of **postwar**

reconstruction. In November, after failing to restore the war-damaged economy and introduce welfare provision,

Neo-realist cinema

Neo-realism in the Italian cinema is reckoned by experts to have lasted for little more than a decade, but the directors who emerged during the immediate postwar years continue to be seen as some of Italy's finest, and the impact of neo-realism on world film-making is felt to this day. Dealing with social and political issues against a working-class or lower-bourgeois background, neo-realism relied heavily on on-location shooting, amateur actors and techniques more usually associated with documentary film-making. Both the earliest neo-realist essay, *Ossessione* (1942), and the film which is seen as an epitaph for the genre, *Rocco e i suoi Fratelli* (*Rocco and his Brothers*, 1960), were made by the same director, **Luchino Visconti**. But it was **Roberto Rossellini** (1906–77) who, in *Roma, città aperta* (*Rome, Open City*, 1945) and *Paisà* (1947), created two of the most compelling and influential examples of the genre, based on the nation's experience of suffering, heroism and betrayal during the years 1943–45, interwoven with deft touches of humour and lyricism.

The evolution of a distinctively Italian national style was only sharpened by the fact that a number of early neo-realist films could not be distributed in Italy until after the war had ended. Under Mussolini, any form of social and political veracity had been withheld from Italian audiences: the lavishly equipped film studios of Rome's **Cinecittà** produced only Fascist bombast. So the realism Italian directors practised – cinema sourced from life in its most ordinary and recognizable forms – was of inherent value in itself. Within Italy, films such as Vittorio de Sica's *Ladri di Biciclette* (*Bicycle Thieves*, 1948) and Giuseppe de Santis's *Riso Amaro* (*Bitter Rice*, 1949) were powerful sources of inspiration to younger directors such as **Pier Paolo Pasolini**, **Ermanno Olmi** and (to some degree) **Federico Fellini**. Neo-realism's influence beyond Italy, meanwhile, may be seen in the work of film-makers as diverse as Satyajit Ray, Robert Altman and Pedro Almodóvar.

Parri and his government are forced to resign. A large-scale **anti-Fascist purge** of state and civic institutions has antagonized many Italians. Various partisan groups organize their own **revenge killings**: as many as 15,000 people are reckoned to have been murdered in this way.

A new government is formed under the leadership of **Alcide de Gasperi**, the first Catholic prime minister since Italy's unification. He restores public confidence by ending the purges and returning most of the state's administrative machinery to ex-Fascist civil servants.

Roberto Rossellini's film *Roma, città aperta* (*Rome, Open City*), set against the background of the German occupation after 1943, establishes a new **neo-realist** style in Italian cinema.

1946 On 2 June, a **referendum** is held to decide whether Italy is to remain a **monarchy** or become a **republic**. A

© THE KOBAL COLLECTION

Still from Vittorio de Sica's *Ladri di Biciclette* ('Bicycle Thieves')

republican majority emerges in northern and central areas. Southern Italy remains firmly monarchist, and this liberal-conservative split will characterize Italian politics from now on. The ultimate result – 54 percent in favour of a republic (with one million spoiled papers) – sends **Umberto II** into exile in Portugal.

Elections held in conjunction with the referendum return de Gasperi's **Christian Democrat** Party to power. The new government, together with an opposition led by Communists and Socialists, drafts a constitution for Italy's restored democracy: a bicameral system consisting of a **Chamber of Deputies** and a **Senate**, both elected. The electoral system is one of **proportional representation**, **ministers** will be responsible to parliament, and the **president** is to be a symbolic elected head of state, intervening in government only when the fall of an administration requires him to nominate a new prime minister. **Judges** will be independent of government control, and a wide range of administrative powers is devolved to the **regions**. One especially controversial article guarantees the close links, established by the 1929 Concordat, between the secular state and the **Catholic Church**.

1947 The **Treaty of Paris**, drafted by the victorious Allied governments, forces Italy to renounce all claims to Libya, Ethiopia and the **Mediterranean colonies** established under Fascism (Albania, Dalmatia, Fiume and the Dodecanese).

Under pressure from the **USA** and **Pope Pius XII**, as well as from right-wing political interests in southern Italy, de Gasperi excludes the **Communist** and **Socialist** parties from a coalition government.

Vittorio de Sica directs *Ladri di Biciclette* (*Bicycle Thieves*), the most successful of several neo-realist films which he describes as 'struggling against a lack of human solidarity and society's indifference to suffering'.

1948 **Elections** establish the **Christian Democrats** as the dominant party of government, bolstered by support from centre-right parties led by **Republicans** and **Liberals**. The **Communists**, led by **Palmiro Togliatti**, will continue to draw their principal support from northern industrial areas and the farming regions of Emilia-Romagna and Tuscany.

1950 Pope Pius XII proclaims the Catholic dogma of the Assumption of the Virgin Mary.

1952 The distinguished literary critic and philosopher Benedetto Croce dies in Naples.

1954 A longstanding dispute with Yugoslavia concerning possession of **Trieste**, now under control of a Communist regime led by **Marshal Tito**, ends with an international commission handing it over to Italy.

Talks in Paris between France, the German Federal Republic, Belgium, the Netherlands, Luxemburg and Italy lead to the establishment of a **Western European Union**.

Italy's first **television channel**, controlled by the state monopoly RAI, begins broadcasting.

1955 At a conference in **Messina**, the six members of the Western European Union discuss terms for an economic pact designed to create a **Common Market**, forerunner of the present European Union.

The Christian Democrat **Giovanni Gronchi** becomes president of the republic.

1956 In a series of articles in the journal *Nuovi Argomenti*, the Communist leader **Palmiro Togliatti** seeks to promote 'polycentrism', the notion of Communist parties existing independently of Soviet control. The traditional **Stalinist** wing of the party reacts unfavourably, and a further crisis ensues when Russian troops invade **Hungary**.

As many as 400,000 members quit the party, but it never-theless manages to recover support over the next decade.

1957 The **Treaty of Rome**, ratified by the six member states, establishes the Common Market.

The 32nd Congress of the **Italian Socialist Party** (PSI) votes for a split with the **Communists** (PCI), their traditional parliamentary allies. This move to the right allows the Socialists to join the **Christian Democrats** (DC) in a coalition.

1958 The 'Merlin Law', named after the politician who devised it, causes controversy by closing down Italy's licensed brothels, an important source of police information.

Appointment and supervision of judges is entrusted to a **Supreme Judiciary Council**, formed by senior lawyers. This ensures freedom from government interference, but divides the judges into politicized liberal and conservative groupings. Judges are free to investigate politicians, union bosses and business leaders, with no control from central government.

Giuseppe Tommasi di Lampedusa publishes his novel *Il gattopardo* (*The Leopard*). Based on the lives of members of his Sicilian aristocratic forebears during the Risorgimento, it makes wider reference to the discontents and baffled expectations of Italy since unification. Selling a million copies within a year and soon turned into an epic movie by **Luchino Visconti**, it becomes the most successful novel in Italian literary history.

Pope Pius XII dies. His reputation as '**Hitler's Pope**', who remained silent on the fate of the Jews in Nazi Germany, will be hotly contested by many Catholics who view him as the saviour of the Church in troubled times. A movement for his canonization begins.

Cardinal Angelo Roncalli is elected pope as **John XXIII**. Though conservative by temperament, he perceives a need for change if Catholicism is to survive, both in Italy and in the wider world.

The period of Italian prosperity known as the '**economic miracle**' begins. Monetary stability, favourable lending rates, low labour costs and the end of state protectionism encourage rapid growth and competitiveness. As a result, this period also witnesses a massive **economic migration** from the backward and impoverished south to the industrial north. The economy additionally benefits from the promotion of Italy as an international tourist destination.

1959 Pope John XXIII summons the **Second Vatican Council** to debate reforms within the Church and to renew its spiritual life.

Federico Fellini's film *La dolce vita* is released. Starring **Marcello Mastroianni** and **Anita Ekberg**, its classic images of glitz and hedonism in postwar Rome give international currency to the word *paparazzo*, used to describe celebrity-chasing photographers.

Michelangelo Antonioni releases *L'Avventura*, the first of four films starring the actress **Monica Vitti** which together offer an extended critique of various aspects of modern Italian life.

1962 The Christian Democrat **Antonio Segni** is elected president of the republic.

The national school-leaving age is raised to 14.

The Second Vatican Council begins its first session, laying its principal stress on ecumenical links with other churches and the ultimate unity of all Christians.

Luchino Visconti's film *Rocco e i suoi fratelli* (*Rocco and his Brothers*), is released. One of the last major essays in the postwar Italian realist style, it tells the story, gloomy and melodramatic, of a family of southern Italians seeking work in Milan.

1963 **Pope John XXIII** dies, having gained the admiration of Catholics and non-Catholics alike for his ecumenical initiatives. His mixture of simple piety with a humane and approachable manner (observing wryly that 'anyone can be pope; the proof of this is that I have become one') has significantly changed the image of the papacy for the better. He is succeeded by Giovanni Battista Montini, as **Paul VI**. A more remote, authoritarian figure, Paul VI will oversee further sessions of the continuing Vatican Council, implementing important changes in Catholic liturgy.

> ❝ It often happens that I wake up at night and begin to think about a serious problem and decide I must tell the pope about it. Then I wake up completely and remember I am the pope. ❞
>
> Pope John Paul XXIII

1964 Antonio Segni retires from the presidency for health reasons. The Social Democrat **Giuseppe Saragat** is elected as his successor.

Palmiro Togliatti dies at Yalta on a visit to the Soviet leader **Nikita Khrushchev**, abruptly ending his highly successful leadership of the Italian **Communist Party**, now the largest in the west. Over a million people attend his funeral.

1965 A law is passed enabling Italian courts to bar suspected members of the **Mafia** from entering or re-entering **Sicily**.

1966 Heavy and prolonged rainfall throughout northern and central Italy culminates in disastrous **floods**, causing serious damage in **Florence** and **Venice**.

Pope John XXIII

1968 Pope Paul VI issues his encyclical *Humanae vitae*, condemning the use of artificial contraception.

The controversial film *Teorema* (**Theorem**) by **Pier Paolo Pasolini** is banned by the government and Pasolini is charged with obscenity. He is subsequently acquitted on **artistic grounds.**

1969 The worst **strikes** in Italy's postwar history take place during a so-called 'hot autumn' of **industrial unrest** and **terrorism**. A bomb containing eight kilos of explosives explodes outside a bank in Milan's Piazza Fontana, killing sixteen and leaving ninety wounded. The outrage is attributed to left-wing activists, two of whom, **Pietro Valpreda** and **Giuseppe Pinelli**, are arrested. Pinelli dies during police interrogation, supposedly as the result of falling out of a window. No satisfactory explanation is given, now or subsequently. Later accusations will shift the blame for the bombing to **neo-Fascist groups** and the Italian playwright **Dario Fo** will later base his surreal satire *Accidental Death of an Anarchist* on the investigation.

1970 In Milan **Renato Curcio**, a 25-year-old sociology lecturer, founds the urban guerrilla group known as the **Red Brigades**.

Work begins on the new port of **Gioia Tauro** in Calabria. Officially intended as an export outlet for the steel industry, it is in fact a ruinously expensive waste of public funds, most of which are embezzled or expropriated by corrupt local politicians and the **N'drangheta**, the local version of the **Mafia**.

1971 The Christian Democrat **Giovanni Leone** becomes president of the republic.

1972 **Giulio Andreotti**, leader of the Christian Democrats, becomes prime minister. A skilful operator with impeccable right-wing Catholic credentials, he has been active in

The Red Brigades

The Red Brigades began as an extreme left-wing group, the Italian equivalent to urban guerrilla movements in France, Germany and the USA, such as the **Baader-Meinhoff** group and the **Symbionese Liberation Army**. Their methods were violent, targeting government ministers, parliamentary deputies, university professors and other establishment figures, as well as an American general. In 1977 Red Brigade members shot **Indro Montanelli**, a veteran journalist and editor of the conservative daily newspaper *Il Giornale*, four times in the legs. Though the capture and subsequent execution, in 1978, of the former Prime Minister **Aldo Moro** was the Brigades' most notorious operation, their activities continued throughout the 1980s. Despite the arrest of hundreds of Brigade members, the authorities have notably failed to identify either the heart of the organization or its real objectives. What is clear is that it continues a long tradition of **political violence** in Italy stretching back as far as the Risorgimento, as well as a national heritage of **anarchism**, dating from the late 19th century. More significantly, it reflects a deep-rooted **popular discontent** with the structures of postwar democracy within the Italian Second Republic. After a period of quiescence in the early 1990s, the Brigades resumed their activity in 1999, killing a PDS politician and, most recently, an economics professor at Modena University.

Italian politics since 1945. Though this particular government is short-lived, Andreotti will remain a dominant political figure during the next twenty years.

1973 Italy begins to experience the effects of the global economic crisis occasioned by the rise in **oil prices** demanded by OPEC. Its **inflation** and **public sector spending** are soon the highest in Europe.

Enrico Berlinguer, Communist Party leader, begins talks with **Christian Democrat** politicians concerned to secure their party's position, threatened as it is by widespread industrial action, terrorist activity and financial irregularities. The **Communists**, concerned at neo-Fascist infiltration of state institutions, are ready to strike a power-sharing deal with the parliamentary right. In a series of articles in the journal *Rinascita*, Berlinguer offers a '**historic compromise**' with the Christian Democrats, designed to save the basic framework of constitutional democracy in a troubled nation.

1974 In a **referendum** on the issue of **divorce**, hitherto prohibited in Italy, sixty percent of the population vote in favour of its legalization. This is a significant defeat for the Christian Democrats and an indicator of the Catholic Church's weakening grip on Italian society.

Renato Curcio, leader of the **Red Brigades**, is arrested, but later freed in a raid organized by his partner **Margherita Cagol**. The Brigades step up their campaign of kidnapping, sabotage and killing.

1975 **Pier Paolo Pasolini** is murdered on a beach at Ostia near Rome, ending a life of alienation and contradictions – whether as a homosexual who angered liberals by his support for traditional Catholic teaching on abortion and divorce, or as the Marxist director of *Il Vangelo secondo Matteo* (***The Gospel according to St Matthew***, 1964), fiercely condemned by the Church but viewed by many as the most moving treatment on film of Christ's life. His film *Salò* used the visual language of pornography to examine Mussolini's post-1943 republic and its effect on Italy. His murder, by a gay hustler, is viewed by some at the time as an establishment conspiracy to silence one of the most outspoken critics of modern Italian government and society. Although the crime is later shown to have no political undertones, this suspicion characterizes the growing mistrust among Italians both of their rulers and of the larger vested interests controlling them.

The poet **Eugenio Montale** is awarded the Nobel Prize for Literature.

Reform of the state broadcasting organization **RAI**, hitherto under Christian Democrat control, allows some measure of **Socialist** and **Communist** influence in two of the television channels.

1976 The Constitutional Court removes the **broadcasting monopoly** from RAI, the state radio and television services, opening the way for private channels.

A new national daily paper, *La Repubblica*, is launched in Rome. It will quickly become Italy's major left-of-centre journal of record, challenging the more conservative *Corriere della Sera* and *La Stampa* for the attentions of an informed and intelligent readership.

In response to the atmosphere of crisis prevailing in labour relations throughout Italy, **Giulio Andreotti** forms a '**government of national solidarity**'. Comprising representatives from almost all the leading parties, Communists included, it represents a triumph for Andreotti as a broker of political deals.

1978 The veteran politician **Aldo Moro**, president of the Christian Democrat party and former prime minister, is kidnapped by the **Red Brigades**. Moro is compelled by his captors to write letters containing a variety of charges against former political colleagues, while the Brigades demand the release of activists currently imprisoned. After considerable deliberation, the government and opposition parties refuse this demand, and Moro is shot by Brigade members.

Pope Paul VI dies and is succeeded by Cardinal Albino Luciani, patriarch of Venice, as **John Paul I**, his double name a tribute to the two previous popes. Having taken office on 26 August he dies on 28 September, as a result of

© CORBIS

Aldo Moro, photographed here during the 55 days of captivity prior to his murder by the *Brigate Rosse*

medical neglect. The Vatican's attempt to conceal both the causes and the circumstances of his death will lead to rumours that he was murdered at the instigation of conservative elements within the Church and the government.

Cardinal Karol Wojtyla, archbishop of Cracow, is elected pope as **John Paul II**. The first non-Italian pope since the 16th century, he embarks on an energetic papacy aimed at reconciling Western and Eastern churches, carrying the Christian message in person to Catholic communities across the world. His profound conservatism is mistrusted by many both within Italy and without, but his role as a charismatic figure dedicated to world peace makes him popular and revered internationally.

The veteran Socialist politician **Alessandro Pertini** becomes president of Italy. He is regarded by many Italians as a 'safe pair of hands', a man of comparative integrity in a political landscape increasingly clouded with **corruption** and **clientelism**.

The film director **Ermanno Olmi** releases *L'albero degli zoccoli* (*The Tree of Wooden Clogs*), a portrait of peasant life in late 19th-century Lombardy which studiously avoids the political stance commonly adopted by other Italian film-makers during this period.

1979 In a general election, the Communist vote suffers a marked decline, prompted by dissatisfaction with Enrico Berlinguer's 'historic compromise'.

Nilde Iotti becomes the first woman to be elected speaker of the Italian parliament.

1980 An Alitalia DC-9 **passenger jet** crashes into the sea off the island of Ustica, apparently hit by a **Libyan missile**. The causes of the disaster remain shrouded in mystery, and many suspect that the true culprit was a **stray warhead** fired from an American naval vessel during a training exercise. A **bomb** explodes in the principal railway station at **Bologna**, killing 85 people and wounding 203 others. The left-wing terrorist organization **Ordine nuovo** claims responsibility.

John Paul II and Italy

Few postwar figures have divided Italians as deeply as Pope John Paul II. On the one hand, the appointment of a **non-Italian pontiff** was resented by many who viewed the papacy as a quasi-national institution and saw no reason to challenge the system that had prevailed for almost 500 years, and which guaranteed an Italian pope in the Vatican. On the other, Karol Wojtyla's election was earnestly welcomed by many who believed that it was precisely the parochialism of the Catholic Church and its 'Rome-centrism' that posed the greatest threat to its survival. What was more, a Polish pope could foster dialogue with **Eastern Orthodox** communions and use his personal experience to bring home more fully the threat posed to western freedoms by Soviet-style regimes.

During his papacy (the longest since that of Pius IX) Italian attitudes to John Paul have remained ambivalent. His world tours and high-profile public appearances are sometimes mocked, and his deep religious conservatism and enthusiastic addition of many fresh saints and martyrs to the calendar are often criticized. He has nevertheless laboured successfully to revive Catholicism's role in the life of the nation. Papal injunctions on **contraception**, **abortion** and **homosexuality** may be out of step with secular law and custom, but charismatic movements such as CL (Comunione e Liberazione – **Communion and Liberation**) have gained a wide following. The role of priests and bishops in the community is a constructive one, moreover, which no longer necessarily indicates a political alignment with the Catholic right.

The charismatic Catholic movement **Comunione e Liberazione**, originally founded in 1969, gains impetus from the mood of renewal within the Church, inspired by the new pope. During the next ten years its membership will substantially increase and its rallies, using American-style evangelical techniques to promote conservative Catholicism among young people, will attract major news coverage in the Italian media.

An **earthquake** in the Irpinia region near **Naples** claims 6000 lives. Of the considerable relief fund allotted by the government, very little will actually reach the homeless population of the area. Towns and villages remain in a ruined condition for well over a decade. The scandal, like that of Gioia Tauro, is seen by some as typifying southern corruption, and by others as symbolizing Italy's wider inability to regulate public life with adequate moral standards.

1981 In Verona, the **Red Brigades** capture the American general **James Lee Dozier**, a high-ranking **Nato** officer, in protest against Nato as 'the multi-national army of the imperialist counter-revolution'.

A Bulgarian Turk, Mehmet Ali Agca, attempts to kill **Pope John Paul II** during a public appearance in Rome. After recovering from the bullet wounds, the pope forgives his attacker.

The failure is announced of **Banco Ambrosiano**, one of Italy's largest banks. Its chairman, **Roberto Calvi**, is prosecuted for fraud. Proceedings are also begun against a high-ranking Vatican cleric, **Archbishop Paul Marcinkus**, whose Institute of Religious Affairs has laundered funds on Calvi's behalf.

A search begins for **Licio Gelli**, a businessman suspected of being grand master of the secret masonic lodge known as **P2** (secret societies are forbidden under Italian law). The lodge, which includes leading figures from all walks of Italian life and has **Mafia** connections, is a right-wing organization dedicated to suppressing the pervasive influence of **Communism**. Gelli flees to Switzerland but is later arrested and detained. The P2 investigation will continue for twelve years.

General Carlo Alberto dalla Chiesa, formerly commander of a special anti-terrorist unit, is appointed prefect of **Sicily**. Shortly afterwards, he and his wife are assassinated in a Palermo street. The crime triggers demands for tougher **anti-Mafia** measures. Police are authorized to inspect private bank accounts, and any link to the Mafia is made a crime.

1982 General Dozier is found alive in Padua and freed by local police.

The disgraced financier **Roberto Calvi**, now identified as a P2 member, escapes to London and is found hanged under **Blackfriars Bridge**. A coroner's jury returns a verdict of suicide, but the unofficial belief of most commentators is that Calvi was murdered, possibly (given certain details of the position of the corpse) at the behest of fellow lodge-members.

1983 Bettino Craxi becomes Italy's first **Socialist prime minister** since the postwar re-establishment of democracy.

1984 Michele Sindona, an Italian banker and former **P2** lodge member serving a jail sentence in the USA, is handed over to Italian justice to serve as a key witness in major investigations into **political corruption**.

1985 Alessandro Pertini retires as president and is succeeded by the Christian Democrat **Francesco Cossiga**.

1986 Nineteen members of the terrorist organization **Ordine nuovo** are arrested for involvement in the Bologna bombing. Tried and sentenced to life imprisonment, fifteen of them are later acquitted.

Bettino Craxi's **Socialist coalition** collapses, following three years in power which have made it Italy's longest-lasting government since 1945. After 35 days of political crisis, Craxi re-emerges as prime minister.

Michele Sindona is reported as having committed **suicide** by cyanide poisoning in his prison cell. Murder is suspected, but so far not proven.

A series of high-profile arrests and trials c.
begins in **Sicily**. The presiding judges inclu⌐
Falcone and **Paolo Borsellino**, both noteɑ
assiduousness and determination. Intense media ι
will focus on these trials. Their process and outcome
viewed as an indicator of the Italian state's ability to preserve the rule of law amid a growing atmosphere of scandal
and corruption within a stagnant party-political system.

1987 **Bettino Craxi** is forced to resign once more, amid
rumours of involvement in **financial corruption**.

The Mafia boss **Salvo Lima**, former mayor of **Palermo**, is
murdered. The crime is linked **by several newspapers**
with his political associates in the upper echelons of the
Christian Democrat Party.

1988 After posing nude in Venice's Piazza San Marco, the
'porno-diva' Ilona Staller, known as *La Cicciolina*, is
denied official immunity as a serving member of parliament
(to which she has been recently and controversially elected
on a Radical Party ticket).

1990 The **Leaning Tower of Pisa** is closed to tourists by
the municipality, in response to concerns at the speed at
which it appears to be tilting. An international team of
experts will eventually rescue the medieval structure by
means of a system of braces and underpinning.

1991 **Gianfranco Fini**, new leader of the neo-Fascist MSI
(Movimento Sociale Italiano, Italian Social Movement)
relaunches the organization as the **AN** (Alleanza Nazionale,
or National Alliance). The image he adopts of a sharp-
suited businessman is calculated to appeal to a younger,
more affluent breed of far-right voter. His programme will
continue to stress traditional Catholic values, together with
an 'Italy for the Italians' policy with regard to asylum-
seekers and immigration.

The Mafia

... described by one of Sicily's leading
...scia, as less an organization than a state of
...owever, it is still very much alive. Although
... its first known appearance in a document
... rabic derivation from *mu'afah*, meaning
...k', suggests that it has much older roots in
the Musl... ...the Middle Ages. From shielding peasants
against bailiffs, tax collectors and the demands of absentee
aristocratic landlords, the Mafia, known as **Cosa Nostra** in
western Sicily and **Stidda** in the south, had by the early 20th
century become such a significant force in the island that
Mussolini devoted special resources to its extermination. The
Allied invasion in 1943 was able to exploit American Cosa Nostra
connections, and in the postwar period the 'honoured society'
held the island as a **Christian Democrat** fiefdom, with occasional
turf-wars between *mafioso* families.

During the 1980s, as the Mafia became more heavily involved
with the **drug market**, it was glamorized by Hollywood in the

1992 On 23 May, **Giovanni Falcone**, one of the judges in
the continuing Mafia investigations, is assassinated outside
Palermo.

Giulio Andreotti, on behalf of Italy, signs the **Maastricht
Treaty**, under the terms of which Italy is compelled to adapt
its financial practices to agreed European Union standards.

Oscar Luigi Scalfaro is elected president of the republic.
A 74-year-old Christian Democrat, he has a reputation for
integrity: parliament's choice of such a figure reflects the
widely held view that Falcone's murder represents a threat
to democracy.

On 25 July, Falcone's fellow judge **Paolo Borsellino** is
murdered by the Mafia.

famous *Godfather* movies. As the organization extended its activities in Italian mainland cities, demands for stricter government action multiplied. A series of **arrests** and **trials** began under a strong media spotlight, culminating in the murder of judges Falcone and Borsellino and the arrest of Giulio Andreotti, charged with direct links to the organization. **Antonino Giuffre**, second-in-command of the **Cosa Nostra**, turned 'supergrass' after his arrest in 2002. Known as *'Manuzzo'* ('The Hand': his right hand is crippled by polio), he has implicated one of Silvio Berlusconi's closest aides, **Marcello dell'Utri** (who was also one of the founders of Forza Italia), as having offered to rein in the police, soften jail conditions for *mafiosi* and alter laws regarding the confiscation of Mafia property, all in return for the Mafia's electoral support. But despite legal sanctions, police trawls and multiple prosecutions, the Mafia nevertheless remains a powerful force in Sicilian life, with its close-knit clan values enforced by women as much as men. Perhaps Leonardo Sciascia was right after all in identifying it as 'a mentality, and by the same token much harder to destroy'.

The *Mani pulite* (**Clean Hands**) operation begins, an attempt by members of the judiciary, led by **Antonio di Pietro**, to purge the state of the **corruption** and **clientelism** which have undermined public confidence in government during the previous twenty years. A number of politicians are investigated, including **Bettino Craxi** and his justice minister **Claudio Martelli**, as well as prominent businessmen. Multiple arrests lead to several suicides, but for the time being a groundswell of public opinion continues to support di Pietro and his fellow judges.

A period of **disillusion** with traditional Italian political alignments begins. **Local elections** demonstrate the dramatic decline of the **Christian Democrats** since the end of the Cold War and its accompanying threats of

Communist hegemony. Voters are instead moving towards new parties such as the **Northern League** (described by a Council of Europe report as 'racist and xenophobic'), the **Greens** and the neo-Fascist **National Alliance**.

The veteran politician **Giulio Andreotti** is accused of involvement with the **Mafia**, and his political immunity is lifted. The judicial enquiry is stalled at an early stage by obstructive tactics at a number of levels, and the case against Andreotti, which alleges links with the *mafioso* mayor of Palermo **Salvo Lima**, does not proceed to trial.

A **referendum** on the **electoral system** shows the nation to be broadly in favour of a move from the current proportional 'list' to majority voting. Other proposed political changes include the abolition of the ministries of agriculture and tourism (80 percent in favour), legalization of drugs (55 percent), and stricter government controls over environmental pollution (82 percent).

1993 In April, **Carlo Azeglio Ciampi**, governor of the **Bank of Italy**, becomes prime minister at the head of a **coalition**. At least twelve of the ministers in his cabinet are, like himself, extra-parliamentary. The three members of the PDSI (**Social Democratic Party**, formerly the Communist Party) who are included resign in protest when the Chamber of Deputies votes to block the prosecution on corruption charges of the disgraced former prime minister **Bettino Craxi**.

The right-wing **Northern League**, led by **Umberto Bossi**, proposes a federal division of Italy into three separate states. Capitalizing on the resentments felt in **Lombardy** and the **Veneto** against southern economic migrants and foreign asylum-seekers, the League has gathered considerable support and now becomes an important force in national politics.

Salvatore 'Toto' Riina, the *'capo di tutti capi'* ('boss of bosses') of the Mafia, is arrested and convicted. He receives multiple life sentences for crimes including the murders of Falcone and Borsellino. Although he has been previously convicted twenty years ago, and was supposedly a fugitive, he has lived a life of luxury in Sicily untroubled by the police.

Salvatore 'Toto' Riina, shortly after his arrest in Palermo

1994 A general election is won by **Forza Italia**, a brash new right-wing party, the brainchild of the businessman and media tycoon **Silvio Berlusconi**. He heads a coalition which includes the **Northern League** and the **National Alliance**.

> ❝ I begged him [Berlusconi] not to go into politics. 'If I don't, they'll tear me to shreds,' he replied. 'They'll tear you to shreds if you do,' I said. ❞
>
> Indro Montanelli, former friend and staunch critic of Berlusconi, in the daily newspaper *Corriere della Sera*

Silvio Berlusconi

The success story of Silvio Berlusconi is one of the more remarkable phenomena of Italian politics during the 1990s. How, non-Italians ask, can a man accused of involvement in various kinds of **financial malpractice** and associated with the **P2 masonic lodge** whose existence seemed to threaten the very fabric of the Italian state, coast so easily through troubled political waters to become one of his country's most popular prime ministers? As a businessman he was a shrewd operator, buying the **Standa** department store chain in 1979 and building up his **Fininvest** conglomerate empire with the acquisition of various television channels, the newspaper *Il Giornale*, the respected publishing house **Mondadori** and the **AC Milan** football club. The

Silvio Berlusconi at the Italian Senate

© CORBIS

latter gave him a name for his political party ('*Forza Italia!*' being the national soccer rallying cry), a streamlined version of the former **Christian Democrat** alignment, stressing law and order, Catholic family values and a clampdown on **immigrants**. With characteristic swagger, he heralded his sideways move from media mogul to politician with the announcement, 'I am tired of being Silvio Berlusconi: I want a heroic life.'

Berlusconi's first administration, which took office in 1994, failed to deliver on its promise of dramatically lowering **unemployment**, and was seen as trying to ride roughshod over legal and **constitutional processes** to attain its goals. But in 2001 the Italian electorate was prepared to forgive him, returning his right-wing coalition to power once more. To many conservatives he represents the triumph of the typical Italian entrepreneur: smart, dapper and resourceful, putting family first and careful to be seen as a respectable churchgoer. To the more sceptical, his ascendancy merely underlines the reluctance of Italians to mature politically, their inherent unease with democracy and their preference for simple answers and firm leadership over the complexities and blurred edges of consensus politics. They condemn what they see as Berlusconi's deliberate manipulation of the judicial system so as to save his own skin: in November 2002 a law was approved allowing defendants to have their trial moved to a different court if they suspected presiding judges may be prejudiced against them. This would, conveniently, further delay Berlusconi's own trial on charges of corruption, specifically for bribing a judge during a corporate takeover battle in 1986. His megalomania (he described himself on one occasion as '**the Lord's anointed**') and the crass vulgarity of his personal style have also infuriated his opponents. Such misgivings have been echoed abroad, notably by the *Economist* magazine, which raised a storm in Italy by pronouncing him 'unfit to lead the government of any country'.

Bettino Craxi escapes to Tunisia and is sentenced in his absence by the Milan judges.

Berlusconi's government falls after only a year in power. His personal style, dictatorial and impatient when confronted with the constitutional process, has embarrassed and antagonized voters. The '**Clean Hands**' judges have earlier announced that they are investigating him and other family members on fraud charges.

1996 The establishment retaliates against 'Clean Hands' with accusations of abuse of power directed at **Antonio di Pietro**. The court hearings and investigations have struck hard at the infrastructure of favours and patronage underpinning Italian life. Having initially welcomed the judges' initiative, Italians now show themselves reluctant to abandon these traditional behaviour patterns in favour of greater integrity. Di Pietro resigns, though subsequently deemed innocent of the charges against him, and the 'Clean Hands' initiative collapses.

Venice's 200-year-old **Teatro La Fenice** is destroyed by fire during restoration work. Initially believed to have been an accident, the fire is later found to have been started deliberately by builders anxious to avoid a heavy fine. Premature announcements of imminent and rapid reconstruction lead to angry recriminations within the city. Rebuilding eventually begins, but the failure of two successive municipal authorities to speed up the process is taken by many as symptomatic of a wider Italian malaise, and the ruin, with its weed-grown scaffolding, becomes a symbol of a culture of blame and buck-passing now prevalent in public life.

Left-wing parties score notable success in **local elections**.

At a general election a **centre-left government** sweeps to power, led by the economist **Romano Prodi** and dedicated to reducing the budget deficit and privatizing state monopolies. His cabinet includes Carlo Azeglio Ciampi and Massimo d'Alema, leader of the PDSI. The left-wing coalition is known to voters as the *Ulivo* ('olive tree'), while the right-wing Berlusconi-Bossi-Fini axis is dubbed the *Polo delle Liberte* ('pole of freedoms').

1997 Increasing numbers of **immigrants** are now entering Italy, principally via southern ports and their adjacent coastlines, from northwest Africa, Tunisia and Morocco, as well as from Albania. Right-wing fears of criminal activity and erosion of the job-market lead to demonstrations and sporadic violence in northern areas.

The **Northern League** calls for the Po valley area, which it now refers to as 'Padania' (after the Latin name for the river) to be separated from Italy.

1998 A new **left-wing government** takes power, headed by PDSI leader **Massimo d'Alema**. Its survival is immediately threatened by challenges from the unreconstructed Communist Party known as **Rifondazione Communista**.

2001 The d'Alema government falls, and in the ensuing general election the Polo axis, led by Berlusconi's **Forza Italia**, emerges triumphant. **Silvio Berlusconi** becomes prime minister for the second time.

2002 Controversially, **Padre Pio** is canonized by Pope John Paul II in June. Pio, born **Francesco Forgio** in 1887, was a Franciscan friar who died in 1968. He had been investigated twice by the Vatican for alleged fraud and sexual misconduct, and had been banned from saying Mass in public for a decade in the 1930s.

In November **Giulio Andreotti** is found guilty by an appeal court of ordering the murder of **Mino Pecorelli**, a journalist and editor of the magazine *Osservatore Politico*: in

1979 Pecorelli was shot dead by the Mafia in Rome. Andreotti is sentenced to 24 years' imprisonment, pending the hearing of his case in the **Supreme Court**. At the trial, Berlusconi refuses to testify.

2003 Giovanni Agnelli, chairman of **Fiat**, dies of cancer. The iconic **Fiat Autos** has long been locked in a downward spiral. Declining demand, criticism from both trade unions and Silvio Berlusconi over massive redundancies, and plummeting share prices have all increased the likelihood that Italy's largest company may pass into the hands of America's **General Motors**.

Italy's **Supreme Court** rejects Berlusconi's appeal for his corruption trial – he stands accused of having bribed a judge in Rome in 1986 – to be moved to **Brescia**. Berlusconi had alleged that Milan's judges were politically biased against him.

> **❝** If, in taking care of everyone else's interests, I also take care of my own, you can't talk of a conflict of interest. **❞**
>
> Silvio Berlusconi

books

books

Certain periods of Italian history have inevitably commanded more attention than others. The Renaissance has, understandably, inspired a copious literature, whereas it is harder to find an in-depth work on the 17th and 18th centuries even in English translation from the Italian. A well-stocked library is obviously the best starting point for serious study but most of the books recommended here are easy enough to find. Where a book is published under a different imprint in the UK and US, two publishers are listed; where a book is currently out of print it is marked o/p.

General histories

Christopher Duggan *A Concise History of Italy* (Cambridge University Press). An excellent outline of Italy's overall historical development, although the author does specialize in the 19th and 20th centuries and, accordingly, much of the book focuses on this period.

Denys Hay (ed.) *The Longman History of Italy* (Longman). The best available historical survey in English, it is divided into eight volumes by different authors (most, but not all, listed separately in the sections below). The series has the admirable aim of embracing cultural as well as historical developments, and chapters are devoted, where relevant, to individual cities and states.

George Holmes (ed.) *The Oxford Illustrated History of Italy* (Oxford University Press). Somewhat impressionistic in certain areas – notably when covering the Roman empire and the 17th and 18th centuries – this is nevertheless a useful and absorbing overview. The chapters on the medieval and Renaissance eras, and on Italy post-1870, are particularly good, whilst the illustrations are striking and original.

Ancient Rome

E.T. Salmon *The Making of Roman Italy* (Thames & Hudson; Cornell University Press o/p). A comprehensive account of the ways in which Rome conquered and absorbed Italy's various peoples and cultures to create the unified political state which became the world's first superpower.

Ronald Syme *The Roman Revolution* (Oxford University Press). Originally published in 1939, this remains the classic analysis of the crucial events surrounding Rome's passage from republic to empire, culminating in the triumph of Augustus Caesar.

Peter Garnsey and **Richard Saller** *The Roman Empire: Economy, Society and Culture* (Gerald Duckworth & Co; University of California Press). How the empire as a social and administrative concept succeeded and endured forms the basis of this shrewd structural analysis of Rome's power over her subject peoples.

Robin Lane Fox *Pagans and Christians* (Penguin o/p; Knopf o/p). This brilliant study of the spread of Christianity through the Roman empire is authoritative and challenging, its serious engagement with the world of late antiquity offset by the writer's eye for telling detail and sly sense of humour.

Edward Gibbon *The Decline and Fall of the Roman Empire* (Everyman's Library; various unabridged US editions). This monumental 18th-century history addresses the causes and traces the course of Rome's decline. Its six volumes are enjoyable as much for the grandeur and beauty of their style as for the author's caustic wit and notoriously cynical view of the impact of religion on humankind.

The Middle Ages

Chris Wickham *Early Medieval Italy: Central Power and Local Society 400–1000* (University of Michigan). The ongoing struggle in Italy between local power and central government is traced back to its origins in this important book, one of comparatively few in English to provide a general account of the centuries following the fall of Rome.

Walter Ullmann *A Short History of the Papacy in the Middle Ages* (Routledge). Ullmann, a refugee from Nazi Germany who spent some time working as a garage mechanic, became an almost legendary figure while teaching at Cambridge University. His sharp, matter-of-fact overview remains central to an understanding of the medieval papacy.

Edward Burman *Emperor to Emperor: Italy before the Renaissance* (Constable). A sequence of individual case-studies looks at the broad diversity of Italian medieval culture, from early Benedictine monasticism and the creation of townscapes to Frederick II's castle-building in Apulia. Burman's text is well served by helpful illustrations.

John Larner *Italy in the Age of Dante and Petrarch* (Longman). A volume in the Longman *History of Italy* series, the book counterpoints the complex manoeuvres of late medieval Italian politics with the flourishing cultural life of the city states.

The Renaissance

Lauro Martines *Power and Imagination: City States in Renaissance Italy* (Pimlico; John Hopkins University Press). The author is a distinguished American historian working in the UK. His stylistic fluency and elegance have been admired as much as his intense feeling for the period under discussion. An essential work.

Denys Hay and **John Law** *The Age of the Renaissance: 1380–1530* (Longman). This offers the best general outline of Italian history's richest and most absorbing epoch. It also pays a welcome, rare attention to Sicily and the south.

George Holmes *Art and Politics in Renaissance Italy* (Oxford University Press). Holmes is a thoughtful and meticulous analyst of the crucial relationship between Renaissance artists and the rapidly changing, unpredictable political climate of the time.

Michael Baxandall *Painting and Experience in 15th-century Italy* (Oxford University Press). The classic 'slim volume', this book's brevity is deceptive. Renaissance painting in the age of Masaccio, Piero della Francesca and Botticelli is concisely contextualized in a work which justifiably remains one of the most admired studies of Italian art.

Niccolò Machiavelli *The Prince* (trans. W.K. Marriott, Everyman's Library). Machiavelli's manual of statecraft, originally written as a warning to republican governments, remains eminently readable and magnificently controversial after nearly five centuries.

Francesco Guicciardini *Selected Writings* (ed. & trans. Cecil Grayson, Oxford University Press o/p). Guicciardini was not just Florence's greatest historian but a stylish prose writer, a statesman, and a major political theorist during the early years of the Medici ascent to power in the 16th century.

James Hall *A History of Ideas and Images in Italian Art* (John Murray). Understanding the Renaissance passion for emblems and symbols can be a tricky business. Hall's book is structured for handy, easy reference, and is an indispensable aid to 'reading' paintings and sculpture.

Piero Camporesi *The Land of Hunger* (Polity Press). The writer is a social historian, concentrating here on a brief but detailed, sometimes harrowing, survey of feast and famine among the poverty-stricken underclass of Renaissance Italy – whose diet forms the basis, ironically, of the 'poor man's' Italian cuisine that is nowadays so highly valued throughout the world.

J.R. Hale (ed.) *A Concise Encyclopedia of the Italian Renaissance* (Oxford University Press). John Hale had a rare combination of scholarship and enthusiasm as a historian. Anyone using this book will want to go on to explore his individual studies of 16th-century Italian government, patronage and warfare.

Giorgio Vasari *Lives of the Painters, Sculptors and Architects* (trans. G.C. Du Vere, Everyman's Library). Often extremely partisan and highly selective, Vasari's book nevertheless offers vital insights into Renaissance art and imagination, making use of his own experience as a painter to assess the achievements of Italian masters from Giotto to Titian.

Bruce Boucher *Andrea Palladio: the Architect in his Time* (Abbeville Press). A fitting tribute to Italy's most influential architect by an acknowledged expert, who is also a fine writer on Baroque sculpture.

Paolo Fabbri *Monteverdi* (trans. Tim Carter, Cambridge University Press). Fabbri uses new documentary evidence to reconstruct the long and busy career of the first genius of Italian opera, and the volatile historical background of the era in which he lived his life.

Italy in the 18th century

Stuart Woolf *A History of Italy 1700–1860* (Routledge o/p). This book is steeped in the Marxist tradition in British historiography, but its broad chronological sweep is particularly useful in revealing the origins of 19th-century Italy's movement towards unification in the ideas of the 18th-century Enlightenment.

Franco Venturi *Italy and the Enlightenment: Studies in a Cosmopolitan Century* (Longman o/p). Unfortunately, Venturi's major work, *Settecento riformatore da Muratori a Beccaria*, a study of the Italian Enlightenment in several volumes, still awaits a complete English translation. The book recommended here is a shorter expression of his argument that Italian 18th-century writers and thinkers ought to be considered more seriously as significant influences in shaping modern European ideas.

Giuseppe Recuperati and Dino Carpanetto *Italy in the Age of Reason 1685–1789* (Longman). A richly layered examination of a comparatively neglected period of Italian history, it reveals the remarkable diversity of initiatives and personalities of an age that has often been written off as merely decadent and intellectually exhausted. Strong on the socio-economic background, the book mystifyingly ignores, however, the wider political dimension (either in Italy or further afield in Europe).

The Risorgimento

Derek Beales *The Risorgimento and the Unification of Italy* (Longman). Beales has since written classic studies of Habsburg emperors Joseph II and Maria Theresa: his understanding of the Austrian imperial context of the Risorgimento is better than most. A reliable account of issues, events and personalities.

G.M. Trevelyan *Garibaldi and the Making of Italy* (Phoenix Press). This study of the Sicilian expedition, along with its companion volumes on 1848, was written during the 1900s, but Trevelyan was more closely in touch than we are with the spirit of Garibaldi's age, and the clarity and verve of his writing make for a vigorous, exciting historical narrative.

Dennis Mack Smith *Cavour* (Routledge o/p; Knopf o/p). Also notable for his studies of Mazzini and Garibaldi, Mack Smith is acknowledged as the expert's expert on 19th-century Italian politics, not merely in the English-speaking world but among Italians as well. This biography of unified Italy's chief architect reveals Cavour to be a restless, multi-faceted, extraordinary man. Though currently out of print, it has been published by several major imprints over the years including Random House and Weidenfeld & Nicolson so can often be tracked down second-hand or online.

Harry Hearder *Italy in the Age of the Risorgimento 1790–1870* (Longman). Hearder adds a valuable final chapter on the early years of unification to his chronicling of the government and economies of the various Italian sovereign states during the Risorgimento. It is also insightful on the conflicting revolutionary ideologies of the period.

Frank Walker *The Man Verdi* (University of Chicago Press o/p US). The best portrait of 19th-century Italy's most inspiring composer, placed vividly in the context of his times, his cultural circle and his personal relationships.

The turn of the century

Benedetto Croce *A History of Italy 1871–1915* (trans. C.M. Ady, Oxford University Press o/p). A significant examination of the aspirations and achievements of the newly unified nation, powerfully focused for having been written under the shadow of Fascism, to which the author, doyen of Italian intellectuals, was bitterly opposed.

Dennis Mack Smith *Italy and its Monarchy* (Yale University Press). Mack Smith's view of the royal house of Savoy and its effect on Italian politics is refreshingly dispassionate and fair-minded. If the four kings do not emerge with much credit, then neither do the politicians who served them.

Martin Clark *Modern Italy 1871–1982* (Longman). As with other volumes in this series, the book assumes some knowledge on the reader's part of contemporary politics and world events. It is particularly good on issues such as relations between church and state and Italy's industrialization.

Caroline Tisdall and **Angelo Bozzolla** *Futurism* (Thames & Hudson). Easily the liveliest and sharpest outline of this extraordinary art movement, the book duly celebrates Futurism's originality and ruefully documents its ultimate decline.

Mussolini, Fascism and World War II

Adrian Lyttelton *The Seizure of Power: Fascism in Italy 1919–1929* (Weidenfeld & Nicolson o/p; Princeton University Press o/p). How Mussolini gained control of the political system and tightened his grip on the nation, written by a historian with an impressive understanding of the driving forces within Italian society of the period.

Christopher Hibbert *Mussolini* (Penguin o/p). The most easily accessible study of a figure who delighted in baffling his contemporaries. Hibbert's is a dispassionate portrait which, while critical, neither demonizes nor vindicates the *Duce*.

F.W. Deakin *The Brutal Friendship: Hitler and the Fall of Mussolini* (Phoenix Press; Sterling). A classic analysis of the destructive relationship between the two dictators, culminating in the *Führer*'s humiliation of his former role model.

Richard Lamb *War in Italy 1943–1945* (Da Capo Press). Written in a rigidly pedestrian style and with little obvious feeling for matters Italian (the partisans surely deserve a better account than they receive here), this is nevertheless a reliable record of the two most fateful years in the country's 20th-century history.

Eric Newby *Love and War in the Apennines* (Picador; Lonely Planet). Newby, a distinguished travel writer, spent three months in 1943 hiding in the Italian countryside after escaping from a prisoner-of-war camp in northern Italy. *Love and War* blends autobiography with travelogue, and describes at first-hand the lifestyle of Italy's mountain communities.

Modern Italy

Carlo Levi *Christ Stopped At Eboli* (trans. Francis Frenaye, Penguin; Noonday Press). Published after the war, as a memoir of the author's 'internal exile' under Fascism, this is a classic portrayal of the apparently timeless problems besetting the *Mezzogiorno*, the Italian South.

Stuart Woolf (ed.) *The Rebirth of Italy 1943–1950* (Longman). Italy's initially painful reconstruction following Fascism's fall is examined from a variety of viewpoints.

Paul Ginsborg *Italy and its Discontents 1980–2001* (Penguin; Palgrave Macmillan). Ginsborg, an expert on the Risorgimento, trains an unsparing gaze on the condition of modern Italy and the strangely potent consensus which has guaranteed the triumph of Berlusconi.

Paul Furlong *Modern Italy: Representation and Reform* (Routledge). Essential reading for those interested in the complexities of Italy's political system and its management within the framework of a modern democracy.

Steven Gundle and Stuart Parker (eds.) *The New Italian Republic, from the Fall of the Berlin Wall to Berlusconi* (Routledge). A rewarding collection of essays presenting recent political developments in Italy within their deeper historical framework.

Tobias Jones *The Dark Heart of Italy* (Faber). Written during a three-year period in Parma, Jones addresses various aspects of modern Italian society, from the legal and political systems to the media and football. He reveals a culture in which evasiveness and ethical malleability are as significant as the much-celebrated virtues of vivacity, charm and sophistication – a culture exemplified above all by the character of Silvio Berlusconi.

Italian literature in translation

Dante Alighieri *The Divine Comedy* (trans. John D. Sinclair, Oxford Paperbacks). Originally published in 1939, this remains the most reliable version of Dante's three-part classic poem.

Giovanni Boccaccio *The Decameron* (trans. George Bull, Penguin o/p). The famous medieval collection of tales, mixing romance with adventure and ribaldry, from which Shakespeare and others drew inspiration.

Michelangelo *The Complete Poems* (trans. Christopher Ryan, Weidenfeld & Nicholson). Ryan has also produced an independent critical study of Michelangelo's poetry. Here the texts are given in the original with parallel English versions.

Leonardo *The Notebooks* (trans. Irma A. Richter, Oxford World's Classics). Italy's prodigal genius of the Renaissance left voluminous notes on everything from anatomy to flying machines. This is an absorbing and tantalizing selection.

Giacomo Leopardi *The Canti* (trans. J.G. Nichols, Carcanet). Melancholy and introspective, Leopardi's odes reveal him to be Italy's greatest Romantic poet. This edition supplements his poetry with selected essays and extracts from his notebooks.

Alessandro Manzoni *The Betrothed* (trans. A. Colquhoun, Penguin). The first major Italian novel, profoundly influential on its author's revolutionary generation and compelling enough to survive its subsequent role as a compulsory text for Italian schoolchildren.

Giuseppe Tomasi di Lampedusa *The Leopard* (trans. A. Colquhoun, Everyman's Library). Source material of Luchino Visconti's classic movie of 1963, Lampedusa's fictionalized account of his Sicilian aristocratic family during and after the Risorgimento also offers an ironic commentary on Italian attitudes in the late 20th century.

Primo Levi *The Periodic Table* (trans. Raymond Rosenthal, Abacus). Levi is better known for his survival narratives of Auschwitz, but these sketches of Italian contemporaries under Fascism bear equally powerful witness to his times.

Giorgio Bassani *The Garden of the Finzi Contini* (trans. Isabel Quigly, Penguin). Love and politics mix uneasily in the memoir of a Jewish student in 1930s Ferrara – a fictionalized episode in the writer's own life.

Alberto Moravia *Two Women* (trans. Angus Davidson, Steerforth). Moravia describes the experiences of a mother and daughter as they struggle to survive in post-1943 Italy, posing important questions about the individual's relationship to history.

index

Entries in **colour** represent feature boxes

b

e

f

h

i

m

n

o

t

W

Y

Z

around the world

Alaska ★ Algarve ★ Amsterdam ★ Andalucía ★ Antigua & Barbuda ★ Argentina ★ Auckland Restaurants ★ Australia ★ Austria ★ Bahamas ★ Bali & Lombok ★ Bangkok ★ Barbados ★ Barcelona ★ Beijing ★ Belgium & Luxembourg ★ Belize ★ Berlin ★ Big Island of Hawaii ★ Bolivia ★ Boston ★ Brazil ★ Britain ★ Brittany & Normandy ★ Bruges & Ghent ★ Brussels ★ Budapest ★ Bulgaria ★ California ★ Cambodia ★ Canada ★ Cape Town ★ The Caribbean ★ Central America ★ Chile ★ China ★ Copenhagen ★ Corsica ★ Costa Brava ★ Costa Rica ★ Crete ★ Croatia ★ Cuba ★ Cyprus ★ Czech & Slovak Republics ★ Devon & Cornwall ★ Dodecanese & East Aegean ★ Dominican Republic ★ The Dordogne & the Lot ★ Dublin ★ Ecuador ★ Edinburgh ★ Egypt ★ England ★ Europe ★ First-time Asia ★ First-time Europe ★ Florence ★ Florida ★ France ★ French Hotels & Restaurants ★ Gay & Lesbian Australia ★ Germany ★ Goa ★ Greece ★ Greek Islands ★ Guatemala ★ Hawaii ★ Holland ★ Hong Kong & Macau ★ Honolulu ★ Hungary ★ Ibiza & Formentera ★ Iceland ★ India ★ Indonesia ★ Ionian Islands ★ Ireland ★ Israel & the Palestinian Territories ★ Italy ★ Jamaica ★ Japan ★ Jerusalem ★ Jordan ★ Kenya ★ The Lake District ★ Languedoc & Roussillon ★ Laos ★ Las Vegas ★ Lisbon ★ London ★

in twenty years

London Mini Guide ★ London Restaurants ★ Los Angeles ★ Madeira ★ Madrid ★ Malaysia, Singapore & Brunei ★ Mallorca ★ Malta & Gozo ★ Maui ★ Maya World ★ Melbourne ★ Menorca ★ Mexico ★ Miami & the Florida Keys ★ Montréal ★ Morocco ★ Moscow ★ Nepal ★ New England ★ New Orleans ★ New York City ★ New York Mini Guide ★ New York Restaurants ★ New Zealand ★ Norway ★ Pacific Northwest ★ Paris ★ Paris Mini Guide ★ Peru ★ Poland ★ Portugal ★ Prague ★ Provence & the Côte d'Azur ★ Pyrenees ★ The Rocky Mountains ★ Romania ★ Rome ★ San Francisco ★ San Francisco Restaurants ★ Sardinia ★ Scandinavia ★ Scotland ★ Scottish Highlands & Islands ★ Seattle ★ Sicily ★ Singapore ★ South Africa, Lesotho & Swaziland ★ South India ★ Southeast Asia ★ Southwest USA ★ Spain ★ St Lucia ★ St Petersburg ★ Sweden ★ Switzerland ★ Sydney ★ Syria ★ Tanzania ★ Tenerife and La Gomera ★ Thailand ★ Thailand's Beaches & Islands ★ Tokyo ★ Toronto ★ Travel Health ★ Trinidad & Tobago ★ Tunisia ★ Turkey ★ Tuscany & Umbria ★ USA ★ Vancouver ★ Venice & the Veneto ★ Vienna ★ Vietnam ★ Wales ★ Washington DC ★ West Africa ★ Women Travel ★ Yosemite ★ Zanzibar ★ Zimbabwe

also look out for our maps, phrasebooks, music guides and reference books

ROUGH GUIDE **HISTORIES**

£7.99 each

The Rough Guide
History of
SPAIN

JUSTIN WINTLE

The Rough Guide
History of
EGYPT

Michael Haag

The Rough Guide
History of the
USA

The Rough Guide
History of
IRELAND

The Rough Guide
History of
ISLAM

JUSTIN WINTLE

The Rough Guide
History of
ITALY

Uniquely accessible pocket histories
— History Today

**Essential pocket histories for anyone interested in
getting under the skin of a country**

Other books in the series: China, England, France, Greece, India